THE TRAIL PROVIDES

ISBN: 9781723785450

Also available in electronic format.

Cover and Map by Kett McKenna
(kettmckennajr@gmail.com)

Photos by Richard Walker (@relaxedcat)
www.TheFakeFacade.Blogspot.com.au

Edited by Brianna Boes
http://www.BKBoes.com

Typesetting by Jo Roderick
www.BookCover.biz

If you would like to read my blog posts, listen to podcasts, and access extra content, visit my blog at
www.ThinkingWithDavid.com

Send inquiries to **smartdavid@mac.com.**

THE PACIFIC CREST TRAIL

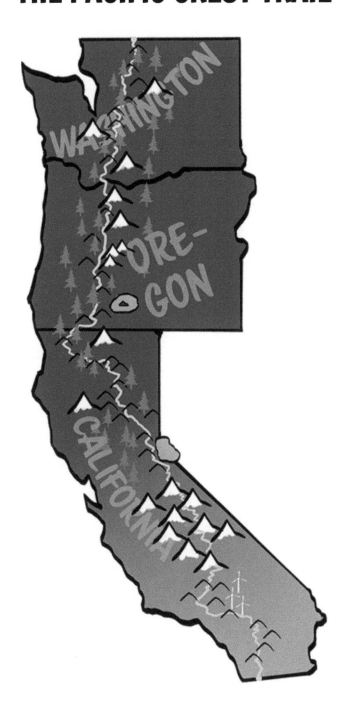

For you—the seeker, soul-searcher, and pilgrim.

"Neither nakedness, nor matted locks, nor filth, nor fasting, nor lying on bare earth can purify a man who is filled with doubt."

–Dhammapada, Verse 141

THE TRAIL PROVIDES:

A Boy's Memoir of Thru-Hiking the Pacific Crest Trail

DAVID SMART

2018

The Trail Provides

PROLOGUE

April 22, 2015
Email Subject Line: And So It Begins
To: <Mailing List of Friends & Family Back Home>

Hello friends! We have arrived in San Diego. We'll be starting a long outward and inward journey tomorrow morning. We'll be thinking of you on our sojourn and providing you with updates along the way.

We would also very much enjoy updates about your lives as well. We are all journeying together, and we are all facing similar challenges. Email is a great tool, but receiving and writing letters has a magical effect.

If you do decide to write or send something, please also include your address so we might have the privilege to write you back. Please use priority mail for more reliant deliveries.

Thank you all so much for your presences. Pray to the rain gods, eh? Major drought over here. Our gift to you is a goofy picture at the airport this morning. Cheers!

Love,
Bradley & David

And so it begins (Bradley & David).

CHAPTER 1

April 23, 2015
Bob's House | San Diego, California

"It's time."

I groaned and turned over as my eyes fluttered open. A man's rounded figure stood in the doorway.

Is today really the day?

Before I could process the thought any further, Bob disappeared, and the door slammed shut.

"Don't forget water," he called out while walking back to the house. "You won't last long without it."

It was the small hours of the morning, but I somehow managed to lift my head from the rickety trailer floor where I had slept the past two nights and glance toward the other end of the trailer. There sat Bradley, sitting cross-legged beside his backpack at the foot of his bed, eyes closed.

I still couldn't believe today was the day I'd anxiously anticipated for the last three months. I was only twenty-four years of age, and my life had changed more in the last ninety days than in all the previous years combined.

The corporate lifestyle just hadn't done it for me. I had been working a digital marketing job since my college graduation two years ago—a fine job with various perks and fancy meals—but I had begun to feel disillusioned by the "real world." Trapped in a nine-to-five cycle of work-hard-play-hard, my life was far from satisfying, and I didn't like where it was heading.

Much of it likely had to do with how I was spending my time. After a long day of meaningless work, my weekday afternoons were filled with workouts, yoga, and other forms of movement simply to keep the stress at bay, and my precious weekends were riddled with poor decisions involving alcohol, hangovers, noisy bars, late night texting, and sleeping with women I shouldn't have been sleeping with given my intoxicated state. But it seemed these activities were the only way to take advantage of my brief time off, a reprieve from the endless cycle that awaited me the following Monday.

What I found most strange about my life was that I had saved up plenty of money, but I didn't know what I was saving for, why I was working, or what I was working toward. It seemed like I had everything I wanted in life, and yet I still wasn't happy. Once money ceased to become my life's objective, I was left to question the purpose of my existence.

My soul was being crushed, my life void of purpose, and I knew it was up to me to find a new direction. My only problem was I had no clue what else I wanted to do. I had no passions to pursue nor any idea what another life would even look like for me. I only knew I needed something different.

So, I began searching for alternatives. My most promising gig seemed to be another marketing job working for a waterpark with a good friend of mine. It wouldn't be the most dramatic shift, but maybe it would be just enough to make me happy! After flying down, meeting the owner, and returning with optimistic ambitions, I decided to take the leap. I quit my job. I hadn't gotten a final offer yet, but I was desperate for change.

It was about a week after quitting and telling all my coworkers I would be working for said waterpark, that I realized there was not going to be another job. My friend called me and told me not to do anything too crazy just yet. I was ashamed to tell him it was already too late.

My unemployment frightened me in the beginning. *How would I make my way in society? How do I spend my time? What should I be working on?* Life was a much different experience when there was no one telling me what to do, and I felt caught in the paradox of choice. Fortunately, I'd saved up a chunk of change and the lease on my room wouldn't expire for another couple of months, affording me time to figure things out day by day. I decided I'd ride it out while contemplating what to do next.

It's been said that humans need a balance between certainty and uncertainty, between chaos and order. Too much of one and the ship begins to sink. After my job had fallen through, it felt like I'd traded a cruise ship with a few small leaks for a bottomless canoe. A week had come and gone, and I was still sitting at my house with no job and no clue of what I was supposed to do next.

That's when I called Bradley.

Bradley was a college fraternity brother of mine. Being two years older than me, he was my grand-big, and I was his grand-little in the fraternity. During college, we were deeply involved in the fraternal lifestyle, playing out all the stereotypes you can think of: drinking, smoking, promiscuity, and plenty of douchebaggery. We shotgunned beers, chugged excessive amounts of hard liquor, and participated in brotherly hazing rituals to gain the affection of our peers.

It may be common for many people to create distance from their college-aged selves, but Bradley's change was especially noticeable, more dramatic than any of my other college friends. Upon his graduation, Bradley had joined the workforce as a junior client representative at a currency brokerage. This didn't last long. Fifteen months to be exact! On a plane flight home from an overseas vacation, he had already set his mind to quitting. No two weeks' notice was necessary. The day of his return marked the beginning of his transient and nomadic lifestyle, which had continued for the past three years, ultimately leading him to the jungles of South America. From what I had heard of his travels, he had spent his time there exploring mountains, traveling far and wide, and even participating in a variety of mind-altering, shaman led ceremonies. Needless to say, he was no longer the same guy from our college days, and at the rate he was going, I couldn't imagine him ever stepping into an office again.

That life intrigued me, and it was when I was sitting at home on my couch that I recalled his story, curious about a man living such a life. I now felt the very same things he must have been feeling when he quit the corporate lifestyle! I found his contact details on my phone and dialed him up.

"You're doing *what?!*" I asked him. My eyebrow shot up. Embarking on a six-month backpacking sojourn and hiking 2,650 miles on a continuous footpath in the wilderness from Mexico to Canada sounded both crazy and irresponsible.

This didn't surprise me. Bradley was the kind of guy who did everything with the greatest intensity. He was, to put it no other way, extreme. To him, quitting a job meant traveling to the edge of the world. Dieting meant days of fasting. And taking a walk meant hiking across the country.

As extreme as Bradley was, I looked up to him. He was older, intelligent, teaming with confidence, mysterious, and much more experienced in the ways of travel and adventure than I was.

I found myself thinking, *as crazy as he is, maybe he has some of the answers I'm looking for...*

"It's called the Pacific Crest Trail, brother!" Bradley said, trying to relax me into the idea.

I'd never heard of it. It sounded like a computer game I'd fidgeted with in my youth called *Oregon Trail* where everyone ends up dying by snakebites and dysentery. But as he began to explain the trail to me, I felt a rush of adrenaline.

Bradley had been planning the trip for months prior, already having purchased all sorts of hiking and outdoor gear, and was soon to finalize the food strategy. Apparently, I had called at just the right time. He explained that the Pacific Crest Trail (PCT) required a resupply strategy to coordinate food shipments to post offices along the trail. We would be hiking in the wilderness, and instead of carrying six months of food on your back—which would be ridiculous and impossible—hikers carried four to seven days' worth of food. They resupplied at post offices and general stores along the way. As for water, hikers picked that up from streams, creeks, and springs.

I'd never done anything remotely like this before. My most outdoorsy experience had been a three-day retreat into Texas' Big Bend National Park during the seventh-grade led by *heavy* adult supervision. If I were to go on this journey, there would be no parents. Only me, my homeless, Jesus-look-a-like, college fraternity brother, Bradley, and whoever else we encountered on the trail. This was a frightening thought to me.

"I'll send you a gear list, and we'll split the cost of food," Bradley said. "Just make sure to purchase everything as soon as possible. My dad will be our quartermaster, so ship your food to my parent's house, and we'll take care of the logistics."

At least he had some things planned out. But a thousand questions still swirled in my mind. The trail sounded, well... dangerous.

"What about death?" I asked, hoping he would immediately scoff at the notion and dismiss the concern. "Is death a possibility?"

"Death is guaranteed, isn't it?!" he snickered. "I'm only joking, of course. Well, sort of. Sure, it's a possibility, but we'll deal with that when it comes."

Nearing the end of our chat, I told him I would need time to think it over and that I'd return his call at a later date.

"The sooner you can let me know the better," he said. "You won't regret this, brother!"

And with that our call ended.

I tried going about my day as usual, but it was too late. Everything had changed, and it felt like a deep and permanent shift had occurred inside me that I couldn't shake. From that minute on, the trail consumed my every thought, and the idea possessed me.

Perhaps this is a sign, I thought. *Maybe this is what I've been looking for. Maybe the trail is exactly what I need!*

It seemed my only other option was to crawl back to my old job, but I was far too desperate for that. I needed something different. Something that would change my life. Even though I had never truly backpacked before, and I'd be hiking alongside the extreme tendencies of my friend Bradley, these were risks I was willing to take. That day I decided the trail would be my next step in life!

I had dialed Bradley back the next day and told him to count me in. I could hear his excitement as he began explaining our next steps.

Thus began my preparations, and telling my parents was first on the list. I had already made the decision, but my parent's support meant everything to me.

"Bears, honey! What about the bears?!"

I could imagine my mother gripping the phone with white knuckles and pacing around the kitchen. To her, the trail was a deathtrap infested with nothing but snakes, mountain lions, and bears! Every day for the weeks leading up to the hike, I received some sort of email correspondence from her containing frightening subject lines and links to articles about trail safety and the dangers of hiking in the wilderness.

I couldn't blame her. It's part of a mother's job to be concerned and protective of her child. And I, too, had had these concerns at first.

How dangerous is the trail?

It was only after a bit of research and numerous phone calls with Bradley that I began to see how hiking the trail was much less dangerous than either my mother or I had originally believed.

Apparently, there would be many other hikers on the trail along with a support network of "trail angels," a name used by the trail culture to designate those who help hikers accomplish their goal of walking to Canada. Trail angels offered shelter, food, water, and transportation. Knowing others would be out there with us helped ease my concern, and so long as we kept our distance from wild animals, kept our eyes on the trail, avoided stepping on any rattlers, and didn't do anything too stupid to get ourselves killed, we'd make it out alive. Plus, after taking into account the probabilities of car accidents in the States, it seemed I was far more likely to die in urban life! It turned out living in the city had an opportunity cost of its own.

Meanwhile, my dad wasn't convinced I'd make it past three days in the wild, offering me the option to return home if the bears didn't get me first. I deserved his skepticism, as I had never really stuck with anything in my youth. I had no credibility or experience to warrant such an endeavor. There was little I had done that a father could be proud of apart from earning a college degree and finding post-grad employment, neither of which were wildly remarkable given my upbringing. And now here I was, leaving all of that behind.

My dad's words echoed in my mind on more than one occasion. "I'm just happy you're exercising that hiking degree that I paid so much money for."

It was a dagger to my heart! But what could I say? He was right. Stepping into his shoes, I imagined it was difficult to see every dollar he spent seemingly tossed into a shredder. To him, I was wasting my education in pursuit of wandering in the wilderness. It was a much different path from the one he must have had in mind for me.

It was my parent's least favorite decision I'd made for myself, perhaps the only one I'd ever made, but in the end,

I had their blessing, even if it was wrapped in fear and disappointment. I could tell they just wanted me to be happy.

So, I'd left everything behind and gone all in to hike the trail. I sold all my possessions, leaving only a small closet of clothes at my parent's house for if and when I returned, and registered for a PCT thru-hiker permit, a permit that granted me access to every national park along the trail. I made many trips to REI, ordered hiking gear online, and watched as boxes and boxes of stuff piled up in my room. I now owned a sleeping bag I'd never slept in, cookware I hadn't the slightest clue how to use, a tarp I didn't have the skills to pitch, and a large backpack to stuff it all into.

When everything arrived, I spread out the gear onto the floor and stared in awe at the simplicity. Having stuffed it all into the backpack, I threw it over my shoulder and questioned my decision more than ever. Is this really everything I'll have for next *six months*? It was the expected timeframe for a hiker to finish the trail, and I hoped I wouldn't have to return before. I had told so many friends about the upcoming trek, and I couldn't imagine the embarrassment if I ended up not finishing the trail.

After finding a friend of a friend to take over my lease, I had no other options or backup plans. I was ready to change my life and find my purpose on the trail.

Hopefully, I thought, *this will be the right place to find purpose… if such a thing exists.*

The day of Bradley's arrival soon came. I picked him up from the Greyhound bus station in Dallas, Texas, three days before our flight to San Diego where we'd begin the trail. Although we'd kept in contact for the last three years since his graduation, I hardly recognized him as he stepped down from the bus onto the sidewalk.

I blinked to make sure it was him. The sharp-dressed guy I once knew now looked… well… *homeless!* His short hair, clean-shaven face, neatly pressed polo shirt, and squeaky-clean boat shoes were nowhere to be seen. In their place was a flowing mane of black hair that fell past his shoulders, a measly beard sprouting from his chin, and janky, home-made rubber sandals with laces crisscrossing up his calves like some ancient Roman gladiator. His only possessions were those stuffed into a white hiker's backpack strapped high against his back. My friend looked like an apostle straight out of the New Testament.

Before we left, we explored Dallas for one night. Multiple people approached him, wanting him to bless them and forgive them of their sins, while others threw him the sign of the cross from a distance. What was I to make of his looks and fashion choices?

I guess that's just what four years of unemployment and living in the Amazonian jungles does to a person, I decided.

PCT Gear.

For better or worse, this guy would be my guide on our upcoming voyage. I was frightened, intrigued, and curious for what lay ahead.

So finally, the day had come as I woke up in that trailer, everything I possessed in piles on the floor. I shoved my life into a backpack, threw it over my shoulder, and followed Bradley out the trailer into the cold, dark twilight.

It was a short walk from the trailer through the side-yard to Bob's house. Bob Reiss was our first trail angel, and for the past few nights, Bradley and I had slept in Bob's trailer. Our days were occupied with helping around the house, meeting other hikers, and preparing for departure. The amount of support, generosity, and kindness distributed by a single individual was incredible.

Bob's cozy home welcomed us as we crept inside. Hikers lay passed out on the floor while others dangled off the ends of the living room couches. They kept still as we filled our water bottles from the sink. They knew today wasn't yet their day to leave.

We headed out the front door where Bob's old van sat in the driveway on the side of a hill ready to shuttle us to the trailhead. The view was great from up high, the city in the eastern skyline and the beach to the west.

I looked away from the scenery, preceding Bradley as we climbed into the van, and buckled up.

Bob gripped the wheel and threw a glance over his shoulder. "Sure you got everything?"

We nodded.

"Good."

And we were off.

Buildings towered over the highway for miles until they didn't, and the city receded in the rearview before disappearing completely. With it went the fresh smell of the seaside air that once poured through the van's air conditioning. I placed my attention on the passing wilderness outside the window as distant red mountains began to surround us all on sides.

We were silent, still drowsy, as we waited for sunrise. I tried forcing my eyelids open, but sleep got the best of me.

My vision faded in and out until the highway turned to rock and gravel and the shaking jolted me awake. The road was precarious and narrow, climbing up the side of a mountain, overlooking the valley below. I tightened my grip on my seatbelt until the path leveled off to split a new desert plateau.

"You two have any final questions?" Bob asked. His bright eyes reflected in the rearview.

None came to mind, but I knew Bradley would think of something. He always did.

Bradley leaned forward in the seat next to me. "Any advice if we're looking to go all the way?"

The car rumbled up the road. We waited in silence as Bob thought.

"It won't be easy," he said, "but the first step is always the hardest. And believe it or not, that step's already been taken."

"Yeah… why don't I believe that?" Bradley laughed.

I didn't believe it either.

Bob chuckled. I sensed we were getting close to our arrival.

"The trail will test you," he said. "You'll change, like it or not. It's a journey unlike any other."

Change stood out to me. I could go for something like that.

It was a grey, cloudy dawn as we reached the end of the road. We stopped there because we could go no further.

"We're here," Bob said, climbing out of the van. "Welcome to Campo, California."

I opened the door and stepped down to the dirt. *Where the hell am I?* Looking around, this was indeed a distant land. Maybe even the middle of nowhere. There was little to nothing here except the border, which was one long wall of barbed wire and another behind it made of corrugated fencing. Each stretched over the desert hills, then vanished.

A few paces north of the border stood a monument. It was four large posts made of wood, each of varying heights, painted white, and grouped together. The highest post boasted the trail's emblem. On another was some writing. I traced my fingers along the smoothed wood-grain indentions and read the markings to myself:

SOUTHERN TERMINUS: PACIFIC CREST NATIONAL SCENIC TRAIL.
MEXICO TO CANADA, 2,627 MILES.

Bradley and David, PCT Southern Terminus.

This was the beginning.

"Hop on up for a picture," Bob said, gesturing for a phone. I handed mine over and climbed the posts with Bradley. "Thanks."

When I took back the phone, the battery was nearly dead, which was strange as I'd made a point to charge it overnight.

I shrugged it off for the moment as it was time to hug our photographer, say goodbye, and begin the hike.

"Now, before you head out," Bob said, "I want to tell you something. As you already know, I don't ask much from hikers. Just pay it forward. And mail me a letter if you make it to the end."

He looked into our eyes and smiled. "The gravity of this situation will hit you once my tail lights disappear. You'll wanna go that way." He grinned, pointing away from the border. It was obvious which direction to walk, as there was only one direction we could possibly go, but I smiled as I could tell he found a certain pleasure in saying this.

We waved as Bob's van passed from sight over the horizon, a trail of dust rising and disappearing into the air.

We were alone.

Bradley and I stood silent and still. Everything had happened so quickly! I looked off into the desert, wondering about the last time I'd seen anything so foreign.

It was then that Bradley reached down, untied his sandals and placed his bare feet against the earth.

I gawked at him. *Is he actually going to do it?*

"Feels good?" I asked.

He exhaled deeply, his eyes narrowed, and his cheeks slid into a grin. He nodded convincingly.

Bradley told me the day after I had committed to hiking the trail with him that he would be walking the trail barefoot.

"Are you serious…?" I had first asked him. The idea seemed both irresponsible and insane!

What kind of crazy hippy hikes the trail barefoot? I thought.

At the same time, I knew this was Bradley I was dealing with, so I wasn't too surprised.

He'd told me hiking barefoot wasn't a big deal for him. During his time in the Patagonia Mountains, he had often hiked barefoot, and the feeling had put him in touch with the earth.

He proceeded to riff on various facts and figures about how the earth emits an electromagnetic charge that offers a host of benefits like improved sleep, disease-prevention, and pain relief to those who participated in "grounding," and how modern society had lost this vital connection to the earth.

"In the grand scheme of human history," he mentioned, "shoes are a relatively new invention."

To each his own, I had originally thought. But the more Bradley talked about it, about his confidence in his abilities, the more it made me think.

Can I do that too...? The thought intrigued me. *What better way to connect to the earth? What better way to embody a pilgrimage?*

Each of us had packed shoes just in case of emergency situations, but I hadn't fully committed to barefooting just yet. I'd told myself I'd set the decision aside until we reached the trail, waiting to see how I felt the day of our arrival at the southern terminus.

Watching the expression of relief on his face after removing his sandals was the final push I needed. *Maybe I'll try this thing out after all and see how it goes!*

So, I reached down, untied my sandals, and set my feet against the ground. The earth was cool from the night before, and the dirt was soft beneath my soles. It was decided. I too would hike the PCT barefoot. If Bradley could do it, I could, too!

I packed away the shoes, hooked my backpack on my shoulders, buckled my chest and hip straps, and tightened them to a snug fit. The pack was heavy with a week's food and four liters of water, but I felt ready as ever to begin this walk.

"Mind if I say some words before we set off?" Bradley asked.

"Sure."

He grabbed my shoulders, bowed his head, and closed his eyes. I did the same. He took a deep breath. "We're grateful to walk a new path. May our steps bring insight. May we be granted safety, carrying only what serves us. We ask that we grow, remain pure, and whatever it is we are looking for, may we find it on this journey. Cheers."

Silence followed.

"Ready?" he asked, opening his eyes and nodding.

"Ready."

"Here goes nothin'!"

As he turned and took his first northbound steps on the trail, I hung back and gave my attention to the wilderness. It was expansive. The footpath before me seemed painted by a brush, running across the hills, and chasing the northern horizon.

Desert surrounded the path—desert and nothing more. But it was much lusher than I had imagined. Instead of life-less dunes, the landscape was littered with green patches of spiky plants, cacti, and small chaparral bushes.

The scene surprised me because I had intentionally lim-ited my research of the trail, wanting to leave the novelty to my direct experience. With Bradley as my guide, I figured I'd do just fine with the lack of information.

A morning breeze brushed my face. Gone were the sounds of the city, the clacking of keyboards, the chatter of office conference calls. The loudest thing for miles was the sound of the wind. Reality sank in like coins to a wishing well.

"You coming?" he yelled, already a short distance down the path.

"Coming!"

I headed up the trail as a nervous excitement swelled inside me. Everything I'd ever wished for, worked toward, or worried about was a distant memory living a thousand miles away. I was free. Truly free. All that mattered in my life were my steps.

As I caught up to Bradley, he looked back and grinned.

We burst out laughing.

"Has this trail really been here this whole time?" he asked.

I smiled and breathed in the early morning sky. This was a new life, a new start, and I didn't think once to look back.

CHAPTER 2

April 23, 2015
Mile 0, U.S./Mexico Border (2,650 miles to go)

"What's the plan again?" I asked. I was already dragging behind Bradley. His legs were like stilts compared to mine. I hadn't anticipated the extra effort it would take just to keep pace with him.

Barefooting.

He cocked his head to the side while walking so as not to break his stride. "We have two days to hike twenty miles to reach the PCT kickoff at Lake Morena Campground. It's a big deal and a good time, supposedly. Lots of other hikers, free food, vendors, and presentations—but remember, we're signed up to volunteer, so we can't be late."

I'd nearly forgotten Bradley had volunteered us for kick-off. The opportunity to serve was important to him, which was another huge departure from his college days. I decided it must be a part of this new spiritual path of his. But ever since the trail had turned from sand and dust to hardened earth, my feet were beginning to grow sore, and the idea of holding to a timetable twisted my stomach in knots, making my feet ache even more.

"So," he continued, "let's aim for twelve miles today and cruise into kickoff on an easy eight tomorrow. What do you say?"

I shrugged. "Uhh… yeah. Sounds good." It seemed like a far distance, but I really had no idea. Either way, it didn't matter. I just had to keep up with Bradley. Barefooting seemed a non-issue for him as he flew over the trail with ease.

When the clouds cleared from the morning sky, heat sunk into my skin. The trail turned simmering hot, requiring a faster hiking pace to keep my feet from burning against the ground. It was challenging, but the discomfort was… tolerable.

At first.

Where things really started going south for me (not literally, of course, since the trail continued its seemingly infinite northern pursuit) was when I stopped and glanced upward. The trail twisting through the desert was a now a minefield of thousands of jagged rocks.

I eyed the situation carefully. There was no going around it, and the only way out was through. I wobbled and winced as I went along, my walking turning into more of a stumble. My soles were growing ever more sore, dirty, and tender as the miles passed, but I somehow reassured myself that this pain was a phase all hikers had to endure, shoes or no shoes.

Thankfully, the rocks ended, giving way to hard earth, but this time the trail began climbing upward. With every step, the hill grew into a mountain. We trudged higher, the weight of my pack pushing against my sweaty back and dragging me down toward the earth.

My trekking poles!

I'd forgotten they were strapped to the side my bag. I took them out and leaned against my newfound third and fourth legs, each stabbing of the earth lunging me forward. I felt like an old man leaning against his walker while heading up the ramp to his retirement home. The feelings of support only lasted so long. Soon, the rocks returned, and my feet buzzed with piercing sensations as I tried to walk over them. I could only hope more forgivable earth would be coming sooner rather than later.

What am I doing? I wondered as I continued to climb. It felt like I'd placed myself in a worse hell than the one I'd escaped two months ago.

Although I hadn't told many people about my grand adventure, I'd told enough. My close friends and family knew. And what would they think of me if after all that talk I didn't even make it past the first few days?

I'd look like a stupid, irresponsible failure! I imagined the mockery and pity from friends and family. If I left now, I'd have to move in with my parents until I picked up the pieces and found myself another one of those corporate jobs...

Nope! I couldn't let that happen. I wouldn't. At least... not yet. Maybe I just needed a quick break.

"Hey," I said, "I'll meet you up ahead." I walked off the trail and threw off my backpack.

Bradley halted and turned. "You sure?"

"Yeah." I could already tell my slow pace was annoying him, and I didn't want to slow him down any further.

He nodded. "I won't go too far ahead."

"See ya soon."

With that, he turned and continued onward.

I found a flat dirt patch beneath the shade of an overgrown shrub that made for a fine seat to drink water and inspect my dirty feet.

The situation didn't look good.

Three blisters, each still in adolescent stages but bulbous and filled with fluid nonetheless, were bubbling up on my toes and soles. The largest blister protruded from the outside of my right big toe. I considered wrapping it with bandages from my first aid kit, but the thought of unpacking my bag and losing further ground didn't settle well on my mind. It surely wouldn't settle well with Bradley.

Better ignore it for now, I thought.

As I drank, the sound of chatter approached me from the south. A middle-aged couple wearing sunglasses, wide-brimmed hats, and huge backpacks came up over the trail. The man immediately stared at my feet.

"Are you hiking the PCT barefoot?" he asked. He looked to be both shocked and awed.

I glanced around for Bradley but remembered there was no one to answer the question but me.

"Yeah," I said with a laugh. "I have a friend who's doing the same thing. You'll probably meet him up ahead."

I figured I had to mention Bradley so it didn't look like I was the only fool in this desert.

Their eyes widened, and the woman turned to the man. "I don't think anyone's done that before!" she said in astonishment.

"You'd be the first!" said the man.

"Really...?" I asked. This was news to me!

So what made Bradley think this was possible if no one had ever done it before?

"From what I know," he said. "It's an impressive feat. Won't be easy, that's for sure, but we'll be rooting for you."

At this point, I felt like I was all in. After all, you can't tell someone you're doing something and then not do it... right?

We exchanged pleasantries, shook hands, and I watched as they trudged forward in a way that only shoes could manage. I envied their pace.

As I got up and continued on, the news that very few people, if any, had ever hiked the PCT barefoot weighed heavy on my mind. Considering an elderly couple had now passed me, it was time to get moving. Plus, Bradley would be waiting and no doubt wondering where I was.

I stared at the footprints in the dirt to distract myself from my foot pain. The path was covered in shoe prints of various patterns, the steps of hundreds of people who had walked it before me. It was easy to follow because of this. Every now and again I'd catch the fresh and unmistakable indentions of toes. *Bradley*. I followed them north one step at a time.

They ended around a bend where I found him resting beneath the shade of some larger shrubs.

Bradley was scowling, and I knew why. I hobbled over, threw off my pack, and sat down beside him.

"You been here a while?" I asked, hesitant to hear his response.

He sighed. "Yeah."

"More than an hour?"

"Doesn't matter..."

I nodded. It had been at least that amount of time. "Sorry, man. It's tough for me."

He nodded slowly. "It's fine. But we should probably set up camp earlier than planned."

He glanced upward at the sky.

"The sun sets soon, and it's best we're ready before dark. We'll just swap the mileage of our original plan. Eight miles today and twelve tomorrow."

I sat in silence, soaking in the day's failure, my feet buzzing. I wanted nothing more than to remain seated for the rest of the day. I shut my eyes and took in a breath.

"Let's go," Bradley said. "You lead."

I nodded. He knew we would only be as strong as our weakest link. We stood and continued up the path, Bradley following closely behind me.

An hour passed before we had climbed over the desert mountain. Our procession came to a stop.

"Hold on," he said, stepping east of the trail and scanning the flat terrain. "Let me check the map."

I waited as he did so, steeping in my uselessness, examining the scene. It was a small, dry clearing of flatland amid gnarled and thirsty plants.

"We're a bit short of eight, and this land isn't marked as a campsite, but it seems flat and nice enough. It's exposed, but the weather's clear. You saved enough water for dinner, right? There's none nearby."

I nodded and threw off my pack. A sense of relief washed over me. The day was done. And I was ready to eat.

"Should we set up the tarp?" I asked.

Bradley examined the sky. He shook his head. "We won't need it."

No tarp? What about all the animals and bugs?

"Oh, well… we should probably set up the bug bivy then?" It was a piece of gear I had championed for in the final days before leaving. The last thing I wanted was to wake up to spider and scorpion legs crawling into my mouth.

"It'll be too cold for the bugs."

"Ah." I guess that made sense.

Bradley unpacked his bag and blanketed the earth with a wide groundsheet—a thin, durable piece of Tyvek, a paper-like material used to line walls during construction.

"This'll be your first time cowboy camping, huh?" he asked.

"Yeah, I guess so."

"You'll like it. There's something special about sleeping under the open sky. Just wait till you see the stars."

I arranged my spot near his, throwing away the rocks that occupied the plot of land and noting the flatness of the earth. After an inspection for ants and other insects, I too laid out my groundsheet.

It had been an unreasonably difficult and disturbingly loud piece of gear in the days before the trail, but on Bradley's advice, a rinse in the wash had softened it and made it quiet. It fell against the ground, twice the size of my body in width and slightly taller in height. It allowed enough space for everything I had to be kept off the dusty ground.

In the middle of my new home, I unfolded my sleeping pad—a thin piece of foam that stacked like an accordion atop my backpack for easy access since it conveniently doubled as a sit pad. This would be my mattress. Finally, scrunched down at the bottom of my pack, I yanked up my sleeping bag and tossed it on top of the pad.

My bed was set.

The light was waning, and the temperature was dropping. We changed into wool thermals and puffy jackets, and I opted for socks to keep my toes warm.

As we were changing, I noticed Bradley's tattoo. It was a massive snake in a figure-eight, and it covered almost the entire left side of his body. The snake's head rested against his chest then curled down his side where it twisted into a loop on his ribs, framing a strange flower bursting of reds, yellows, and oranges. The snake continued its journey, traveling up his back and wrapping his shoulder, entangling his arm to form the upper loop where the snake was devouring its tail with open jaws.

There was something mystical and mysterious about that tattoo. Traveling had changed Bradley in some way, some way that I too wanted to experience.

"Oh," he laughed. "Yeah, I forget it's there sometimes, too. It's called an Ouroboros... the snake that eats his own tail. The flower is the seed of life."

"What's it mean?"

He shrugged. "It keeps changing for me. It used to be this idea that things are cyclical. Then it was about the integration of the opposite, of the shadow."

"The shadow?"

"Yeah, the confrontation with one's dark side. We all have one, and it's only through really knowing it that we become whole. So they say. But more recently it's been the eight-fold noble path. It's always changing. You don't have any tattoos, do you?"

I shook my head. "Nah."

"I didn't think so. I would have remembered. Hey, hand me the cookpot, would ya? Let's eat."

It was about time he mentioned it. A long day's hike had stirred up a monstrous hunger in me. I reached into my bag, unsheathed the titanium pot from its mesh sleeve, then handed it over. He balanced the pot atop its handles like stilts in the space between our groundsheets then slide the stove under.

"Mind pouring in some of your water?" he asked.

I glanced at my supply.

"Sure," I said, filling the cookpot to match Bradley's offering.

Although water seemed like it would be incredibly sparse, I felt hydrated enough to contribute my fair share. I had enough left over to last me the night and some of tomorrow morning. Plus, as we'd discussed beforehand, we'd be sharing basically everything with each other. It was something I would have to get used to doing.

Bradley poured distilled alcohol into the stove then leaned down while holding his lighter. Some hikers at trail angel Bob's house had informed us that alcohol stoves weren't permitted in the desert, but it was all we had brought, and we'd have to make due until a gas stove presented itself to us.

It took some time to light the stove as the wind wouldn't give the lighter a chance, so we turned our backs to the gusts and shielded the attempts with our hands. Finally, a small blue flame emerged from the stove, flickering in the evening light.

My stomach grumbled as I waited for the water to boil. The flame was weak, at least compared to the high blast of my good old kitchen stove, and amid the growing cold I found myself shoving more and more of my body parts into my sleeping bag.

Is the stove even lit? I tilted my head for a better look at the flame.

I could barely make out its figure, but it was there. This was how we'd be eating our meals from here on out. Quite the change from cooking in a kitchen…

When I looked up, Bradley was digging into his food bag and pulling out Ziploc bags.

"Cornmeal, powdered potatoes, amaranth, brown rice farina, millet, oats…?" he asked, raising the Ziploc bags then placing them between us as if we were at a buffet. I added what I was carrying into the pile.

I hadn't heard of half the options. They were all Bradley's pre-trail choices, as I'd piggybacked on his planning late in the game when the food strategy had already been set. With each option sounding as equally questionable and unappetizing as the last, I went with what I knew.

"How about cornmeal tonight and oats in the morning?" It was a fair offer considering he carried the cornmeal while I was burdened with that huge sack of oats. The quicker I could rid myself of that oat bag's weight, the better.

He smiled. "Wise decision."

The water was now boiling. Bradley stirred the cornmeal with his titanium spoon.

"Ah," he said, reaching into his food bag. "I forget to tell you about these." Ceremoniously, he placed three smaller bags in front of me.

"These are our spices. Cinnamon. Pink Himalayan sea salt. And this one," he said, shaking the bag of yellow powder, "is where the real magic happens." He opened the bag and smelled it. "Turmeric. It has anti-inflammatory properties perfect for joints and recovery."

That sounded okay since my feet felt like they had been crushed beneath a steamroller.

"Is it good?"

He nodded. "Try it."

I cautiously dipped my finger in the bag and brought some to my tongue. The awful, bitter taste spread throughout my mouth and made me want to puke.

"Mmm," I said. "… Maybe just a little?"

He laughed, then dumped it into the cornmeal.

"Trust me. We'll need it."

I stared wide-eyed as heaps of turmeric spilled into the dish. But I didn't say anything. He'd done too much work, and I still felt useless, a feeling that stopped any further complains.

"Get your spoon ready," he finally said. "It's time."

He carefully lifted the pot by its handles, scooped out a bite from the mush, and nodded as he chewed. It looked like the best meal the man had ever tasted! I was surprised drool wasn't leaking from the edges of his mouth from enjoyment.

I furrowed my brow. "It's that good, huh?"

More heavy nods. He took one more large bite before passing me the handles.

"Be careful. It's hot."

Finally, it was my turn! I smelled it, as is my habit with food. Passing a smell test, I slowly lifted a spoonful into my mouth and began to chew. Then I stopped chewing. My cheeks briefly inflated as I barely resisted the temptation to retch.

It took a full minute for me to process that bite, still aware I couldn't offend his cooking after all he'd done to put up with me. As we traded spoonfuls from the pot, my bites grew smaller. I couldn't stand the yellow gruel.

"I'm good," I finally said, holding my hand up to the pot.

Bradley scowled, glancing at the remaining cornmeal. "Really?" he asked. "We gotta finish what we cook, man. There's no tossing this into the desert, not unless you want coyotes visiting us tonight. Eat up, brother."

Choosing between coyotes or cornmeal was difficult. Eventually, I chose the latter. But my bites remained so small, Bradley nearly finished the entire dish by himself.

"Look," he said, edging out the dregs of the remaining specks with his titanium spoon. "I'll be on scrape duty tonight, but if I'm scraping, you're washing. Try and help out more next time, too."

Maybe if there was less turmeric, it wouldn't have been a problem...

I nodded, and he showed me how to wash the pot by pouring water into it and scraping the edges fully clean with his fingers. He looked barbaric doing so, and I'd rather not have had his dirty appendages pressing up against our eating bowl, but it was quite evident there would be no dishwashing machines on this trail.

Afterward, I staved off my remaining hunger with some handfuls from my feedbag, a large Ziploc filled with granola, dried fruits, nuts, and seeds. It did the job well enough.

"Here, take this," he said, handing me something small and soft. "A nightly treat."

It was a coconut rolled date, and it looked delicious. "Thanks."

He nodded. "Yeah, man. What's mine is yours."

My teeth sank easily into the chewy delight, and I smiled. I could have eaten fifteen more.

By now, night had blanketed the desert. I brushed my teeth by the light of a headlamp and crawled into my sleeping bag, stuffing my jacket behind my head to use as a pillow.

Bradley stood at the edge of the campsite overlooking the terrain, brushing his teeth with baking soda. He had explained the powder's purpose to me at Bob's. It was free from fluoride, a chemical that supposedly calcifies the brain's pineal gland, or the third eye, as he called it. I guess I would have to make due with a calcified pineal until I could find some powder of my own.

After a long brushing, he began combing his hair with a small bamboo brush. The teeth passed through his long, black mane with difficulty as he fought against the knots, tossing the fallen strands to the wind. I wasn't watching him per se, but one can't help but notice what another person is doing when there is absolutely nothing else to do.

Nevertheless, the littering concerned me. Bob Reiss had explained to us an important rule of hiking: *leave no trace.* The rule was sacred, one hikers supposedly paid careful attention to, making sure never to leave any evidence of their presence whether it was trash or the coals from a campfire the night prior. If anything, nature should be left in better condition than how it was found.

I had to probe further.

"So, you're just gonna throw those hairs into the wild?" I asked.

"Bro," he scoffed, "hairs are nature's tumbleweeds." He cast another few strands to the breeze, which vanished into the darkness.

"Right..."

After further thought, I realized that actually, tumble-weeds were nature's tumbleweeds. But I didn't care to press the issue any further. In fact, as I ran my hands through my own shoulder-length hair in an attempt to untangle it, I couldn't help but think that bringing the hairbrush was a good idea.

I was ready for bed but penned a short journal entry, recalling the difficulties of the day. There were too many to recount and sleep was approaching fast.

The urge came to check my phone. Of course, it had died, probably hours ago. If the overnight charging hadn't worked, then something was likely wrong. And if that was the case, my phone would be of little use for the rest of the journey. Hopefully, I wouldn't need it but for the occasional check-in with family and friends when we reached town every four to seven days.

I flicked off the light of my headlamp. The world went black, and the light of the moon shone down on the desert. The sky was vast. Thousands of stars filled the heavens, more than I'd ever seen before. Bradley was right about one thing—there was something special about the night sky. The stars demanded my attention for some time. I was small in comparison, compared to it all, compared to what lay ahead.

Even though dinner was a disaster and barefooting had hardly gone any better, at the very least, I was grateful Bradley had put up with me for the first day. Maybe with some luck tomorrow would be better, but I had a feeling it was going to be twelve more miles of limping across rocks.

I rested my feet against the top of my backpack as did Bradley. He'd told me new blood would flow to the legs to heal the feet. I'd try anything if it meant feeling like my feet weren't breaking.

"Night," I said.

"Goodnight, brother."

Just as I began drifting to sleep, a loud, guttural snore erupted a few feet from me.

I turned over. *How did he already fall asleep? It's only been a couple of minutes since we spoke.*

I waited, hoping he would stop. In my experience, people stop snoring if given enough time. But Bradley wasn't like other people. The sounds only grew louder and more bizarre. I reached over and shook him.

"You were snoring."

"Thanks."

It was a surprisingly polite thing to say after being woken. Time passed, and the quiet returned. He soon fell asleep, this time silently.

A rustling came from the bushes nearby. My eyes opened wide.

What was that?

I sat up and glanced around the campsite before burrowing back into my mummy bag, straining my ears to the outside world. Everything was hushed.

A chorus of howls echoed in the distance.

Are those coyotes?

Sleeping so exposed to the wild, not knowing what surrounded me, sent my heart beating against my chest.

I prayed for a coyote, snake, and spider-free night. And above all, I prayed I would survive this journey alongside the guy sleeping beside me.

CHAPTER 3

April 24, 2015
Mile 8, Desert Campsite (2,552 miles to go)

I felt as if I had only just shut my eyes before I woke up the next morning. As I peered out to the sun peaking over the horizon and the clouds floating along the morning skies, the bones in my feet still felt as if they'd been crunched from the inside out.

The air was cold, so I donned my jacket-pillow and began to stand. The process had never taken as long as it did today, and an aching inferno ignited in my feet before I returned to a sit, massaging them with my thumbs.

The thought of walking twelve miles across a rock-laden earth loomed over me like a storm cloud. I gazed over the landscape, taking my first heavy, conscious breaths.

When I finally found the strength to stand, I headed out into the desert and took a leak among the cacti.

Bradley made oats for breakfast. I had high aspirations for the meal, but it tasted like bland Styrofoam. Perhaps they hadn't been cooked thoroughly, he suggested. A few ample dashes of cinnamon convinced him the dish was much improved. I thought the opposite, forcing myself to consume what was planned as our staple breakfast meal for the rest of the trek. I hardly spoke as we ate.

Our packing routine followed. It always took time packing away one's life. I crammed in my sleeping bag before preparing my groundsheet, shaking it hard with both hands to rid it of dirt before shoving it to the bottom. Warmth was returning to the desert, and I changed back into yesterday's clothes then packed away my clothes bag. The stove and gas canister fit into the cookpot, and the food bag was packed last for easy access to snacks. I cinched the mouth of the pack taut, folded down the lid, and then clipped and tightened the pack cover. After one last look around the campsite, we nodded and set up the trail.

"Remember," he said, "we've got to reach kickoff before the day's over."

I could have done without the reminder.

As I had feared, the minefields returned and my pace slowed to a crawl. Bradley forged ahead, again leaving footprints at which to stare. Glimpses of his silhouette came into view every now and again. I stopped for a moment, sniffling and holding back my tears.

"Hey," said a voice.

I turned my head to see someone behind me. I put myself together and stepped off the trail to make way for the coming hiker as was customary.

"You're good," he said. "I like this pace."

It was then I noticed his massive backpack—a ridiculous amount of weight for anyone to carry—and the way he hunched over as if he was about to topple forward. He seemed to be enjoying his hike just as much as me.

"My name's Eedahahm," he said.

"David."

We shook hands.

"Good to meet you, David. It looks like I'm not going much faster than you. Want to walk?"

I looked up to the distance. Bradley was nowhere to be seen, and it was probably time to get moving.

"Yeah, man."

Eedahahm was similar to me in height and age but slightly pudgier compared to my wiry frame. He panted as we walked, describing to me his Asian heritage, the concepts of Kintsugi, the practice of repairing broken pottery with gold, and Wabi Sabi, the acceptance of imperfection. They were particularly interesting ideas, and it was most comforting being around someone who was struggling just as much as I was.

"So, what's in your backpack?" I asked.

"Mostly gear," he said.

"That's a lot of gear."

He laughed. "Yeah, it's pretty heavy... I brought my laptop, camera, and chargers, so I may have to get rid of something... eventually."

Something told me he wouldn't be able to carry any of it to Canada, but as a barefoot pilgrim, who was I to judge? I didn't press his situation any further. Nor did he press mine.

There was rarely shade to be found beside the trail, so we stopped in the sun to drink water in a clearing beside some rocks. The surrounding desert was boundless, hills crawling across the landscape, and I soon found myself in one of those positions where I could lay unmoved for many eternities.

"I'm glad we met," he eventually said, throwing his fifty-pound backpack around his shoulders. "I think I'm heading out now, but I'm sure we'll see each other again."

I thanked him and waved goodbye as he vanished around the bend. At my pace, I figured that was the last I'd see of him.

The day was long, night was nearing, and I hobbled up the mountain switchback realizing this would be the way of the trail: gradual and sustained elevation changes upward over the mountains, traversing across the sides of mountains, and slow sloping descents into valleys. If there was a climb, it usually continued for a good while, at least long enough to make me rethink everything about my life. But the climbs always came to an end, and a descent awaited me. During this downhill trod, I thought about how there was surely another climb right at the bottom. Of course, sometimes it went flat, and all I could do was hope for rock-free, dirt stretches of trail.

When the uphill trek finally leveled off, I stepped forward to overlook the ridge. Darkness covered the lake, but I knew it was my destination.

Lake Morena. The flickering lights and faint noises coming from the basin confirmed my suspicions.

I descended the trail, which sloped down to reach a gravel parking lot filled with hundreds of vehicles. I traveled through the lot toward a group of people sitting around a campfire. Taking a deep breath, I approached thinking Bradley had to be there somewhere.

"It's you!"

I looked up. A woman sat beside the fire, her eyes fixed on my bare feet.

"We've been seeing your tracks for the last twenty miles. Look, Sherpa. It's one the barefooters!"

A wild, grey-haired man glanced up from his food preparations, staring at me as a child would an animal at a zoo exhibit.

"I'll be damned," he said, reaching out his hand.

We shook. I still had no idea what was happening.

"Great to meet you," Sherpa said. "I've been wonderin' if you were human or Sasquatch! There should be two of ye' from the tracks—one big and one small. So, where's the other?"

I sighed and feigned a smile. "Yeah, that's Bradley. Have you seen him? Tall, skinny guy with long black hair and… barefoot."

"Nope," he said. "But yer welcome to sit with us."

"Oh… sure."

Might as well. I couldn't set up camp until Bradley came around.

After chatting with the couple for some time, the thought of looking for Bradley lingered in the back of my mind. Just then, a figure emerged from the shadows.

"Found you," Bradley said.

The man glanced up from the fire. "Are you two brothers?!" Sherpa blurted out.

We laughed.

"Just trail brothers," Bradley said.

The man chuckled. "Based on the tracks, I figured you two would be father and son. You two will be gettin' a wild trail name, no doubt. Something like... the barefoot brothers!"

We laughed and rolled our eyes. *Please, anything but that...*

We'd been chatting with Sherpa for quite some time, and it was getting late.

Bradley stood, signaling that we should get moving. "Do you happen to know of a good place to set up camp?" he asked.

"We're in the van tonight," Sherpa said, pointing to the lot, "but the hiker campsites are past the bathrooms... that way. If you ever need anything, please come on by."

We thanked them and departed into the darkness.

Led by the light of our headlamps, we weaved up the road, passing campsites and tents and a structure that must have been the restrooms before coming to an open clearing among the trees which was quite a distance from the parking lot.

"Should we try setting up the tarp?" I asked.

Bradley looked up into the sky. It was filled with clouds. "Yeah."

We had arrived in camp at a much later time than the night before, but we drew the tarp and stakes from their stuff sacks and spread them onto our groundsheets.

"So where do we start?" I asked.

Bradley grabbed the tarp, shook it confidently and walked over to a grove of trees. "Come," he said. "It should fit between these trunks. Find the tie outs and stake down the corners."

"Sure."

We got to work, but I had no idea where to start. I held the string in my hand wondering how the knots should be tied to the tarp and where the stakes went. Long minutes passed, but after numerous tries, our tarp lay flat atop the grass.

Knowing how little research I'd done on shelters, I wasn't prepared to see Bradley fumbling with what was supposed to be our home for the next six months.

I narrowed my eyes and looked at Bradley sidelong. "I thought you said you'd done this before?"

He turned and stared at me. "Just give me a second," he hissed. "I'm trying to remember how he did it in the video…"

I took a step back and watched. It seemed there was nothing else I could do.

"Maybe we should just forget it?" I regretted the suggestion as soon as it left my lips.

"Wasn't this your idea?" he shot back. "Now lend me a hand. Or at least grab your light."

Reluctantly, I held the tarp and shone my light while he tried looping some sort of knot.

As the struggle continued, the sound of footsteps approached. Light poked through the trees, becoming brighter as it came near.

"You guys need any help?" asked the voice. It was a middle-aged woman and her husband.

"That would be amazing," I said.

We all set to work together. With the couple's help, the tarp stood taut and hovered above the ground with impromptu knots. At least it was something livable. I wish I could say I'd retained the information, but I was so exhausted that everything flew right by me. I feared Bradley was in the same boat.

We thanked the couple as they disappeared back into the campground.

Tossing our belongings beneath the shelter, we readied ourselves for bed and collapsed into our sleeping bags. My eyelids were half-closed by the time I zipped it up to my shoulder. Two days of barefooting had taken its toll. I was too tired to journal. At least tomorrow was kickoff, which meant there were no trail miles to walk.

What could possibly go wrong?

I shut my eyes and slept despite Bradley's snoring.

CHAPTER 4

April 26, 2015
Mile 20, Lake Morena Campground PCT Kickoff (2,640 miles to go)

I shifted uneasily as the morning's warmth woke me from slumber, filtering down through the overstretched tarp hovering above me. A dull chatter filled the campgrounds. Bradley groaned and stretched, which was my signal to rise.

I changed clothes in my sleeping bag before attempting another long journey from lying down to standing. It was even more difficult than yesterday. My legs were noodles. My feet had somehow worsened. I grabbed my Jesus sandals and tied the laces around my legs. Since we weren't on the trail, I'd told myself the miles didn't count so I could wear shoes. It didn't surprise me that Bradley opted for bare feet.

"Let's go," he said, stepping out into the sunlight. "We have to check in and find out where we're needed for volunteering."

We rolled out into the morning, decided to leave the tarp up in case we'd need it that night, left our things, and then followed a flow of hikers toward a nearby field.

I was hobbling even while wearing sandals. Stares followed us on our walk, but we met them with smiles.

The flow led us to an open field filled with hundreds of hikers amid rows of vendor tents. We were two pilgrims among many. Four thousand hikers were attempting the trail this season, and a few hundred of those were in attendance at this year's kickoff.

Class of 2015 PCT hikers pose at kickoff. Bradley and I missed this photo!

Late April was a critical start time. Bradley had explained that it allowed the snow to melt in the Sierra Mountains of central California and provided enough time to outrun the winter snowfall in the Washington Cascades, which would shut down the trail. We'd soon be starting the trail alongside the herd, this mass of hikers surrounding us in the field.

The place was like a fairground, and we walked along the alleyways of canopies where vendors sold goods, gear, books, and guides on our way to the check-in line. We waited before receiving our nametags and volunteer assignments; we were both on breakfast duty. It was another short walk across the field toward our designated canopy: the outdoor kitchen.

"How goes it, boys?" asked a round man with a tall white hat. "I'm Chef Paul. You two volunteers?"

"At your service," Bradley said.

"Good. Follow me."

He turned and led us beneath the canopy. Others were already hard at work behind rows of tables filled with massive cans of beans and cheese.

"It's not the healthiest food, but it'll feed the masses," said the chef. "Nobody will supervise you. This way."

Following him, I leaned over to Bradley. "Did he just say nobody is supervising us?"

"I think so…"

Chef Paul halted in the back of the canopy beside the stoves where a middle-aged man with leathery skin and sunglasses toiled over rows of huge boiling pots.

"Nobody will help you from here," the chef said, turning to leave.

"Huh?" Bradley asked.

The man reached out his leathery hand. "The name's Nobody."

"Oh," I said. "Good to meet you."

We were still getting accustomed to the fact that everyone who hiked the trail got a new name called a trail name.

"We've got to get to work," he said. "We're running behind. Take these, and choose your positions."

Nobody turned and handed Bradley a giant spoon while I was given a can opener.

With little more instruction, we got to work. Hundreds of cans needed to be cranked open and passed to Bradley, who then poured the contents into pots for stirring. A delicious aroma filled the canopy.

I handed a can to Nobody, who then smashed it into a round disk with some flattening contraption.

"This your first thru-hike?" he asked.

"Yeah," I said with a smile. "What about you?"

"Won't be hiking this year. I hiked it many years ago. Ages ago, it seems."

My eyes lit up.

Someone who has hiked the trail! I hadn't yet met a finisher before and had a thousand questions for him.

"Do you have any advice for new hikers?" I asked.

He crunched another tin can and threw it atop the others. "One step at a time," he said.

I nodded.

"What did the trail teach you?" I asked him.

He continued his work and shook his head. "A lot. I remember the trail like it was yesterday. And yet it seems the whole thing was just a dream."

Just a dream? What did he mean by that?

"Let's go, everyone!" shouted Chef Paul. "It's time to serve breakfast!"

When I looked up from my work, I noticed a long line of people forming across the field. Everyone in this entire kick-off was now waiting on us.

"Who needs help?" Chef Paul repeated as he moved about the canopy.

We continued our work until a voice shouted from just outside the canopy.

"Are you shittin' me?!" The words rang loud beneath the canopy, and everybody glanced up from their preparations.

A man had stepped out of line, and his face was red with anger.

"What's taking so long? I've been waitin' here for goddamn twenty minutes now, so where's the damn food?!"

Chef Paul met the man in front of the canopy with long strides.

"Sir," said the chef. "It'll be ready when it's ready. We're doing the best we can."

The man's stare was frightening and firm, but Chef Paul held his gaze. Finally, the man turned and retreated back into line.

I turned to Bradley. "Did you just see that?" I was amazed at how Chef Paul had handled the situation.

He nodded. "The man's done work on himself, that's for sure."

It was the sort of demeanor I wished to one day cultivate when presented with such a tense situation.

We picked up the pace, and ten minutes later the long foldout tables outside the canopy were lined with hundreds of tin foil wrapped bean, cheese, and lettuce burritos. A single burrito would be enough to fill any reasonable human's stomach, but in a world of hikers, most would eat two or three.

After breakfast had been served and cleanup was finished, Chef Paul assembled us around the tables to dismiss the crew. "Enjoy your evening and be sure to check out the tents. You may find something there of interest…"

Free at last, we thanked our chef and made our way to the tents to join in the day's festivities, which were now in full swing.

My attention soon fell on an unusually large crowd surrounding a group of conjoined canopies. The banner draped across the booth read: The Wolverines. We approached with curiosity.

Sitting tall in her chair across from her latest volunteer, the wolverine was in the midst of her work as we approached. A middle-aged woman shifted in her chair before her vast assortment of possessions, which were spread out in the space between them. The wolverine scanned the items thoroughly and carefully.

She bent over and picked up a stack of paperback books and laughed.

"Four books?" she asked. "A bit much, don't you think?"

The woman cringed and shrugged. "Well, my daughter gave me this book… and my brother told me I had to read this one… and this one—"

"You get to pick one!" the wolverine said firmly before turning to the audience. "Even one's too many, but we have to start somewhere."

We continued watching as the wolverine grilled the hiker, tossing more and more items into a shed pile to be sent home or given away.

Bradley looked at me. I already knew what he was thinking. This was exactly what we were looking for. If we could shed more pack weight, imagine how much easier barefooting would be!

"Who's next?" shouted a large man beneath the awning next to us. "Who's ready for a shakedown?"

Bradley stepped his way to the front. "We're ready for you… if you're ready for us."

The man scoffed and ushered us into his canopy. We sat in the hot seats, ready for scrutiny.

"Steve Climber," he said, extending his hand. "I'm here to help you today, boys. Unload your packs and let's shed some weight."

After organizing our belongings into piles, we looked up in anticipation.

Steve started with Bradley. He scanned his belongings until his eyes narrowed. He picked up Bradley's homemade rubber gladiator sandals. "Do you think you'll need two pairs of shoes, bud?"

A deep smirk dug into Bradley's cheeks. "That's my only pair," he said.

Steve's gaze fell to Bradley's feet. His eyebrow rose. "Hold on… no shoes?"

"Yes, sir," Bradley said. "We decided we're hiking the trail barefoot."

Steve's eyes widened. The small crowd gathered around our canopy grew slightly larger.

"For real?" Steve asked.

We nodded.

"Well, that changes everything," he laughed. "In that case, you'll need to go as close to ultra-light as possible. Let's go through this again."

Steve shuffled through our belongings, and the quest to go ultra-light grew our shed pile significantly. We shed blankets, sleeping bag liners, books, extra clothes, external chargers, and the bug bivy. Glancing at the pile made me nervous, but lifting my remarkably lighter backpack brought a smile to my face.

My stomach sank when Bradley offered up his first aid kit and water filter, knowing I'd have to match his boldness. Steve reminded us that if we insisted on shedding these items, to do so at our own risk and to borrow from other hikers if needed. It seemed there would be plenty of others on the trail, so it wouldn't be an issue.

As our discussions continued, a lanky man wearing a wide-brimmed hat stepped his way into the canopy.

"Hold up there, Steve," the man said. He was glaring in our direction. "So, these are the barefoot guys, huh? You're not helping them, are you?"

Steve chuckled. "That's how they said they want to hike it, Bill."

The man removed his hat and held it against his hip. "They won't last a day out there, Steve. Just look at 'em! You there," he said, gesturing at me. "How much barefooting experience do you have?"

His stare was penetrating, but I wasn't about to say what he wanted to hear. I was committed to barefooting the moment that elderly couple passed by in the first few miles. I kept silent, hoping the others might speak up.

"Who knows if they will or won't make it all the way, Bill," Steve said. "Anyway, I don't know if it's much of your business."

"Oh, it *is* my business, Steve," Bill said. Sweat was beginning to run down his forehead. "This is damn right foolish.

You're putting yourself at risk, these boys' lives at risk, and I'm not going to have it."

Steve stood slowly and calmly, his eyes locked onto Bill's. "These are two grown men making their own life decisions. I'm sure as hell not going to stop them from hiking the trail. Are you going to stop them, Bill? You're damn right I'm going to help them. I'm going to make sure they're as safe as they can possibly be."

A timeless stare passed between the two men before Bill scoffed and turned away, a trail of murmurs following him out the tent.

Steve sat back down. He placed his hands on his knees and sighed.

"Listen, boys. If you're doing this, you should commit. But you must promise me one thing... keep one pair of shoes. Trust me, you don't want to be stuck out there without them. Don't worry about Bill. You'll find plenty of re-sistance along the trail with or without shoes."

We nodded, shook Steve's hand, and returned to our campsite to discuss the event. Since there was no post office at the campground, we'd have to hike another twenty-one miles to Mount Laguna, the next town, before we could send anything home.

Another two days and twenty-one miles to town? I couldn't stand the thought of venturing back into the desert, but the promise of sending home our excess belongings motivated me. Going ultra-light meant smooth sailing all the way to Canada.

We were served dinner back at the kitchen canopy among the hikers as the sun set over the horizon. Sensing sleep was coming soon, we headed back to our campsite.

"Boys," whispered a voice, "check this out."

It was Chef Paul and Nobody. They were standing be-neath a tree beside two chairs and two large pots filled with water. Steam was rising from the pots.

"Thanks for your hard work this morning. I thought you two might enjoy this. We were going to pour out this water but figured you two could put it to use first. Go ahead, take a load off."

Our faces lit up as we headed beneath the trees. We eased back against the lounge chairs and dipped our toes into the hot liquid. A warm rush spread through my body from toe to head as I sank further back into the chair and plunged the rest of my legs in.

I closed my eyes. I guess service really did have its perks. As my feet soaked in the hot water, I thought about how I'd sleep more soundly that night.

CHAPTER 5

April 28, 2015
Mile 40, Mount Laguna (2,610 miles to go)

I stepped the white-painted line along the interstate highway, trying my best to avoid the scalding hot blacktop. My trekking poles (or what was left of them... the tips had nearly worn down into nothing) clicked against the pavement, barely holding me upright. Bradley walked the pavement beside me as though walking on comfy kitchen tiles.

Two days had passed since leaving kickoff, two days that had dragged on infinitely longer than the days before it. Bland meals, blaring heat, and blistered feet were now my life. They were all I knew. And to cap it off, a searing pain throbbed ceaselessly against the front of my skull as if my brain was going to explode at any moment.

My only saving grace was that supposedly we were nearing Mount Laguna's post office. I'd been searching the rows of pines lining the highway for this allusive building for hours, seeing only houses buried deep within the woods. Leaving the desert brush for the forest was a welcomed change of scenery, but I was more than ready for town and the chance to rid myself of our extra weight.

"Hey!" shouted a voice. It had come from the woods. We stopped and turned our attention to the west.

The yell came again. "What on earth are you two doing? Get back here!"

Between the gaps in the pines, I spotted an old woman waving her arms on her front porch.

One of my eyebrows shot up. "Is she yelling at *us*?"

Bradley looked away and walked on. "Don't have time for that," he laughed. "The post likely closes soon."

I started after him. "Yeah."

The amount of attention and the diversity of reactions we were attracting by barefooting were both strange and warranted. As we meandered up the highway, her shouts fell silent behind the pines.

Before long, the trees opened, and a large general store emerged in the distance.

Relief poured over me. It was Mount Laguna.

Ten to fifteen hikers sitting beneath the shade of a porch greeted us kindly, many glancing at our feet as we hobbled up the store's front steps. The place was like a mini-mart inside, stocked with aisles of snacks and fridges of cold drinks.

A group of hikers was gathered in the corner of the shop, ruffling through large boxes filled with clothing, gear, and food.

"Whoa," Bradley said as we approached. "What's going on here?"

"Hiker boxes!" said one of the hikers as he continued his hunting. "If you're carrying something you don't want, you can leave it here. Someone will take it."

"So, everything here is fair game?" Bradley asked.

"That's right."

Our eyes widened. The boxes were overflowing with all kinds of foods, offering some much-needed diversity from our diet of cornmeal and oats.

Thus my attention became transfixed on the food boxes. Hikers had their own cuisine, and the various bags of colored powders and dehydrated foods were all but foreign to me. While I was most interested in what was most evidently edible and properly labeled, Bradley was busy studying the unlabeled Ziplocs and sealed bags. This would become one of his favorite games, identifying what he called 'the hidden gems.'

How he had learned this skill I wasn't quite sure, but he could easily identify most baggies at first glance. Others required further study. A sniff test sometimes did the job, but if that didn't work, the taste test would. And Bradley wasn't afraid to try anything, even if I thought the contents looked beyond sketchy.

After scoring a few precious gems and a fair number of other meals, we decided to deposit our cornmeal and oats into the hiker box.

Maybe someone will be really desperate, I thought.

Next, it came time to shed our excess belongings. After donating some items to the boxes, we headed to the front desk where the gentleman behind the counter handed us empty boxes to ship home the rest.

We kept only the absolute bare minimum of things, even going so far as to break our toothbrushes in half, an ultralight tactic we'd seen used by other hikers.

The most difficult items to relinquish were the water filter and tarp. Bradley was confident the water filter wasn't necessary, reasoning that if we were filtering out the harmful particles, we were also filtering out the beneficial particles. I hadn't done any research on the topic, and I doubted he had either. However, his reasoning seemed to make perfect sense to me at the time.

Sending home the tarp was my greater fear, an idea we'd been toying with for the last couple days. But after six nights of safe sleeping beneath open skies and six days of carrying it around in my backpack without using it, I finally placed it in the box and sealed it shut.

We grinned as we lifted our backpacks. Mine felt like a sack of feathers. Maybe barefooting *was* possible.

Items sent home: Nalgenes and Platypus water bag (replaced with Smart Water bottles from the general store), water filters, adventurer's hat, camp towel, passport, bandana, beanie/balaclava, toe shoes, extra socks, Jesus sandals, gloves, pants, shirts, sleeping bag liner, underwear, swimsuit, external battery, first aid kit; also sent home, but not pictured: our tarp.

Smiling, we walked out the front door of the post to the evening sun and rested beneath the porch shade while chatting with other hikers. Others remarked how small our packs looked, and many believed we were crazy to send home our shelter.

"What if it rains?" they asked.

"We've got groundsheets," Bradley said. "We'll just wrap ourselves up like burritos."

It wasn't ideal, but it was what barefooting was requiring of us! Plus, what were the odds of heavy rainfall in the desert?

We hadn't sat long on the porch before a sedan came roaring up into the parking lot. Everyone turned at the screeching noises and out stepped a familiar presence.

It was the angry front porch lady from the miles before reaching Mount Laguna.

Noticing her presence, I shuffled behind a few wide-eyed hikers holding back their laughter, but it was too late for Bradley. Her attention was honed, and her eyes were fierce with determination.

"You're making a huge mistake, young man!" she shouted before walking around her car, yanking a pair of shoes from the trunk and marching toward him.

"Wear these," she said, holding them out with outstretched arms as she continued her lecture.

Bradley remained still, taking the abuse with dignity, trying his best to calmly and politely refuse her offering. But with one last-ditch effort, she shoved them to his chest and drove away. There he stood, alone in the middle of the parking lot, the pair of shoes dangling from his fingertips.

He checked the shoe size beneath the tongue and rolled his eyes. They would fit him perfectly. He walked over to where I sat among the other hikers and tossed them on the ground.

"Anyone need some shoes?" he laughed. As committed to barefooting as he was, there was no way he was going to wear them.

We snickered and made it clear we wanted nothing to do with the shoes. He then proceeded to pace the general store premises trying to pawn them off onto another in-need hiker, eventually discarding them in the hiker box.

"Did I hear someone say they had an extra pair of shoes?" another hiker finally piped up. "Mine are too small. My feet must have grown from all this walking."

"Thank God," Bradley said, snagging them from the hiker box and handing them over. After finding they were a perfect fit, the man graciously accepted them. At least someone had been helped by the day's events! Although the old lady wouldn't have approved of the re-gifting, in some small way Bradley felt like he'd done the guy a favor. And he had!

Bradley sat down next to me. "Do you think it was a sign?"

"To put on shoes?" I asked.

"Yeah."

"Maybe…"

Even in the shade, I could feel the heat of the sun simmering off the concrete lot. I wasn't ready to go back onto the trail and neither was Bradley. It didn't help that my brain was still pounding against the back of my head from our latest two-day stint in the desert. In search of cold water, we headed down the road and found a table at the Mount Laguna Café.

It felt nice to escape the sun. The blades of the ceiling fans cast shadows against the walls and filled the room with a gentle breeze. A waitress came by and served us pitchers of ice water. We chugged glass after glass. The cold liquid slid down my throat, chilling my insides and lightening my forehead. Strength was slowly returning to me. I found an outlet beside our table, plugged in my phone, and decided it would be a good time to email our friends and family back home with an update.

April 28, 2015
Subject: "Shedding Skin"

We have spent a week on the trail thus far, and it has been challenging, exhausting, and deeply rewarding. We are finding our rhythm and embracing all the necessary changes: expected and unexpected. We expected we would need to drop weight from our packs but didn't expect the extent of the weight to be so large. Our bodies simply can't carry some of the comforts our minds desire. We realize this journey is about putting one foot in front of the other. It is no different from your journey. Dropping weight and comforts will accelerate our pace, and we shed not just physical pounds but emotional tons.

Being without you has amplified our appreciation for you, and we hope this message is received in good faith. No matter how stressful our day can be, we realize it is paramount to appreciate the moment and whatever unfolds in front of us. May you be happy in your moment.

Love,
Bradley & David

I enjoyed writing these emails to friends and family back home. I felt closer to them in those moments. Bradley did, too. He was a skilled writer, and the shared reflection helped us reconnect, take a step back, and uncover new insights.

I took another gulp of water, crossed my arms on the table, and rested my head. I'd given up so much so quickly, and the first few days seemed like a blur. The trail was forcing us to let go of everything: comfort, friends, family, shoes, and shelter. I closed my eyes and took a breath, hoping I had made the right decision by coming on the trail.

CHAPTER 6

April 28, 2015
Mile 40, Mount Laguna (2,610 miles to go)

The pulsing against my skull settled as the two of us sipped water in relative silence. As I lifted my head from the table, I noticed Bradley's gaze locked on our waitress as she re-filled our pitcher. I understood his intrigue. After all, she was noticeably beautiful, strong, and fair skinned.

Striking up a conversation, we discovered her name was Kitty. She was a veteran hiker who had spent the past few summers living in the van parked in front of the café.

When I asked her how she got the name Kitty, she laughed. "Well, I started eating organic cat food on the trail. I swear it doesn't taste nearly as bad as it sounds! Plus, it's affordable and packed with protein, so why not?"

It sounded like something Bradley would say.

As she turned and left for the kitchen, Bradley's stare turned back to me.

"She's cute, huh?" I asked.

He nodded. Kitty came back out, making her rounds, re-filling drinks. Bradley seemed to watch her out of the corner of his eye the whole time.

"So, what do you think, David?" Bradley asked after placing his empty glass on the table. "My feet are telling me they need another night's rest before we head out again."

I nodded emphatically, unable to agree more. Although my headache was passing, the knots in my feet remained just as tight as ever. I'd do anything to delay putting in more miles.

Kitty had overheard us from a nearby table. Her face lit up, and she approached us. "Oh! You two should camp at the nearby campground then," she said. "There should be other hikers there. I'll probably stop by too."

Bradley smiled. "Works for me."

"Let's do it."

The sun sank beyond the trees, and we set out down the highway, which was now shaded and cool. The white painted line was still a much smoother walk than the blacktop.

A map mounted on a display at the campground entrance showed a winding road lined with campsites, one of them reserved for thru-hiker camping. I laughed. The hiker's campsite was separated by some distance from the others. I figured it must either be our stench or our noisiness.

The road bent around the corner and the rich, oaky scent of a campfire reached my nostrils. We followed the smell and evening chatter to a group of hikers sitting around a fire.

A familiar face stood out to me. "Eedaham!"

He shot to his feet with a bright smile.

"David!" he said. "You two made it!"

I laughed, shaking my head and heading over to join them. I thought I'd never see him again. It took a while to reach them as the sharp pine needles littered about the campground pricked my feet.

A boy named Ben was the first hiker we met beside the fire. A thick, black beard hung down from his chin, and a small backpacking guitar sat in his lap. He smoked a joint with one hand and shook hands with the other.

"You boys want a puff?" he asked.

"I'm good," I said.

"No thanks," Bradley said.

"Suit yourself…"

The end of the joint glowed a bright red as he inhaled and passed it to his right.

I was noticing that smoking was prevalent among this counterculture of thru-hikers. Tobacco and weed were both readily available, but Bradley and I had discussed our shared desire to abstain entirely from these substances in an attempt to distance our new selves from our college selves.

In so many ways, the trail was a spiritual journey for us, and while we held no judgment toward any other hiker, these substances reminded us only of our old, miserable selves. If we could help it, they wouldn't play a role for us on this pilgrimage.

More hikers soon gathered around the circle to kick back, relax, and chat. Ben's fingers began moving along the frets of his guitar, and we quieted down to listen. As he increased his tempo, the strumming set the tone for the evening. Pretty soon everyone had loosened up and joined in with improvisational song, humming, clapping, or beat-boxing.

As our music spread through the woods, another two figures joined us around the campfire: a middle-aged man and a young girl. They clapped when the song ended.

"You guys are so rad!" the man said. "What are your names?"

We welcomed them with a new round of introductions.

"I'm Canyon, and this is Rabbit," said the man. "Good to meet you."

"Likewise," I said.

The two were a father-daughter hiking team, a duo I was surprised to see. Rabbit in particular looked remarkably young, still a child, but differences between people were beginning to carry less and less importance on the trail.

Chapter 6

"How old are you, Rabbit?" Bradley asked.

Her shoulder-length mop of blond hair bounced as she glanced up. "Nine," she said confidently.

I pointed at a small green backpack sitting next to her feet. "Is that your backpack, Rabbit?" I asked.

"Yep."

"Rabbit carries all her own gear," Canyon said.

"Daaang, Rabbit!" Ben said. "Are you two going all the way to Canada?"

"Yep," Rabbit said with a soft laugh.

"Daaang!" Ben repeated. "You're a badass, Rabbit!"

Canyon laughed, and Rabbit nodded.

"Our crew is one man—I mean woman—down at the moment," Canyon said. "Rabbit's mom, Sky, is joining us around mile three hundred."

I wondered if we'd ever get to meet Sky, imagining how cool a mother she might be given her name and her family.

The group's attention shifted toward Canyon and Rabbit. They were gems among the many twenty-something-year-old guys. The presence of a father figure, and the bright spirit of the young girl brought us comfort.

"How did you get into backpacking, Rabbit?" I asked.

"We hiked the John Muir Trail last year," she said.

"It's a 211-mile trail through the Sierra Mountains," Canyon responded. "It was Rabbit's Christmas wish to hike the PCT. So, here we are."

"Wait," Bradley said, shaking his head in disbelief. "This is too cool. You guys are incredible. What's your story, Canyon?"

He laughed. "I'm a Jewish scientist raised by hippies in a teepee. Explains a lot, doesn't it?"

"I'm excited to hear more about this," Bradley said.

We continued chatting until the night grew dark and it was time to cook dinner. Further discussions revealed Canyon as a wellspring of knowledge in the realms of religion and philosophy, and we soon discovered one of the hikers, Chris, was a Christian. Everyone seemed to be opening up.

Bradley turned to Chris. "You don't have a trail name yet, do you?"

Chris shook his head.

"How about... Transformer?" Bradley asked. "I think you'll be making some big changes on this trail."

He smiled, pleased by the suggestion. "I like it."

Bradley grinned. It was the first trail name I'd seen doled out successfully.

During our meal, I couldn't help but want to learn more from Rabbit. She was mature for a nine-year-old, and I imagined it took courage to embark on a trail with few, if any, other kids her age. If this bothered her, she didn't let it show. I watched as she picked up some twigs and began leaning them against one another.

"What are you building?" I asked.

"Houses," she said.

"That's pretty sweet," Bradley said, picking up a few sticks of his own. "Who are the houses for?"

"Fairies."

Our eyes grew big, and we nodded.

"Have you seen any yet?" Bradley asked.

"Nope," she said, dismissive of the idea.

We laughed.

"Give it more time," Bradley said.

After the meal was over, Ben picked the guitar back up, and we erupted into song. I noticed Kitty was watching over us from the shadows. Bradley must have noticed too as he went to talk with her.

It was fascinating how quickly relationships formed on the trail, but it wasn't a surprise. There was nowhere for us to hide. Devoid of the distractions, routine, stress, numbing, escapes, and addictions surrounding modern society, openness and vulnerability flowed easily. Everyone was a seeker, and there was always the chance that we might find something in these strangers turned friends.

The singing and chatting stretched late into the night before everyone decided it must be bedtime. Departing to our sleeping spots, the campground fell silent.

"How was your talk with Kitty?" I whispered to Bradley with a grin as we climbed into our sleeping bags.

Bradley shot me a sidelong glance and laughed as he shoved his legs into his blue sleeping bag. "Good. She told me that in all her years of working the café, she'd never seen a group connect so quickly and as close as ours."

I nodded.

"I guess that means we're doing something right."

"I think so too."

Stars filled the sky above. I missed my friends back home, but I was grateful for new ones, too.

"Night, brother."

"Night."

Sleep took hold when my eyelids shut.

CHAPTER 7

April 29, 2015
Garnett Peak, Mile 50 (2,600 miles to go)

Light shone golden all around the campsite as I squirmed from out the depths of my sleeping bag. I cringed while rising to my feet, but there was no more time to waste. It was time to walk.

Bradley and I packed up and headed north onto the trail. As much as I wanted to hike with our new friends, my pace wouldn't allow it. As we bore up the path, the trees vanished, and the trail led us back into the desert.

We came to a fork in the road after a long day of hiking. I looked out across the landscape, surveying the two options. One path continued along the PCT, and the other led toward a mountain peak rising in the east. Bradley stared at the distant mountain.

I glanced at him. "You're not thinking…?"

He smiled and turned to me. "What's being avoided must be confronted, right?"

I sighed.

"You have an aversion towards it, don't you?" he asked.

"I mean…"

"I say that's even more reason to do it."

He was right. I wasn't a fan of heights, and the last thing I cared for was to hike extra miles. However, the challenge had been presented, and I knew he wanted to confront the peak.

What am I supposed to do otherwise... wait for him?

"Alright," I said. "Let's do it."

Immediately, the path climbed upward, and soon the dirt trail turned to nothing but boulders. Realizing we should have left our backpacks at the fork, we set them down beside the trail and continued upward. Crawling on hands and feet atop the rocks toward the peak, I glanced up. The summit had seemed so close before, but the nearer we drew, the higher the peak rose into the sky.

My hair flapped as we climbed. Bradley was gone by now, likely already sitting at the top. My breath was heavy, and my mouth was dry. I pressed upward against the rocks with my hands to ease the pressure on my feet.

Finally, I reached the summit. Careful not to fall or slip, I nestled myself into a few boulders just below Bradley. He had been waiting for some time.

It was silent atop the peak, and I peered at the world below with tired eyes. Mountain spines curled in all directions but the beauty meant little to me in my delirium and thirst. I only wished I had brought water.

My crawl down the mountain began soon after reaching the top, knowing I'd need the head start to keep Bradley from having to wait.

It was a grueling climb down before we finally arrived at our backpacks. With a dried tongue and parched mouth, I reached for water and brought the bottle to my lips. It was empty.

A wave of panic crashed over me.

"I'm out, too," Bradley said. "But we'll be fine. Humans can go days without water."

I rolled my eyes. "What do the maps say?" I asked. "How far are we from water?"

Bradley reached into his hip-belt pocket for the papers and studied them for a moment. "We're miles away."

"Miles?" I asked. "How many?"

"Two or three."

I closed my eyes and massaged my fingers into my temples. Three miles wasn't a long way to hike for the casual hiker, but for the shoeless, three miles was a third of a day's work.

"Let me see."

Hoping he was wrong, I took the maps and tried to decipher the distance until we would reach water. My eyes drew a blank stare at the pieces of paper. Until this moment, I'd only cared about the elevation charts, a simple line graph that clearly showed how much uphill or downhill climbing lay in front of us. The topographical maps had been Bradley's assumed responsibility. I handed the maps back to Bradley.

"What do we do then?"

"What do you mean?" he asked. "We walk. There's no other choice."

I hated the answer, but he was right. Buckling our backpacks, we slogged toward the horizon.

Heat simmered from the desert floor, and dizziness began creeping over my field of vision. I looked into the distance, but something wasn't right. Instead of being on the ground, I was astonished to find myself much higher than expected, floating and suspended in mid-air.

Wondering how this had happened, I glanced around me, further confirming I was indeed standing in the sky. I looked down. A ring of vultures circled beneath me, and in the middle of that was a small corpse, still and lifeless on the desert floor.

Well... that doesn't look good! I thought.

I could see the body was burned and blackened, its eyes fathomless like the holes in a mask, and although it was dead, surrendering to the desert heat long ago, I felt a strange love for that body and a longing to return to it. I then realized that body was *my body*.

I blinked my eyes hard and shook my head furiously, and I found myself back on the ground, still walking steadily on the trail. I waved my hands in front of my face, never before so grateful to see hands. Thankfully, I was alive, but returning to the middle of an endless desert seemed barely a better fate.

My existence retreated into a narrow frame. I tried focusing on one step at a time. This was all that mattered, and it would be the only way out. The last thing I wanted was to end up like the barefoot Christopher McCandless—the thought of being found dead and barefoot, with shoes in my backpack, was quite possibly the most embarrassing thing I could think of. I marched forward, reaffirming my sureness in my steps.

Just this step. Now this one.

Realizing I'd lost track of time, I looked up. Bringing my hand to my head to shield the sun, Bradley was nowhere to be seen. In a panic, I turned to survey the desert behind me. Hanging his head and trotting forward was a slow-moving Bradley. For the first time, he seemed to be suffering just as much as I was. How I came to lead our two-man procession was a mystery to me, but I was amazed I'd built up so much steam during my hallucinations. I stopped, waiting for him to catch up.

"Keep going," he said. "I'm fine."

Now would probably be the right time to put on shoes, but then again, just a mile more and we would reach water... hopefully. I resisted the urge and continued north.

Time passed slowly from that point onward. Thoughts swirled in my head about how I wished to see my family and friends. There was so much I had to say to them, about how

I was sorry for the littlest things I'd said or done yet grateful for everything we'd been through. The preciousness of life dangled before my eyes. There was so much left undone that I had always dreamed of doing but never had. It made sense that no matter how long I lived, there would always be things left undone. The faces of family members and friends and the desire for life kept my legs moving.

When we climbed over the hill, we noticed two workers and a truck parked near an outhouse. I felt relieved to see people but our approach was met with blank stares.

"Water?" Bradley asked. It was all he could muster.

The two men turned to each other and shrugged.

"Don't have any," said one of them.

"Sorry."

"Isn't there a water source around here?" I asked.

They glanced at each other. Nothing.

For some reason, I imagined water bottles rolling around the truck's floorboards or propped up in the backseat cup holders, but I was too tired to ask anything more of it.

Searching the grounds for a spigot or a spring, we found nothing.

Is there really no water here?

Bradley pointed to a patch of grass beneath the shade of a tree. There we lay down, exhausted and dehydrated. I gazed thoughtlessly above into a tangled web of branches and sunbeams, studying the patterns to take my mind off the thirst. The limbs twisted and turned into a crooked mess, and I thought if I were to stare long enough, I might discover something about branches no one ever had before.

My studies were interrupted when music approached from the near distance and a woman hiking the trail emerged over the hill. When she reached us, we sat upright.

She took out her earphones and smiled. "Are you guys okay?"

We nodded unconvincingly.

"Do you know if there's any water nearby?" I asked.

She bit her lower lip, glanced into the sky, and fished around in her pocket for maps. "There should be something around here somewhere. Let's see…"

Her calmness alone brought me comfort as she sat down and scanned the papers.

"Oh yeah," she said. "This way."

We followed her west across a gravel road. Although I looked ridiculous stumbling across the rocks, my existence brightened when I saw water flowing from the spigot.

I could hardly wait for my turn to chug.

We thanked the hiker, filled our bottles, and drank endlessly before returning to the shade. The water cooled my throat and made my belly heavy. Lying back down on the grass, I was thankful to be alive. Before I knew it, the earth pulled me into sleep.

It was bright when I awoke. *Maybe an hour has passed?*

But what was time anyway? Less than a week had gone by since we began the trail, but the week had felt like an eternity.

"Let's go," Bradley said, strapping on his backpack. "We still have a few more miles before camp."

I lay unmoved beneath the branches a few more precious moments, readying myself for another round of pain and suffering.

As I began to stand, Bradley headed up the gravel road and, making quick work of the rocky climb, disappeared around the bend.

Slow and steady, I continued as gravel crunched beneath my feet. I had been able to manage the pain before, but suddenly something struck me like an arrow. An intense pain pierced my foot. I threw off my backpack and plopped down in the middle of the rocky trail. I was on the brink of tears.

Inspecting my foot, blood was flowing from a popped blister over my dusty and dirty sole. Clenching my teeth,

I poured water over the wound, slid on socks and sat in the heat of the sun, gazing out to the desert.

Everything was quiet.

I couldn't help but wonder why I was still putting myself through barefooting. I looked up to Bradley as a person, but was I trying to be like him instead of making decisions for myself? And if that was the case, how much of myself was I willing to sacrifice to become someone else? How much more pain would I have to endure before I learned to walk my own path?

I couldn't help but laugh, sigh, and shake my head, knowing how long I had dragged out my own suffering. As I stared into the wild, my life slowly began to make a bit more sense. I realized that the more you try to be like others, the farther you stray from yourself. And desires to please the expectations of others end up pleasing no one. But sometimes we're blind to what's obvious, to our own limitations, to all the opportunities that await us beyond what we can see, and it takes us sinking low enough before the need for change becomes most clear. A part of us might even feel emptier than when we began, but we're not. It's in those moments that we're one step closer to finding ourselves.

Shoes would be a good first step.

I found my shoes and tightened the laces around my feet while sniffling. As I made my way up the mountain, the socks felt like clouds around my toes while the sturdy layer of rubber cushioned my every step. The difference between shoes and bare feet was… laughable.

Bradley stood waiting around the bend. I met him with shoulders slumped and a downward gaze, unable to bear the sight of his face, to show myself as someone who had failed, but when I looked up, he was smiling. I shrugged, and we embraced.

"I decided on shoes," I said, as if it wasn't obvious.

He smiled. "Yep."

"If you want to keep barefooting, I know you can make it."

"Thanks."

He nodded, and we continued up the trail. I led the way for only the second time on the hike.

The desert took on new beauty almost instantly. As it turned out, this place wasn't entirely filled with death, suffering, and barren nothingness. It was equally filled with bright, vibrant, and colorful life. The sand glimmered and shined in the sunlight, the mountains casting shadows onto the valley below. An excited energy surged through my body.

I felt grateful to have hiked fifty miles barefoot, but the challenge was too difficult for a tenderfoot like me. I imagined hiking the entire trail barefoot would be near impossible without years of prior barefooting experience.

Only two days later, at mile seventy-five, Bradley took out his homemade sandals and wrapped the laces up his legs. Relief washed over me as I watched him put on his Jesus sandals. They weren't nearly as durable as my trail runners, but at least they were... something.

He looked at me and nodded.

There was lost ground to make up and a new life to live. I smiled and stood. Free of the baggage of barefooting, we walked further into the desert, reborn and ready for whatever adventures lay ahead.

CHAPTER 8

May 2, 2015
Mile 90, Julian (2,560 miles to go)

Tired and hungry, we stopped mid-switchback high on the mountain ridge. It was night, and it was dark. The spot wasn't a designated campsite, but it would have to do. There was no way we'd make it the necessary miles toward the next one.

It had taken us three days to reach this spot since putting on shoes. The trail had led us through a valley, stopping briefly at a highway where we caught a hitch into an old gold-mining town called Julian. Shortly after, the path climbed beyond the mountain ridge behind the town, leading to more hills and mountain ridges. Each ridge rose into the horizon like crusty anthills spread beneath the sunlight.

My entire body was still sore to the bone, even while wearing shoes. Instead of hobbling for a measly ten miles a day, we could now walk for fifteen or more if we started early. It seemed like fifteen to seventeen miles was a good number to walk in one day for novice hikers. Twenty miles was an excellent day, and we knew it would take us some time to work up to that amount. At our current pace, we could walk about two or three miles in one hour.

Shoes helped, but my feet were not free from pain. My blisters were thriving, and my feet ached endlessly at the beginning of each day. It was only after walking a few miles that they began to lighten up, although a dull pain never subsided.

Having settled down for the night in what seemed to be a crevasse tucked into the mountainside, I plopped down in the darkness to pour out the accumulation of dirt that had some-how found its way into my shoes from the past miles.

I beat my socks against my backpack. Dust clouds rose into the air, and I turned them inside out to dry. My feet were still blistered, but my wound was healing nicely. But, oh man, did they smell. It was a foul stench, one that had per-meated my body, clothes, and gear. Although I was days from my last shower or laundry, I was quickly becoming ac-customed to it and even found myself enjoying my own scent.

It was every other hiker that smelled terrible. Bradley more than most, it seemed to me. Yet this was the least of my concerns, especially on a night like tonight. Both of our food bags were empty, and we were still a day's hiking dis-tance from Warner Springs, the next closest town.

Our capacity to eat had grown substantially since we'd started the trail, and we hadn't expected to so quickly con-sume our entire resupply and all the food from the Julian hiker box. What remained between us was one serving of oats. It was an unfortunate predicament to say the least. My stomach grumbled and tightened, knowing sacrifices would have to be made.

"We've got two options," Bradley said while unpacking his bag for the night. "We can either eat the oats tonight and go without food tomorrow morning, or we can go to bed hun-gry and eat in the morning."

I thought long and hard. With oats as our only option, both choices seemed equally dreadful. "I guess I could wait until tomorrow."

"Same."

As we prepared for a night's sleep without dinner, Bradley's flashlight must have caught a glimpse of the distant plants surrounding the edge of the trail. His eyes lingered on them steadily.

What is he thinking about?

"Hold on a sec..." he said, eyeing a tall plant surrounded by Spanish dagger. "I think that's a yucca plant. And if I'm not mistaken, those pods are edible."

I was as equally skeptical as I was starving. Searching the dark, we managed to snag a few pods that had fallen to the desert floor.

We went back to our campsite and studied the green and warty pods.

"Are you sure they're ripe?" I asked.

"Look fine to me."

He dug for his pocketknife and split the pods revealing their seeded chambers. I took one in my hand.

"You sure about this?"

He rolled his eyes. "Food is food, brother. Are you hungry or not?" He popped one into his mouth and nodded as he chewed. It had become a theme with him. The crunch of the pod seemed like the most delicious treat his tongue had ever known.

I bit into the pod, chewed, then nearly barfed. *What is this thing?*

It was hard and crunchy, a thousand times worse than turmeric cornmeal. But it was too late to go back now. Knowing this was my only sustenance for the evening, I decided not to spit it out. Chewing thoroughly, I gulped it down and crammed one more pod into my mouth, forcing it down my gullet in order to last me the night.

That night was one of the longest of my life. I spent most of it lying around in a sweat, trying to decide if and when I was going to vomit. My stomach could not be less happy that it had been involuntarily recruited to work the night-shift, forced to endure hours of churning, squeezing, and contracting against what felt like pins and needles poking my insides. I breathed heavy and lay still until my eyes shut once again.

I woke the next morning starving but without appetite, a feeling I hadn't thought possible.

"Do you feel sick?" I asked.

"There's some rumblings," Bradley said. "But I'll be fine."

I could hardly stomach the morning oats. My forehead felt unusually hot, and one more bite would no doubt lead to a purge. Miserable, I packed up and continued north.

My day of sickness was juxtaposed with nice, cloudy weather. I walked slowly behind Bradley who had finally confirmed his stomach pains. I hoped my walking would send signals of strength to my stomach.

Our procession halted suddenly where some rocks had been organized to form the number one hundred on the side of the trail.

I cocked my head. "One hundred?"

Then it hit me. This was the one hundredth mile marker. We had walked one hundred miles. A small note was left beside the rocks: "Only twenty-five more of those to go," it read.

Wait a second... twenty-five more of those?!

My heart dropped, and my mind nearly exploded. The last one hundred miles had been the longest days of my life, and to think I would need to endure twenty-five more of those lifetimes suddenly put the trail's end completely out of reach.

Yet on second thought, I'd never dreamt of walking one hundred miles when I was struggling back at mile twenty. I decided as long as I wasn't thinking too much of the future and kept walking, the miles would take care of themselves.

I wished my phone was working to take a picture of the milestone. It was funny how in the past, documenting a moment had taken priority over experiencing one. Maybe my mind always worked like that, wanting to hold on to the old instead of letting go to make room for something new. With my phone battery dead, a fleeting memory would have to do. After soaking up the experience, I smiled briefly then continued up the trail, sickness still dwelling inside my stomach.

I was hungry now. With every step, fantasies of resupplies, hiker boxes, and coconut-rolled dates danced in my head. My thoughts were mostly about food on the trail, but that day was the worst it had ever been. I grabbed my stomach. Town couldn't come soon enough.

Before long we came across a hiker named JungleGym, a smiling, bright-eyed, carefree man about our age or a few years older, hiking with a reflective umbrella he used for shade. They seemed to be worth their weight in gold, doubling as both rain and sun protection. I was jealous of this umbrella as the sun was a worthy adversary for us hikers.

JungleGym was a musician and teacher by trade and a Christian by faith. I tried my best to chat with him, but he must have noticed my sluggish demeanor.

"You okay, man?" he asked.

"Yeah, I'm fine…" I said at first, but when he asked again, I told him the truth, explaining how we'd run out of food, eaten yucca pods… the whole spiel.

"I think I've got something for you," he said. "It's not much, but…" He stopped, reached into his pack, and handed us a snickers bar.

Our eyes brightened. I was a sucker for these chocolaty, milky treats. It seemed to be twice the size of a normal chocolate bar, and I hadn't eaten such a tasty morsel in ages.

"It's not the most nutritious thing, but I hope it helps."

"Wow!" I said. "Are you sure?"

He nodded. "Of course," he said. "Pay it forward."

We thanked him, and he went on his way as we chose to break for water.

Bradley turned to me. "That was nice of him."

"No kidding."

I couldn't help but recall those words... pay it forward. We had offered our help in various ways so far including cleaning around trail angel Bob Reiss's house, volunteering for kickoff, and donating shoes to an in-need hiker, but all these kind gestures were continuing to pile up. I knew we had to find more ways to give. The thought was brief as my attention fell back onto the wrapped chocolate treat in Bradley's palm.

He raised his eyebrow. "You know the drill, right?"

I nodded. It was time for the ceremony to begin. The two of us had devised a set procedure for splitting food, the fairest way known to man, and this was the perfect opportunity to execute it.

Here's how it worked. If a food item required sharing, one person was designated the splitter and the other the chooser. It was the splitter's job to slice, tear, or separate the dish in half as best he could. Afterward, the chooser then selected their desired half. Such a process ensured a fair share of the dish while any shortcomings in the splitter's efforts would be his own.

Since it was my turn, I assumed the role of the splitter, first eyeing the chocolate bar carefully and then tearing it in two with the utmost precision before presenting Bradley with the two halves.

He narrowed his eyes on his options, reaching for the half he believed to be just slightly larger, and his choice sparked debate over who was the true winner. As we continued up the trail, I savored my portion knowing the bites would be my last before Warner Springs. I allowed ample space between bites and let the thick chocolaty goodness slowly melt in my mouth. I felt much better after eating the chocolate and that much more grateful to JungleGym for his kind offering.

As the trail descended, the world fell flat. Where the trees ended, a wide plain spread out across the valley. So many times on the trail, it felt like walking down a hallway and discovering the different rooms of nature's mansion. This room was particularly spacious, beautiful, and filled with life. The path ran arrow-straight through the middle of the grass that fanned the valley, and we walked in awe of the plains.

Just when things couldn't possibly become any lovelier, a light mist began falling from the heavens, cooling my skin, emitting an earthy scent of fresh dew while a double rainbow shimmered in the distant blue skies. I couldn't help but realize how quickly life could change.

The rain passed for clearer skies, and we soon came upon a huge mass of rocks to the east of the trail that resembled an eagle. A hiker stood there and offered to photograph us, saying he could send us the picture at a later time if we gave him our emails. We accepted, returned the kind gesture, then continued onward. I hoped his picture turned out as well as ours did.

Eagle Rock, Mile 106. Bradley & me.

Later that afternoon, I exhaled as we passed a sign for Warner Springs. Apart from my constant thoughts of food and feasting, I had grown curious about what I might have missed from the outside world. Being in the wilderness was rewarding in its own right, but I hadn't yet lost my appreciation for the worldwide web. Hopefully, there would be somewhere to charge my phone, check in with my old life, and see what had happened.

Surely I've missed something of importance!

We entered Warner Springs through a chain-link fence. It was less a town and more a small park with a community center sitting atop a concrete lot with patches of grass and a track field nearby.

Hikers sought shade beneath trees like herds of mountain lions and cheered as we entered the gates. We smiled and waved before heading into the building. A rush of cold air-conditioning rushed over my face. I stood there a while, lifting my chin and letting my jaw drop open.

Apparently, this location was a satellite to the actual town and reaching the post office and hiker boxes would require a short hitchhike.

Hitchhiking was commonplace on the trail as the path often bisected a highway at a remote location. To reach the nearest town without a long road walk, it was necessary to hitch a ride. As we had done to reach Julian, someone would need to find a hitch into Warner Springs proper.

Bradley volunteered to make the trek, and I decided to stay, opting to plug my phone into an outlet near the corner of the trailer and reconnect with the digital world.

As he was walking out the door, I called to him, "Should we ask your parents to send the tarp back?"

"Depends," he said. "Do you wanna carry it?"

I sighed. "Nah."

He walked back over to meet me. "I say we have it sent to us at Kennedy Meadows. That's the start of the High Sierras in Central California, and we'll need shelter high in the mountains. Until then, I think we'll be fine in the desert."

I gave him a thumbs up, and he walked out the door into the sunlight.

My phone picked up cell service, and I waited attentively to see the incoming activity. There was a text from a friend wondering how everything was going and three responses to our last email. I smiled at the messages. Few things brought me more joy than hearing from friends and family. I browsed social media to see what I had missed, if anything, but none of it interested me. Compared to all that had happened and what was happening around me, the curated pictures and stories seemed altogether superficial. The sight of the glowing screen strained my eyes and staring at the device began to feel oddly unnatural. I could sense my brain beginning to shut off and drift into mindlessness.

I turned off my phone and traded it for a notebook I found sitting on one of the tables. It was a trail log, a special note-book signed and dated by each hiker who passed through town. I recognized some of the names as hikers we'd met at kickoff and smiled knowing they were still on the trail. In looking at the dates, however, I was startled to see how many days ago they'd passed through and how much barefooting had delayed us.

Setting aside the trail log, I killed the afternoon with a thirty-one-year-old named Gandalf while waiting for Bradley's return. Gandalf was a friend I'd met in the few miles right before Julian. His trail name was fitting as a long beard hung past his neck, and he carried an enormous hiking staff carved of wood. Gandalf had begun the trail with a friend named Clay, but he hadn't seen him since kickoff. He seemed assured they would meet up eventually. I guess he wasn't as closely tied to Clay as I was to Bradley.

Apparently, the last section of trail hadn't been kind on Gandalf. He told me he had just endured a thirty-two hour stint where he had woken up with a splitting headache, retched, and decided to keep walking since he'd had migraines before. But this one only got worse. He hid underneath a bush, hung some clothes for shade, and dumped water on his chest, trying to keep the heat down and his breathing under control.

That didn't help. He ended up calling 911 after writing his GPS location on his arm, which he got from the Halfmile app on his phone, and was helicoptered out of Scissors Crossing, the section of the trail before Julian. Turns out he wasn't eating enough sodium and potassium.

With my mouth still gaping, I felt briefly thankful for Bradley's choice of Himalayan sea salt.

"Geez man, that's quite the experience. I'm glad you're okay."

"Yeah, just be careful… stay hydrated. You never know what could happen."

I nodded, thinking back on our barefooting days, grateful it hadn't come to helicopters.

Gandalf let me know about his new trail name: Gandalf the White.

I laughed as it was a reference to *Lord of the Rings* and the great wizard's (spoiler alert) resurrection.

As we sat in the cold air of the community center, I noticed how it was pleasant to speak to someone other than Bradley. Not that I disliked him by any means, but these past hundred miles was nothing short of living like a married couple, except without all the best perks… if you catch my drift. The constant presence of the other required more of everything—effort, attention, patience, and negotiation. Conducting a relationship with myself was already hard enough.

Bradley returned no more than an hour later, proudly carrying our resupply. We anxiously cut it open to reveal the box's predictable contents: sacks of granola, dried fruits, banana chips and nuts, canned sardines and tuna, instant mashed potatoes, and blocks of cheese. Then there were some new items that pleased us: peanut butter and chocolate-chip oat bars, summer sausage, pasta sides, and nut butters.

He also waved a few unlabeled bags of powder and dried foods in my face. He had identified them from the hiker box and proudly reminded me of his ability to find the hidden gems.

Reaching into our resupply, I lifted up a most unfortunate bag and laughed. "More oats?" The bag was by far the largest of any we'd received.

Bradley narrowed his eyes and raised an eyebrow. "Hey, don't look at me. You're more than welcome to plan the food strategy next time around, brother."

I sometimes forgot how he had planned virtually this entire trip and that I had merely piggybacked on his prior efforts. Still, the oats had been a waste as we had yet to figure out how to properly cook them, so we found an empty cardboard box and decided to start a new hiker box with our maps and oats as the first contributions. The maps, as we discussed, wouldn't be necessary since the trail's emblem seemed to pop up often enough on iron posts and trees, always guiding us in the right direction. Bradley seemed rather confident in shedding the maps, but I still wondered if it was the right decision.

As for the oats, although I had developed a deep hatred of the bland chow, it still pained me to give them up, knowing I'd spent a good chunk of change to buy eighteen pounds of the stuff before the trail had started. But given their taste, it was all for nothing. The bags of brown rice farina and cornmeal, while equally unappealing in my eyes, would remain in our diet for the journey north. I guess something had to stay.

I wasn't sure about our food strategy thus far, and there was still much to learn. For instance, most of our meals required water to cook, a sparse resource in the desert terrain, and the activity was far more time consuming than we had anticipated. The utility of snacks over meals was clear, and stocking up on ready-to-eat foods seemed like the best route for the future. But if we wanted to make changes, I would have to take the lead. Regardless of what we ate, Bradley would still act like it was the best meal he had ever tasted.

With our food ready and water filled, we crafted a message for our email list before setting out, recalling a story set in Julian I had skipped for the purposes of telling it in this email...

---

4 May 2015
Subject: "A Small (Milkshake) Story for You..."

Famished, dehydrated, filthy, and stinky, we walked into a local diner of an old gold mining town called Julian [at PCT mile 77]. Being on a budget, we decided instead of ordering a $7 milkshake, we would gather the remnants of other customers' unfinished malts. Soon, there was a milkshake graveyard at our table. Those around us were intrigued, disgusted, embarrassed, and supportive. We ordered our food, a juicy burger and salad, and at the end when expecting our tab, our waitress told us it had been picked up. We were overwhelmed with gratitude, and we still have no idea who paid for our meal.

Support flows in from all directions, seen and unseen, and we can't help but think independence is a myth. No man is an island. With this insight, instead of seeking to be supported, we ask ourselves: "who can we support?" We all have resources we can share. And here's the kicker: the more we give, the more available we are to receive. Whether it's a meal or a smile, may we continue to share our resources unconditionally, and if possible, anonymously. Unless of course, you want to send us some goooodies... :)

Scavenging was the new norm. Leading up to the trail, we'd discussed the reality that our hike would last only as long as the money in our bank accounts. Going broke ends a thruhike, and our best bet for finishing was to adapt to a resourceful lifestyle. Thankfully, most hikers seemed to rival our level of budget consciousness, and the mindset was supported and encouraged by much of the trail culture.

After sending out the email, we packed up and headed out the gates of Warner Springs, waving goodbye to the packs of hikers in the shady grasses.

The next forty miles after leaving Warner Springs were more of the same—a slow three-day trod north through the desert before reaching mile 152. There, a trail angel named Devil Fish offered us a ride in his van to a nearby restaurant.

While it may sound sketchy to hop in the car with a stranger, Devil Fish was a well-known trail angel and had been giving rides to hikers for years. We couldn't pass up his offer, which came with a gentle smile. Other hikers surrounding the junction felt the same. Seeking town food, we hopped into the van and started down the highway.

My mind melted moments later. From out the window, I could see the desert rushing by. I clenched my seatbelt. It was as if we were blasting through space and time in a rocket ship, completely ripping apart my previous days understanding of time.

The speed of travel made me think. *Is hiking all these miles a waste of time if the drive to Canada could be made in a day or two?*

Well, one thing was for sure, the driving was far less fulfilling than the walking. In a way, it felt like cheating, but I wasn't complaining. As my belly rumbled, I was grateful we'd soon reach the highly anticipated destination of the Paradise Valley Café, more than ready to feast on some proper town food.

Upon our arrival at the café, we met a hiker named Patch lying around with his German Shepherd, Sophie, who was tied to the railing next to him.

"Hey," he said. "You mind watching my dog for just a sec?"

I didn't mind at all. Although I had none of my own, I loved dogs, having grown up with them in my youth. I looked over Sophie as Patch disappeared into the café. She looked tired but happy, panting rapidly, occasionally lifting her head to lap water from a small bowl.

Patch returned from the café soon after he had gone, holding a small carton of food.

Bradley's mouth fell open. "Patch, is that a burger?" he asked. "How'd you manage to score that? We know you didn't pay for it."

"Of course not!" he said with a grin. "I told them Sophie was hungry."

He slid down the railing beside Sophie, petted her head, and sank his teeth into the juicy burger. Sophie stared at him and whimpered.

"Sorry, Soph. But thanks, girl."

"What's it like hiking with someone who doesn't speak?" I asked, smiling at Bradley.

Bradley inclined his head and playfully narrowed his eyes.

"Oh, she's lazy as shit," Patch said. "She doesn't carry any of her own stuff. I even bought her a backpack—a nice, expensive one, too—but she just whines when she sees it. Not to mention I have to carry her on my shoulders when she gets tired. But I wouldn't have it any other way. She comes in handy every now and again, don't you, Soph?"

As Patch polished off the last bites of cheeseburger, he stuck out his hand so Sophie could lick his fingers. It was a fine consolation prize for Sophie and a clever tactic on Patch's part, one Bradley and I didn't have the resources to pull off.

We sat outside in a silent, hungry stupor as hikers and patrons devoured huge plates of fatty foods and creamy malts from behind the café window.

Devil Fish's van pulled up, and a new group of hikers spilled out the car doors into the café. The window rolled down, and he looked at us from behind his sunglasses and nodded.

"You two ready to head back to the trail?"

We had hoped for town food, but our luck had run thin. Bradley and I glanced at each other and stood, wedging our packs in the trunk before hopping in. Later that night we would settle instead for a measly dinner of turmeric noodles and sardines.

It was a few days later before we ran into something we had not expected.

CHAPTER 9

May 5, 2015
Mile 155, San Jacinto Mountains (2,495 miles to go)

The trail climbed through the mountain pines toward an overcast sky. My hair and windbreaker flapped in the wind. This place was nothing like the desert. The elevation had taken us higher into the San Jacinto mountain range, into the cold, thin air of the woods.

The cold and climbing was made tolerable by the fact we'd been hiking with Canyon and Rabbit, the father-daughter duo we'd met at the Mount Laguna Campground. We spent our days discussing our lives before the trail, philosophizing on the meaning of life, and exchanging all we knew of religion and science.

Then Rabbit halted and looked into the sky. "Is it going to rain?" she asked. The clouds along the horizon had thickened, their underbellies darkening and spreading across the sky.

"It might be too cold for that," Canyon said.

Before I could make my own deductions, something cold splashed onto my face. "Did anyone else feel that?"

"I think I just felt something," Bradley said.

We glanced upward. Snowflakes fluttered from the sky in droves. At first, the snow was a glorious reprieve from the heat,

97

and we tried to catch them on our tongues. But the snowfall grew unexpectedly heavy. Sheets of white swirled around us on all sides.

"It's not looking good," Canyon said. "I think Rabbit and I are going to play it safe and set up camp here for tonight. Hopefully, we'll run into you guys tomorrow."

"No problem," we said, waving goodbye to our friends and continuing up the trail.

"Stay safe!" they shouted.

What's wrong with a little snow? I wondered. I really had no idea what we were walking into.

The winds grew cold and icy as we hiked the path lined by trees. The weather began to concern me, and I wanted to check our distance from town.

I stepped beneath a pine for coverage and rummaged my pack for my phone. We had gotten rid of our paper maps, but I recalled other hikers were accessing the trail maps via an app.

My gloveless hands shook as I dug into my backpack. It was a regretful reminder of all the cold weather gear I'd sent home.

It was hardly a surprise to me that my phone was dead. I wondered why I had checked in the first place. At that moment, the woods seemed to dim a shade darker.

Thankfully, I had kept my puffy jacket and my thermals. I decided to wear the jacket but not the thermals, since the clothes I was wearing were already damp from the snowfall, and I knew at least one pair of clothes should be kept dry for sleeping.

It was while slipping on my jacket that an unfortunate thought hit me. *We sent home our tarp...*

A snowy night without a shelter wasn't something I looked forward to experiencing. My pack felt lighter from sending home the tarp... but at what cost? I threw my pack on and mushed through the white flurry to catch up with Bradley.

"Should we turn back?" I asked.

No reply. He didn't even bother turning around. His steady steps lurched forward leaving tracks in the snow.

Is he mad at the situation or at me? I summoned up the courage to try again.

"What are we going to do without our tarp?"

"Walk," he said.

I tilted my head. "What about sleep?"

His gaze remained downward, attention focused on the trail. "I probably won't."

No sleep? When I looked up, a rumbling sea of charcoal grey clouds had eclipsed the sky. This was going to be a long night.

A brief moment later, I convinced Bradley to take a break to eat and discuss the situation, but we couldn't sit for more than a couple minutes in the cold before forcing our legs to continue onward. It was only enough time for him to change from his Jesus sandals into some proper socks and shoes that he'd kept buried deep inside his pack. He was hesitant to do so, but we hadn't imagined walking through such cold.

The trail stretched on endlessly as darkness fell. The downpour of snow grew heavier, winds rising. The pines were layered in snow, and soon the path was lost beneath a blanket of crystalline powder.

We bore on northward against the wind and cold. My steps crunched in the snow, dampening my socks. My ears numbed from the ceaseless winds. Snowflakes covered my head and clung to my exposed legs. I walked with my hands shoved into my jacket pockets, squeezing them into fists for warmth, occasionally bringing them to my face to exhale through the tunnel of fingers. The body needed to move, or my remaining limbs might end up like my ears.

It was the first time I had ever really considered what it would be like to freeze to death. The thought of my blue and crusted lifeless body buried beneath the snow shook me to my core and made me miss the desert sun.

The snow was nothing either of us could have predicted at the time, and I couldn't help but think we should have been more prepared. Stuck in this mess as we were—and not for the first time on this trip I might add—my initial reaction was to blame Bradley for everything.

First the barefooting incident... and now this? What have I been led into?

Bradley stopped marching. His hand rose, and he pointed to a tree beside the trail.

"There," he said.

I gazed up over his shoulder through the flurry. Carved into the trunk of every few pines was a mark. The markings signaled the trail. At least we knew we were heading in the right direction, as any little bit gives hope even in the worst of times.

We followed the signs, the trees leading us through the forest, until we came upon some fresh footprints. I felt a strange relief knowing there were others who had been caught in the snow, that I wasn't alone with a guy who wanted to walk all night through a blizzard.

Following the tracks, we spotted a figure in the distance. It was a lone girl sitting in a precious plot of dry earth beneath a thick canopy of branches holding back the snow. She wore a puffy down jacket and windpants, but despite her preparedness in clothing, I could tell by her scowl she was just as worried as me.

When she saw us nearing, she looked up and smiled. Her name was HannaSolo.

"Do you happen to know how many miles from town we are?" I asked.

She laughed. "Too far. But we can check the maps again."

Thank God... maps!

We examined the papers, searching carefully for any and all possibilities of hope.

"Wait," Bradley said, pointing to a note on the bottom right-hand corner of the map. "Is that... a cabin?"

"Oh my gosh, guys!" cheered HannaSolo.

"Yeah, and it's less than ten miles away," Bradley said. "If we keep walking, we'll reach it before nightfall."

It was a farther distance than I had expected to hike that day, but we'd freeze without shelter. At least this time we had an aim, a faint glimmer of reprieve. Together, we set back out into the woods, returning to the snow.

Hours later, the world was too dark to see by the light of the moon. Hardly anything pierced through the mass of clouds above.

I pulled out my headlamp from my hip-belt pocket, tightened it around my head, and turned it on. A smattering of light shot out from my forehead, illuminating the back of HannaSolo's backpack and her tracks in the snow. The three of us walked closely together, one in front of the other so as not to lose anyone, stopping only for HannahSolo to pee before continuing on. It was too dangerous for anyone to be left alone.

I kept my attention focused on the trail, fitting my feet into the sets of tracks left behind by Bradley and HannaSolo. Again, my mind found comfort knowing others were suffering the same conditions. I doubted I could have made it on my own.

Miles passed until the trees parted and we walked into a meadow. Our eyes lit up as the silhouette of a structure became visible in the distance.

"Guys, is that the cabin?!" HannaSolo shouted.

We walked toward it with rising anticipation, dreaming of what lay inside. Our hearts sank as we neared. It was an outhouse.

"Well, if that's our only option…" Bradley said.

"Yeah," Hanna Solo said. "I'd be willing to sleep in it."

We yanked at the door. It was locked.

Great.

A desperate search for the key turned up nothing, and we slumped against the side of the shed to escape the snow, hanging our heads.

"Well, I'm going to set up camp here," HannaSolo said. "You guys should probably do the same."

Bradley and I looked at each other.

"We don't have a shelter," I said.

Her jaw nearly fell off. "What?!"

"Yeah, we sent it home in Mount Laguna."

She shook her head. "Well… my tent's only a single. But if that's what it's come to, I'm sure we can try it."

I glanced at Bradley. Three people wouldn't fit a single tent… or could we?

Bradley shook his head. "No," he said. "We'll keep walking. Maybe the cabin is further ahead."

I glared at him from the wet ground as he stood. Recalling memories of the yucca pod fiasco, this was now the longest night of my life, and I was beginning to fear it wouldn't end well. Left with no other choice but to continue, Bradley and I began retracing our footsteps back to the trail.

Just as HannaSolo was unpacking behind us, a bright light was cast onto the snow in the distance. I squinted and traced the light with my eyes to an open door. Two figures stood in the light and above them, the faint outline of a log cabin.

"Over here!" they yelled.

"No way," I mumbled.

All three of us ran toward the light, through the roaring winds, over the porch steps, and through the front door as it slammed shut behind us.

I nearly stumbled onto the stone floor. I blinked hard and looked around. Everything was quiet for a moment. Flames flickered in the fireplace, and at least twelve other hikers, many of whom we knew, were gathered on the floor. I could hardly believe what I was seeing. Had we really gotten this lucky? The hikers cheered when they turned and realized three new hiker friends had just escaped the snow and were set to join them for the night.

"Are you guys okay?" they asked, standing to examine us.

"I'm good!" HannaSolo said, shaking the snow from her hair and smiling.

I was beside myself with excitement. Realizing our good fortune, I wrapped my arms around Bradley to embrace him, but he shoved me away at once. I nearly fell backward before recovering.

"Get off!" he snapped.

What had I done wrong this time?!

"What do you mean?" I asked.

Bradley was silent, his face ghostly white and stricken as he stared at his shaking right hand. "I can't feel it," he said. "I can't feel sensations."

Everyone in the room exchanged concerned glances.

"Is it hypothermia?" HannaSolo asked.

There was no answer.

"Get him to the fire," said another hiker.

We slipped off our backpacks and sat beside the flames. Everyone in the room pulled their sleeping bags from their packs and wrapped them around Bradley, hugging him to offer their body heat. There he shook, and we remained quiet, hoping he would soon recover.

Before long, Bradley's hand settled, and he was able to curl his fingers into a tight fist. His old self and strength were returning to him, and he cracked a smile upon seeing the movement.

Blankets were flung around our shoulders, and we hung our socks and shoes on the mantel before pushing our limbs and faces toward the flames to thaw. The warmth flowed from the fire and into my fingertips. I thought about how fortunate we had been and wondered how this had come to be— the blankets, the fire, the other hikers.

Surveying the room, I noticed a man in the corner sitting in a rocking chair that looked as if he didn't belong. He was much too clean. And there was a woman, who, much like the man, was older and much better dressed compared to us hikers. She approached from the shadows of the side room, balancing a tray stacked with porcelain bowls.

"Here, take this," she said.

We looked with shock from the bowls to the woman. They were filled with steaming hot and delicious smelling noodle soup.

"Eat as much as you'd like. We always bring too much every year anyway."

"Are you two trail angels?" Bradley asked.

"We are now," she laughed. "But we didn't know anything of the trail before today." She looked around the room and smiled. "We book this cabin once a weekend every year for our family reunion. You're lucky everyone else doesn't arrive until tomorrow. So tonight, you're welcome to stay, get some sleep, and head out in the morning... if weather permits."

"Oh, and it's a good thing you hadn't arrived yesterday either," the man in the chair said. "A day earlier, and this place would have been locked. A day later and we might not have had room for you."

We thanked the couple endlessly while sipping soup, eating crackers, and chatting beside the fire. Our antics and silliness amused the couple.

"Wait!" Trampon yelled while sniffing the air. "Does anyone smell something burning...?"

"The sock!" HannaSolo shouted.

We looked toward the mantel. A flickering ember was traversing up the heel of a lone sock, beginning to burn through the wool.

It was Bradley's.

As he leapt to his feet, yanked it down and extinguished it by slapping it against the stone floor, I couldn't help but crack a smile. In the end, the sock's heel had nearly melted off, forming a gaping hole. He glanced at me.

"You think it's a sign?" he asked with a grin.

I knew he was referring to going back to bare feet. His old self had definitely returned.

I shook my head and laughed. I knew he was joking... at least partially. To Bradley, everything in life had meaning. Every moment was a sign or an omen to be heeded. For now, I didn't have an answer for him apart from knowing I wasn't going back to barefooting!

That night, we curled up alongside eight other hikers in sleeping bags on the cold stone of the cabin floor, keeping the fire fed through the night. And we slept.

At dawn, the snow had lifted, and we headed through the woods, anxious and ready to reach town.

CHAPTER 10

May 7, 2015
Mile 180, Idyllwild (2,470 miles to go)

It was days later when we reached Idyllwild, a ski town nestled between the pines and cedars of the San Jacinto Mountains. It felt like the first real town I'd seen since starting the trail.

I walked the streets with wide eyes, staring at the snow-capped roofs of outdoor outfitters, cottage gift shops, and cabin homes that lined the streets. Even the air smelled of freshly baked goods. I was more than ready to enjoy what seemed to be an entirely different realm of the trail experience—town life.

We were hanging out next to a town bakery, reading the trail logs and scrounging through hiker boxes, when a few familiar faces approached us. It was Gandalf, Oz, and Nomad, three hikers we had met from earlier sections of the trail.

"Did you guys hear the news?" Oz asked.

Bradley and I shook our heads.

"Snow for the next two nights," Gandalf said. "It's going to be rough up there in the mountains, so we thought of booking a hotel room for a night—you two interested? We could sleep five in a four-person, maybe even sneak in a sixth to cut down the cost. There's a full kitchen, a shower, a TV—"

Bradley standing atop an Idyllwild monument.

Bradley stood. "What are we waitin' for? Let's go!"

Tired, sore, and ready to relax, we followed Gandalf, Oz, and Nomad to the front desk of the hotel. Apart from kickoff, it would be our first zero-day, a day where a hiker doesn't hike a single mile.

As Gandalf pushed open the door to the small cottage room, my eyes widened. A month earlier, this place would have been nothing special. But now I gazed upon the scene through the eyes of a hiker. Chairs were thrones, sinks were springs, and the carpet was a king bed unto itself! What were once merely essentials had now become luxuries.

First on everyone's mind was the shower, so we scooted across the street to the front desk to ask for some extra fluffy white towels before returning to the room. Having thrown our heap of filthy clothes into a trash bag and donned our towels, a queue for the shower was established through a game of choosing kitchen spoons. I drew fourth, but in the end, it was Oz who had to go last. He also got laundry duty, which required a short walk across the street to the laundry mat. My yellow shirt was browning when I'd thrown it into the bag, and I could hardly wait for the feeling of clean socks.

As our laundry tumbled and the TV buzzed, my friends emerged one by one from the bathroom doorway. Steam poured into the living room as they exited the shower reborn, smiling, and sparkling clean.

When Bradley was done, it was my turn. As the tub filled, steam filled the bathroom. I stood there, feeling a forgotten comfort. For the first time in two weeks, I finally had a space to myself. Privacy was another lost luxury, and I cherished every moment.

I stripped naked, dumped in handfuls of Epsom salt we had found in the town's hiker box, and eased into the scalding hot water. It burned nicely, and the space between my eyebrows melted away as I sank below the surface. A hard scrubbing of my arms, legs, feet, and hair left me steeping in a brown moat. The tub would need a good cleaning before the next person could enjoy it.

When I hopped out, I caught my blurred figure in the mirror. My curiosity was sparked. I took my towel and wiped away the fog. It felt like ages since I'd last seen myself, which had been good for my mind to be free from the concern of personal appearance. Now, I stood there for some time, shocked and perplexed. A whole new person stood before me.

Who is this guy?

His hair was longer and shaggier than I'd ever seen it. A thick beard was sprouting from his face and neck. And his body! It looked stronger than ever before, tan and toned in the stomach. The physical changes were glaringly obvious, but there was something else happening on the inside of that mirrored man that I couldn't yet put into words.

Chapter 10

These two to three weeks on the trail held more challenge, adventure, and meaning than I'd experienced in the previous twenty-four years of my life. This journey seemed to be a lifetime of its own accord, and I wondered what else the trail could possibly have in store for me. I smiled, wrapped myself in a fluffy white towel and headed out the door to join the others.

Once we were done cleaning our bodies, our clothes were returned from the wash only slightly resembling their original colors.

Apparently, the socks had undergone their own wash, but it clearly wasn't enough. We tried for a second round in the tub but it was a mostly futile effort. After ringing them out multiple times, murky brown liquid still flowed from every twist, and we decided they would never return to their original cleanliness.

That night, sheets of torrential snow layered the outside world as we ate a hot, home cooked meal together by the television. The zero-day was like a hook sinking into my mouth, tightening its pull. The body needed rest, but we needed to be aware of the danger of falling victim to this vortex.

In hiker-speak, a vortex is a place with a pull so strong that it keeps hikers from progressing up the trail. Usually, hikers make sure to spread the word of upcoming vortexes, but even with these warnings, some comfort was too great a temptation to resist.

I'd even heard stories of vortexes ending entire thru-hikes. If one became too enchanted with the pleasures and luxuries of town life and allowed oneself to lose track of time, it was easy to fall behind, left with a slowly draining bank account. A week's distance could be made up with hard work, but one too many vortexes, and the problem compounded.

When night came, I noticed Bradley slip out the door of our cabin, and although much time had passed, he still hadn't returned.

Where could he have gone at such a late hour?

109

As insane as Bradley was, and despite all our previous mistakes, there was a strange brotherly interconnectedness between us from the past two hundred miles. It was difficult to sleep knowing he was missing. But, my exhaustion from the days prior demanded rest, and I left the thought at that. The droning of the heater, the chatter of the television, and the comfort of the shag carpet were more than enough to pull me into sleep.

The next day was nothing but wandering the town, meeting hikers, and lying around the hotel room with Bradley, who had finally reappeared. I felt restless knowing we couldn't hike out. And nothing special would be found watching the television, another device that now brought a feeling of disillusionment and a newfound appreciation at the same time. I must have lazily and happily watched two to three movies that day. It was more than enough to get my fill of picture flicks.

Later that night, after we had eaten another home-cooked dinner, I remembered to ask Bradley where he had been last night. The thought had stayed with me ever since, but it was never the right time to ask about it with all of our other hiker friends hanging around.

"I'll show you," he said. "I was planning on returning tonight anyway."

I nodded, and when night came, since it seemed there was nothing better to do, we escaped into the streets.

He led me down the dark, empty, snow-covered streets until he eventually stopped in front of an abandoned shop. It was made of brick, and most of its windows were shattered and boarded up with planks and cardboard. The front door was cracked open.

Bradley turned to me as he pushed it open. "They're a bit crazy, but they're good people. I've heard it said that insanity is a form of wisdom."

I nodded but thought differently. *How could insanity be anything closely resembling wisdom?* It didn't make sense to me, but I put aside the thought as we crept into the building.

The place was in ruins—deserted, dark, and damp. Piles of bricks, fragments of stone, and abandoned tools lay atop the busted tiled floor. The only light I could see was a faint sliver cast down from a half-opened door across the room. The sounds of muffled music coming from behind the door reached my ears.

"This way," Bradley said.

We crossed the room and pushed the door open. The room reeked of nicotine and despair, and a smoky haze lacquered the room. A trail of crushed beer cans led my eyes to a table of five men.

Town vagrants maybe?

They sat around the table holding beer bottles stuffed in brown paper bags while tapping the burnt ends of their blunts into an ashtray. They turned and cheered as we entered the room, greeting Bradley warmly before asking me my name.

"Take a seat," replied one of the kids, a cigarette hanging loosely from his lips as he spoke. "Let's play."

I joined them around the table, and he gazed at me with faraway eyes, shaking the five pairs of dice cupped between his hands.

"Hey," Bradley whispered, placing his hand on my shoulder. "I'll be outside."

I raised an eyebrow. "You're leaving?"

We had only just arrived, and if he was leaving, I had little interest in steeping in smoke for the rest of the night.

"I'll be right outside," he said before sliding out the side door into the alleyway.

With Bradley gone, I wasn't sure why I had come here in the first place. I looked back to the lean man at the head of the table. His eyes were intelligent, but bloodshot red. They rested steadily on mine. He handed me the dice.

I don't remember much more of what was said that night as I played along with the table's dice game. One man, swaying and wobbling in his chair, delivered a grand prophesy about the coming end times that he was sure would soon take place. It was an idea so far out in left field, but I was willing to entertain him, at least for a while. As the night went on, he kept droning on and on about a remarkably complex and elaborate conspiracy. I could understand how one's attention could fall into this hole, but to what end?

Still, I listened to the intoxicated rambling, as was my habit. I tended to give attention to those in need whether or not it served my own well-being. I listened with sympathy and curiosity, aware that, in his state, he would likely forget everything he'd said by morning. All the while, I wondered how and when I would make my escape.

The smoke was getting to me at this point, and I was more than ready to leave. I broke mid-sentence, mumbling something or the other, and headed out the side door to find Bradley to let him know I was heading back.

It was cold and dark in the open air, and I felt a sense of release stepping away from the chaos inside. The relief didn't last long.

Turning to my right, a group of shadows was gathered in the alleyway beneath a dim crimson light, a joint being passed between them. Bradley was in their midst, leaning against the brick wall. He was but a shadow at first until he looked over at me. His eyes were bright red, and he gave me the slightest nod and rolled his eyes before glancing away, handing the joint to the shadow next to him.

My mind's image of Bradley shattered into a thousand pieces. *After all we discussed of purity, of seeking something different from the life we once lived, has he already forgotten what we came here to find? Has my guide been led astray, fallen back into old college habits?*

I thought back on the words he had first spoken before we set out from the southern terminus:

"May we carry only what serves us. May we grow and remain pure in this experience. And whatever it is we are looking for, may we find it on this journey…"

Then it hit me. Before, I had been convinced Bradley was well ahead of me on this path, and if I could become more like him, then I too would reach some sort of advanced stage of existence. But now, I was without my guide. I was lost. I was alone.

I didn't know whether it was the thickening cloud of smoke or my growing disappointment, but my throat tensed and my forehead grew hot. I felt sick and turned at once to hop the fence that led back into town.

As I was halfway over the fence, Bradley looked to me. "You leaving?" he asked.

"Yeah, just feeling… tired." With that, I dropped down on the other side and headed up the icy streets.

The road led me back to shelter, my breath spouting fog along the way. I walked alone, steeped in thought. *Why am I so bothered by another person's actions? He didn't do anything to me.*

Maybe I was bothered because I knew Bradley knew that he was participating in something he shouldn't.

But who am I to judge him? Could it be my judgments were just as harmful to my body and mind than the smoke he inhaled?

And what about the others in the abandoned building?

I had been in their shoes no more than a few months ago. Disillusioned, questioning societal norms, skeptical of the pointlessness of the rat race for more money and materialistic gain, searching for easy answers.

But as for the drinking, smoking, hedonism, and pleasure…

Again, they're a means to what end?

I'd already traversed that dead-end path too many times in my college and workingman days. It brought me no closer to whatever it was I was seeking.

And what am I seeking?

Was it enlightenment or some sort of perfect state? Surely no one in this world was perfect! So why had I expected it of Bradley?

Maybe I just wanted the best for him. Maybe I just wanted the best for myself.

As I walked, I wondered how long the two of us would continue hiking together. Maybe we were on different paths after all.

It made for complicated logistics. We shared a cookpot, a food strategy, and a shelter, although neither of us was carrying the latter.

All of this leisure and these zero-days had brought rest, but new problems seemed to emerge when I least expected them. I told myself things would be better if only we were back on the trail.

These thoughts were my last before finding the cabin and crawling into my sleeping bag. I shut my eyes and fell asleep on the carpet to the dull drone of the heater and the soft stirring of my cabin mates.

CHAPTER 11

May 9, 2015
Mile 180, Idyllwild (2,470 miles to go)

I could feel the morning light leaking through the cabin window onto my face. I yawned and peeled my eyes open. A shadowy figure stood by the sunlit window, staring out across the snowy streets.

It was Bradley.

The urge to discuss what had happened the night before prodded me. But with everyone else around us, it wasn't the time. It was better left for later.

"Anyone know the forecast?" Bradley asked, turning away from the frosted window.

"Snow for the next four days," Oz said after studying his iPhone.

"Guys, check this out," Gandalf said, showing us his smartphone. "This house is for rent for the next five days. It's affordable so long as we can find five more hikers to join us. We'll be set!"

Five more zero-days? I couldn't believe it. What other problems would arise during that time? How much further were we willing to fall behind?

As painful a thought as it was to stay off-trail, I was even less a fan of embarking into the snowy mountains without a shelter. Pulled into the promise of comfort, we found five more hikers and booked the house.

The house was a mile walk from town. After days of being away from the trail, it was welcomed exercise. A herd of backpacks lined the streets as we headed down the road into the woods. When we finally came to the white house with the porch swing, we gathered around the front door. The key stashed beneath the rock fit perfectly inside the keyhole.

Inside, the house was nothing short of spectacular, even more luxurious than our cozy cabin room from the past two nights! The kitchen cabinets and drawers were stocked with proper tableware, silverware, and cooking utensils. A shiny, granite island countertop ran the length of the room with plenty of space to host a grand feast of epic proportions. The living room held multiple leather couches while the bedrooms were stacked with sizable bunk beds, sheets, and pillows.

At once, we rushed to claim our spots, darting from room to room. Somehow, despite being one of the shortest hikers among us, I managed to claim the largest leather couch. After settling into our new home base, we made the trek back into town where we spent the rest of the day.

I still hadn't spoken to Bradley about the night before, mostly because I'd chosen instead to spend that day with my friend, Oz. He was easily one of the most interesting people I had met on the trail thus far.

Oz was a nineteen-year-old cyclist, anarchist, and young intellectual from Florida. For such a young guy, Oz was well beyond his years. At his age, I was but a scrawny, pimply-faced child wondering what video game should consume the next year of my life. Meanwhile, Oz had already committed to a life of adventure. Upon the age of sixteen, Oz had left home, biked across the United States, hiked the Appalachian Trail, and was now walking across the country once again.

Oz had two defining features of which he was most proud: his quads—which I'll admit were both oddly and impressively large for his age—and his appetite. Oz possessed the uncanny ability to consume a gallon of ice cream in a single sitting, attributing his talent to the two-stomach theory.

"The human body has two stomachs," he once explained to me. "A savory stomach and a sweet stomach. That's why, no matter how much food you've eaten, there's always room for dessert."

Oz riding a borrowed town bike.

I was a fan of his two-stomach theory as I, too, had developed a sweet tooth for ice creams and malts, seeking out this treat whenever we arrived in towns.

Oz's real name was Miles, a name already well suited for the trail, but he had been renamed Oz as the abbreviation for ounces, a measurement he paid very close attention to when it came to the contents of his backpack.

"Every ounce counts," he said.

He took the saying seriously. While most hikers hauled twenty-five to forty pound backpacks, the base weight of Oz's pack was a mere seven pounds! And thanks to his ability to craft his own makeshift gear and his willingness to adopt lighter gear alternatives when they became available, his pack weight was in a perpetual state of decline.

For example, he carried a hand-sewn, lightweight down-quilt instead of a sleeping bag that hardly covered his body as he slept. For his tarp, he had cut a large piece of ultra-thin cellophane and added custom tie outs to the corners. Then, there was his spoon, a plastic one taken from a McDonald's restaurant because his titanium spoon was simply not light enough. He was also critical of anyone who carried a spork, stating that such a device fulfills neither the purpose of a spoon nor a fork and should only be used in the most desperate of eating situations.

Oz's favorite theory was that his life's purpose was to fulfill the duty of being a good host for his bacteria. "I live to serve my bacteria," he would say in a robotic voice while inhaling a quart of yogurt and citing the benefits of cultivating healthy gut bacteria.

Most impressively, Oz was resourceful. Having lived as a vagabond for the past year on his bike tour, he had acquired many skills in the realm of purposeful homelessness, a trait that also made him quite mischievous. He knew exactly which roofs were good for sleeping, which parks should be avoided because of sprinklers, and how to be attentive to local law enforcement when making such choices. He fit into our group perfectly, considering we were doing all we could to avoid spending money.

It was the morning after settling into our new home when Oz led me downtown. "The market," he kept telling me over and over again, "the market's where it's at."

He'd been wanting to dumpster dive at the town's grocery store since the day we had arrived, explaining to me the benefits of modern foraging techniques. Although he'd already told me of this desire many times before, he reminded me again just how promising he felt it would be.

"The best time to dive is in the early mornings," he said as we walked along the town streets. "Shops usually lock their dumpsters at night, but it's too late then anyway because the sun spoils the produce pretty fast. There's not much in a dumpster that's good eating after a day's warming. Just imagine them like ovens. Even I wouldn't eat that shit. And that's why we go in the mornings."

I nodded as we came upon our destination.

"There she is," he said.

I looked up. The dumpster was sizeable, larger than most, and it sat right beside the grocery's entrance. The exposure was a bit unnerving to me.

What if people see us? What if we get caught?

But the easily observable location didn't stop Oz. He had no fear of dirt bagging. Walking up to it, he flipped open the bin and pulled himself up and into the dumpster in one fluid motion, steadying himself atop a heap of trash bags. A whiff of the contents filled my nostrils. The smell was wretched even for a dirty, smelly hiker like me. It reeked of spoiled dairy and warm meat, but to Oz, this was merely the price paid for glory. Free food wasn't going to find itself.

He proceeded with his rummaging using precise and calculated movements, first studying the lot, then pushing around the trash bags, narrowing his eyes as he deciphered their contents. He threw aside the white trash bags.

"These ones are no good," he said, "no good at all. Filled with lobby trash. Things like receipts and tissues and paper." He ripped one open to show me, and of course, he was exactly right.

"See these black ones?" he asked, grabbing hold of one and lifting it up. "*These* are what we want."

He hauled it to the edge of the dumpster—which was right where he wanted it—ripped it open and began pillaging.

In the first couple trash bags, he found nothing of use. Then his eyes lit up.

"*Duuuude*," he announced emphatically. "You ain't ready for this, man."

"What?!"

"Grab one of those for me, will ya?"

I handed him a cardboard pallet that was lying on the ground, the sort bunches of bananas might come shipped in, and when I looked back, he held a bright red tomato in front of my face.

"Check these bad boys out! Ain't nothing wrong with these guys."

One by one he began tossing his findings onto our cardboard pallet. Skeptical, I picked one up for examination, but indeed, there was nothing noticeably wrong with them.

"Why'd they throw them out?" I asked.

"Expiration dates, man. It's a dirty rotten scandal and a downright shame," he said. "It's a product of capitalism, dude. I'm telling you, the world would be a much better place if everyone were anarchist. Until then, that's what we're here for, to take back what's ours, to live off the waste of civilization. One man's trash!"

Again, Oz went back to work, digging around, finding new trash bags to loot. Each bag was like a present waiting to be opened on Christmas day.

"No way…" he said.

I gripped the side of the dumpster to peer in.

"What?!"

The rush of the search was making me forget my hunger.

He turned around holding two large avocados in each in hand. As a lover and connoisseur of avocados, I knew at once by the look and feel of them that they were perfectly ripe and ready for eating.

Chapter 11

"That's not all," he said, almost losing his mind at the sight of the contents of a recently opened trash bag. "You gotta get in here, man! Shit's like El Dorado up in here."

Me...? Get in there...? That wretched, smelly dumpster?

My unease since our initial approach had slowly disappeared, but I had watched from a safe distance. The thought of being the one scrounging around in that dump like a rat was a new realm of discomfort.

"But you promised, bro," he said with sad eyes.

I sighed. I had told him I would join him on this adventure, so I decided to go for the full experience.

With nervous energy filling my stomach, I pressed myself up and leapt into the dumpster, finding my balance. I crept atop the trash bags, in some parts sinking like I was walking on a slowly deflating bouncy house. I sifted with bare hands through each garbage sack that looked promising.

What has my life come to?!

Only a couple months ago, I was being wined and dined at the fanciest restaurants in town by vendors looking to court huge marketing budgets. And now, here I was digging for food scraps in a small-town dumpster! Maybe the bigger question was, why did the scavenging feel so much more rewarding?

I noticed the occasional townsperson stopping to watch our antics, their eyes filled with curiosity and judgment, desperately wanting to say something, but they must have thought the subject too awkward to broach. I had felt like them only moments ago. If only they knew how freeing diving could be!

I continued digging and ripping apart trash bags, throwing aside the expired, useless, and rotted items. The more I dug, the more fun it became. Kneeling down, I began to uncover some spoils of my own. I snagged the gems.

"How do these look?" I asked, tossing Oz a couple cabbages.

"What a find!" he said with a proud nod before tossing them onto our pallet. The dumpster was a treasure chest, and our filling pallet was our bounty.

Before long, the dumpster had determined our dinner. Based on the current haul, the plan was to make two large dishes of curry and guacamole. The digging continued, and it only stopped when the take was sufficient to feed eleven hungry hikers. The final count: fifteen avocados, ten carrots, three cabbages, and a few tomatoes and onions, all piled high onto our cardboard pallet.

The walk home was filled with fast-talking, chests held high, yelling, and high-fives. You'd think we had just won the lottery.

"Top five," he said again and again, referring to the idea that it was one of the top five dumpsters he'd ever seen in his life. Those words quickly became his favorite saying for the rest of the day. "It's not usually this easy," he said, "Top five, bro."

We busted through the front door of the house like heroes. The pallet was set on the counter and our housemates' ooh's and ahh's filled the room. A massive pot of curry and a huge batch of guacamole were whipped up on the granite kitchen countertops. The curry was cooked to perfection, and everything was distributed evenly to the crew. And thus, the feast began.

I ate next to Nomad, a thirty-year-old religion and philosophy major who had spent many years teaching English in Taiwan where he met and married the love of his life. You'd never know it because of his silly and vibrant attitude, but Nomad had come to the PCT because his wife grew sick and tragically passed away not long after they married. Afterward, Nomad felt called to the wilderness in search of answers, eventually stumbling across information about the PCT. His plan was to toss his wife's ashes from the peak of Mt. Whitney, the tallest mountain in the contiguous United States, located just a few miles off the PCT. I was looking forward to getting to know Nomad better and hoped he would reach his destination.

After dinner, it was time for dessert. Large tubs of ice cream had been set on the kitchen counter, purchased by the other hikers as a token of their appreciation and desire to contribute. I approached the scene like a lion stalking its prey.

Secretly, I knew Bradley wasn't the only one reaching for indulgence and comfort. He did so through smoking while food had become my vice.

Feeding my vice.

Conveniently, the long days of walking the trail meant I could eat whatever and however much I wanted without the side effects of weight gain. Nutrition took a backseat to caloric content. Whether it was a half dozen donuts, candy bars, or a gallon of ice cream, I easily gave myself to sweets, seeking out these pleasurable sensations in moments of discomfort. The mind was a clever thing in this regard, rationalizing and justifying that one had to satisfy the body's needs and that this food, no matter how poor in nutrition, was energy—energy to be stockpiled and utilized for the up-coming stretch. Each time I brought a spoonful of creamy, milky goodness to my lips, I knew Bradley was watching me with the same eyes through which I viewed his smoking. We still hadn't discussed it, but the silence spoke volumes.

The night unfolded into something like a schoolgirl's slumber party. We nestled up on pillowed couches, wrapped ourselves in blankets, and sprawled out across the floor. To our delight, a Netflix account was logged into the television, and the movie *Wild* just happened to show up on the *recommended for you* queue.

We laughed.

The movie, based on a novel by Cheryl Strayed, was criticized by many in the hiker community for not being enough about the trail. In my eyes, the criticism was unwarranted, as it was more about the story of an individual's inner journey while the PCT was simply a setting, a vehicle aiding in her transformation.

The book and movie played a larger part in my coming to the trail than I had initially realized. Days ago, Bradley revealed that although he had heard of the trail long before he had heard of *Wild*, watching the movie inspired him to finally begin seriously researching the trail. That meant it had played a role in bringing me here, too! I had seen the movie the week before my flight to San Diego, and it planted in me a vague notion of what the trail might be like.

After thirty minutes of endless scrolling, chatter, and debate, we instead watched a movie called Tracks. Yes, we picked the hiking movie. The flick was a true story about a woman named Robyn Davidson and her journey walking across the Australian Outback with only her dog and four camels.

Maybe I could be like her someday...

As the credits rolled and the hikers began another movie, I slipped easily into sleep.

CHAPTER 12

May 15, 2015
Mile 180, Idyllwild (2,470 miles to go)

Snow was piling up outside the window when we woke. From the look of it, the weather wouldn't clear up anytime soon.

That morning, at the center of town, other hikers expressed their impatience, planning to hike out into the mountains regardless of the weather. But returning to a snowy trail without a tarp or tent didn't sit well with me. With the house rented and the chance of being bailed out by another cabin unlikely, we hung back, hoping for clearer weather.

Four days passed. Days of digging through trashcans and dumpsters and asking bakeries about their expired goods. The dumpsters stopped yielding the fruit they once bore. Bakeries grew dismissive and annoyed by our lingering presence.

How quickly the vagabond activities have lost their luster!

It didn't help our spirits knowing the cost of housing was leaving a hefty dent in our finances.

I was quickly finding out how much we would rely on money to continue our hike. We were less than ten percent of the way to Canada, and at this rate, we'd be bankrupt long before the northern border. We'd have to become even more frugal as the miles passed.

When the snowfall finally lifted on the fourth day, I hiked out with Bradley, Oz, Nomad, and Gandalf. Leaving town with the added friends brought me comfort. It felt nice to be part of something bigger, to belong.

My first steps returning to the trail were tentative and uneasy, my legs weaker than I had remembered since our barefooting days. Six zero-days had brought comfort, but how much had my conditioning suffered? My pack was filled with a fresh supply of food and water that pulled me down. I realized how much I relied on momentum for confidence.

As we began our northern climb through the ponderosa pines and up the switchbacks of the San Jacinto Mountains, my confidence slowly returned. The weight of my pack rested heavy but easy on my shoulders and hips.

"Shit!"

The voice came from just behind me. I stopped, turning to see what had happened. It was Gandalf. He was keeled over, grabbing his ankle.

Everyone gathered around him. I clenched my teeth.

"You okay, man?" I asked.

"I'm fine," he said, trying to put weight against his foot.

"Sit down," Bradley said. "Let's take a look."

His ankle had swollen into a baseball. It looked like he had sprained it. He lifted himself up again and took a few steps before sitting down and burying his face in his hands. My heart sank in the silence.

"We're not far from the trailhead," Oz said. "I'll walk you down to the road if you can hold on to my shoulder. We'll wait there until we can find you a hitch back into town."

Gandalf nodded solemnly and stood. Oz slung his ultralight pack across his chest, slid Gandalf's backpack onto his back, and with Gandalf's arm around Oz's shoulder, they began stepping their way back down the mountain.

"Do you want us to wait for you?" Nomad asked.

Oz turned and shook his head. "I'll catch up later in the day. You guys keep moving."

We pressed our lips together as the two hobbled down the mountain and disappeared around a bend.

"Get better soon, brother!" yelled Bradley.

"You'll be back in no time!" yelled Nomad.

I was speechless. I knew Oz would make his way back to us by the day's end, but a sickening, sad thought crept across my mind that we might not see Gandalf again. The whole thing made me want to cry.

To think injury could happen to any of us at any time was difficult to stomach. The thought crept across my mind every few miles. I was falling in love with the trail, sinking deeply into its experience. There was something I still needed to experience before my time here came to an end. And if I could help it, I wanted to finish. I wanted to go all the way.

After a long silence, we turned and continued up the footpath into the woods, trees spreading outward in all directions, a family of deer watching us quietly from a distance. The days of wandering, comfort, and nightly town feasts felt like nothing more than waking from a dream after a long night's sleep.

CHAPTER 13

May 25, 2015
Mile 310, Deep Creek (2,340 miles to go)

There was no snow beyond the mountain ridge, and we were thrown right back into the desert heat. The mountain pines faded to the familiar thorny chaparrals, rocks, and dust.

My yellow shirt was turning brown, so I often went without it, allowing me to showcase my scrawny arms and flat-bodied chest to a female every few miles. We also chose to forgo sunscreen, citing Bradley's pseudo-scientific belief that "after you get a couple of good burn layers out of the way, you've adapted, and the body can endure infinite amounts of sun."

Strangely, the strategy seemed to work. I say *seemed* because I'm sure the exposure was quite detrimental to long-term health, but we weren't so concerned about such things. After the initial burn, the peeling was just a transitory phase, and we soaked in the sunrays, thinking highly of our freshly tanned skin.

It was a drought year for our class of thru-hikers, and the terrain's long stretches of open desert and dangerously few water sources brought cravings of cold water, ice baths, and the chill of standing in front of a freshly opened kitchen freezer. I would have paid rent to live in one of those bad boys ...

Some hikers said the extreme heat was a promising sign for the future. In drought years, there was a reduced likelihood of heavy snowfall in the High Sierra, the mountains of central California. As I had recently discovered, I was no fan of the snow nor could I imagine enduring it in higher altitudes. But the supposed advantage was too far in the future to be thankful for today. My skin was burnt and peeling. The heat penetrated our backpacks, melting everything from the inside out, chocolate bars to cheese.

Water was sparse. Creeks, springs, and rivers were but empty beds   of cracked dirt, and anything listed on Oz's and Nomad's trail maps were usually assumed dry. In this case, carrying the water report became a must. It was a piece of paper, a crowdsourced compilation of water information that accurately provided us with mile markers of flowing springs. It saved us on many occasions, but like many hikers, we continued to rely heavily on the reliable word-of-mouth network of on-trail hikers.

Surprisingly, most of our drinking water came from tarp-covered piles of plastic gallon jugs called caches that were coordinated and maintained by trail angels. Caches were a source of trail controversy. Some believed hikers should be forced to navigate nature as nature intended, without the help of outsiders. Others claimed caches posed a risk to hikers, especially those depending on something maintained by error-prone humans. What would happen if the cache were empty when they arrived? Once a cache is set up, word spreads, and it needs to be kept running for the safety of down-trail hikers.

It was always oddly thrilling in the moments before arriving at a supposed cache.

Will it be there? What will happen if it isn't?

Thankfully, we never had any problems with caches. While everyone likely would have preferred the pristine, cool flow of a natural river compared to the warm jugs, I was grateful for water of any kind, unbothered by the politics.

Shade was equally hard to come by. Most plants surrounding the trail were prickled, dried, and no more than ankle or waist high. Brush, bramble, cacti, and chaparral filled the land. It was simply too hot to walk in the daytime with temperatures teetering above one hundred degrees Fahrenheit most days. Many hikers sought shade in the daytime, hiding beneath their tents or forming canopies atop the bushes with clothes or tarps, opting to only hike the early morning or night hours. Not surprisingly, this problem inspired Bradley, and he suggested that one day, he wanted to hike twenty-four hours straight without stopping.

I cocked my head and laughed. Bradley often conjured crazy ideas like this. It sounded unsustainable and unnecessary, but again, nothing more was said of it. In the end, I feared he would somehow get his way when the time came.

Though Bradley and I had become very close, I still felt tension between us. The trail's high mileage, hot temperatures, and few water sources combined for a difficult environment, which agitated our relationship.

Despite the hot days, we progressed over miles of seemingly endless desert mountains accompanied by Oz and Nomad. They provided a nice balance to Bradley. We even named our wolfpack the Poodle Dog Boys after the Poodle Dog bush, the name of a plant that had infested entire sections of the trail, forcing miles of closures.

At first, we all thought the plant was a dangerous thing with a silly name. It was known to be poisonous if you touched it. The hairs from its buds clung to clothing, and the slightest touch caused bumpy, itchy, two-week-long skin rashes.

It also looked and smelled like marijuana. We heard that someone in years past had tried to smoke it only to earn himself a quick trip to the emergency room.

Another girl we had met along the trail earned the trail name Poodle Lips from a close encounter with the plant. It was something everyone was looking to avoid.

It wasn't until much later that we discovered the story of the Poodle Dog bush, how its seeds lay buried and dormant in the earth for years, awakened only by forest fires. When the forest finished burning, the plant rose like a phoenix from the ashes and acted as a defense mechanism for new plants to spring up and take root. Its poisonous buds defended the burnt land against animals and humans, and once the saplings of the new desert plants are deemed sustainable, the Poodle Dog bush dies, sacrificing itself for the new generation of life. Hearing this story only solidified our decision to take on the name. To us, it implied that although something looks troubling on the outside, perhaps its existence still served some greater purpose.

One day, as the Poodle Dog Boys were walking together, the trail shifted downhill, and we spotted a distant white blob moving toward us.

Bradley turned his head around with wide eyes and nearly burst out in laughter.

"What?" I asked.

As the blob moved closer, the situation needed no explanation. Slowly approaching us was a man wearing headphones, sunglasses, a hat, and nothing else. His flabby, nude, sun-screened body jiggled as he neared.

Why is this dude hiking naked?! I took a deep breath, knowing it was common to greet passing hikers. I didn't want to treat him any differently.

We walked off the trail as was the courtesy for uphill hikers. Just as he passed, I looked him in the eye, about to give my regards, but he continued on without even acknowledging our existence.

It was one of the only times I had passed a hiker without a moment of genuine acknowledgment, an act I enjoyed and even forced upon those who might be trying to avoid it. The gesture differed heavily compared to life in the city where I could so easily move about in a crowd, all of us like ants, going to and from our various tasks without exchanging eye contact or smiling. But as the naked man passed us, I had no issue with him continuing on.

The man is in his own zone! I breathed a sigh of relief, and we had a good laugh before continuing down into the valley.

We headed deeper into the gorge, following the curve of the canyon walls, and when we reached the bottom, we couldn't believe what we saw nestled there.

It was an oasis! Natural hot spring pools overflowed and cascaded gently into a cold bubbling creek. East of this sat a sandy beach with a couple dozen people lounging beneath trees or basking in the open sun. This would be a special place indeed.

There were five familiar faces sitting in the largest tub, all of them naked and bathing in the hot springs.

This must explain that naked guy, I thought. It turned out clothes were optional at Deep Creek Hot Springs…

Among the familiar faces lounging in the hot pool was Saint Croix, a wise, middle-aged man bearing the name of his hometown who looked years younger than his true age. I would later discover his life of adventure was sparked by tragedy. He recounted to me the day his house burned down to the ground and how he stood on his front lawn watching the flames consume the life he had built and known. He lost everything that day, he'd said, and he was only able to salvage a few photos and keepsakes that remained. But he also said that having his house burn down was the best thing that ever happened to him. The change re-ignited his adventurous inclinations. Taking inspiration from a time before when he had set off Huckleberry Finn style to float down the Mississippi River on a handmade log raft, he decided to live a new life and go full-time in his nomadic seeking by thru-hiking the Appalachian Trail. The PCT was his inevitable next step.

Sitting in the cauldron next to Saint Croix was a trail couple, Chatty Kathy and Sacajawea. Chatty was one of the funniest guys I'd ever met. As his name implied, he was talkative and guilty of blabbering. But he was also lovable, laid-back, and sweet. I couldn't help but laugh at everything he said. He carried a backpacker's guitalele, a mix between a guitar and a ukulele, and his playing reminded me of how much I missed hearing music. The last time I'd heard it was two hundred miles ago, back at the Mount Laguna campground. Even though many hikers listened to music from their phones, I had opted not to bring headphones in favor of listening to my thoughts in an attempt to live more in "the present moment" with the surrounding nature. I liked this decision. It forced me to confront what was happening inside of me and made music that much sweeter whenever it came around.

Sacajawea, Chatty Kathy's wife, was a beautiful woman with a confidence that made me want to know her better. Sac enjoyed telling the story of how she and Chatty had met while hiking the Appalachian Trail the year prior. Apparently, Chatty had followed her the entire trail—a claim Chatty didn't deny—and proposed to her from atop Mt. Katahdin, the AT's northern terminus. Instead of taking some exotic, week long excursion for their honeymoon, the two decided they'd hike the PCT together the very next summer. Having thru-hiked before, the newlyweds had a great sense of humor and lightness about the whole situation. Sac in particular was constantly telling jokes about having to "put up" with Chatty, which made everyone laugh.

Soaking next to these two was another hiker couple, a more recently developing "trailationship", Macho Man Randy Savage and DK Shh. They were two of my favorite people, and just like Chatty, I couldn't help but crack up at everything they said. When these three got together, they were a dangerously funny comedy troupe with spot-on impressions and funny accents that killed me every time. I was an easy crowd.

"Velcome to zeh hot springs, boys," Chatty said.

"It's so vunderful in here," DK Shh said.

"Vill you join us for a soak?" Macho asked.

"Must be a cold hot springs," laughed Bradley.

"I'm a grow-er not a show-er, partner," Macho said, tipping his non-existent cowboy hat.

"We're coming in, hold your horses," Nomad said.

As Bradley and Nomad stripped down and jumped in, I stood for a long moment from the outside looking in, hesitant to bear my manhood. Being naked in public was a realm I'd never ventured into, and I sat on the edge of the pool until it was clear that judgment of any sort seemed to be the least of anyone's concerns.

Recalling my experience with dumpster diving, I eased into the idea, slowly shedding my clothes and sliding into the hot cauldron to join the others. The warmth flowed across my body, steeping my skin in a relaxing embrace.

"Apparently, there's deadly bacteria living in that creek," Sac said, pointing to the gentle waterway down below.

Bradley snapped to attention. "Says who?" he asked.

"Didn't you see the sign?"

He shook his head.

"Sounds dangerous," DK Shh said. "But I'm sure we'll be fine… just don't open your eyes or drink the water."

Bradley grinned. I already knew what was coming. He immediately rose out of the water, stepped to the edge of the hot tub, and dove into the creek. He emerged moments later with wide eyes and an open mouth.

"Cleanest water I've ever tasted!" he announced.

"Eww," Sac said.

I laughed and soon dove into the creek to join him. The water was frigid and took my breath away while the shift in temperature woke me right up. Hours passed of us cycling back and forth between the hot pool and the cold creek. Settling into the hot spring, Bradley and I looked at each other, rolled our eyes, nodded, and laughed. It was easy to get along when everything was going well.

"Hey, want to stay the night here?" he asked.

I squinted, unsure about spending any more time away from the trail.

"Just one night…" he said, "We'll head out bright and early in the morning. Experiences like this don't come around often."

I felt uneasy considering how many zero-days we'd spent in Idyllwild. We were falling farther and farther behind schedule, and I knew winter would arrive sooner than we might like to believe. But looking around, I must have been the only one even remotely concerned about time or destination. Everyone was too busy enjoying his or her nakedness, relaxing and splashing in the waters of this oasis.

What harm could there be in staying just one more night?

"All right," I said. "One night."

Bradley smiled. He stood on the rock shelf and launched himself into the creek once more.

I remained captured by my surroundings for some time. The shadow of the canyon cliff was cast against the river like a curtain, shading the willows and grasses rising between clusters of white boulders. Town life was luxurious, but this place was paradise.

I don't recall who had offered them to me, but at some point shortly after Bradley had left, I was approached with the opportunity to take magic mushrooms.

The sight of the mushrooms made me laugh. It reminded me of just how much my mindset had changed over the years. I had taken magic mushrooms a handful of times in college, the first of which transpired during my freshman year. And come to think of it… it was at Bradley's house, no less!

It was a dark and rainy night, and the living room was musty and smelled of smoke and days of partying. Seated in a leather recliner and having taken the shrooms some time ago, my chair was no longer a chair but a boat, and the wood panel flooring had transformed into a great ocean! Back and forth I rocked amid the storm through crashing waves, holding onto the sides of the deck (which were actually armrests) brimming with fear and excitement, not knowing the difference, left to the mercy of the suburban tides. I learned little from this experience other than how the mind could experience fleeting states of consciousness much different from the reality I usually experienced in my day-to-day life.

I'd taken magic mushrooms three more times since the first, finding there was much more to myself I didn't yet know. The debate remained...

Which state of being is actually closer to reality?

Either way, after voyaging through these trips, I was left to drift back into my old life, easily taken by negative emotions, ego, and pleasure.

At this moment, taking mushrooms was a phase of life I had already passed through. There was no reason to stumble through that door again.

And if I take them, wouldn't that make me a hypocrite? Wouldn't I be swimming in the same waters that I despised seeing Bradley in? And all those days of accumulated efforts in purity... wouldn't they be lost in seconds, leaving me to start over from the very beginning?

But then new thoughts surfaced. I had come a long way since my college days. Maybe things would be different this time...

Maybe because so much time has passed in my current state, there is something different awaiting me on the other side. And if I don't take this opportunity now, will it ever come again?

Curiosity got the best of me. I took the mushrooms and ate them.

The sky was empty and blue as I floated in the creek. Nothing changed for some time, and I had accepted that maybe nothing would happen. Maybe they were just ordinary mushrooms! Or maybe I hadn't taken enough. Either way, I was okay and more than happy to simply enjoy the water.

Just then, a light pressure settled against my forehead. I had felt the feeling before, and it was definitely of the magic sort. Time began to slow. The world around me grew shades brighter, and before long, I seemed to fill spaces I didn't normally occupy, as if I was becoming integrated into my surroundings rather than separate from them. I stepped out of the creek and made my way to the sandy shore nearby.

The sand was warm beneath my toes, and I settled on a nice spot to lie down under the sun. Stretching my body out in every direction, I began noticing neglected tightness, remembering long-forgotten body parts—the hips, the side body, spine, and back. My yoga practice came rushing back to me. It was something I had been ignoring on the trail, despite the critical role it played in relieving stress during my nine-to-five.

Yoga at Deep Creek.

The passing hours felt timeless and were spent stretching, working through every inch of my body. By the time it was over, I wondered what—if anything—I had learned from taking the mushrooms. If they had taught me anything, it was only a reminder that somehow the answers were inside of me, inside my own body, and that even during the most difficult times, the body should not be neglected. It was my most important asset. It was remarkable how much tension I had been holding in my body, and yoga allowed me to release those channels inside of me. I stood, walked over to the cold, flowing creek, and dove in head first. I decided spending any amount of time in this place, so long as it was for the benefit of my body and mind, was well worth the investment.

Night came, and all the hikers at the creek stayed up late, soaking in the hot springs, chatting, and playing music until it was time for bed. We slept on the sand with the sound of the bubbling creek echoing into the canyon. Town awaited us the next day, and even though I was ready to move, it was difficult to leave paradise.

The one thing that pulled us forward was the promise of a McDonald's fast food restaurant waiting for us at the next pass. The only reason to leave one paradise was the pursuit of another.

The Poodle Dog Boys, along with a few new friends, departed the hot springs at sunrise and walked seventeen miles that day, climbing out of the canyon to eventually reach Cajon Pass at mile 328 by the afternoon.

The trail winding its way to Cajon.

We could hear the humming of engines and honking of horns along the six lanes of bumper-to-bumper interstate traffic from miles away. I was excited upon hearing the noise, knowing we were close to town and grateful we were separate from it.

To our good fortune, the McDonalds was not a myth. There stood the golden arches with backpacks lining the outside walls of the restaurant. It felt nice to escape the heat.

Inside, the place was a haven for hikers. Hiker trash, an endearing term for hikers, had taken over nearly every inch of the restaurant space. We filled booths, created long queues, plugged our devices into every available outlet, and carried ungodly sacks of food on trays overflowing with dollar cheeseburgers, fries, and pies. Bradley and I caved. We each bought a milkshake while friends offered us fries and bites of their burgers.

We exited the McDonalds with our savory and sweet stomachs filled but curious if any known hiker boxes existed in the area.

My feet had been killing me during the past miles as their swelling had caused my toes to press up against the front of my shoes. They just didn't fit like they used to, and I was afraid that injuries and blisters might start cropping up once again. It also didn't help that the shoes were already ruining, the tread wearing down completely and the front end of the shoe beginning to peel open at the seam.

Wearing proper footwear was an essential part of the trail journey. I still couldn't believe Bradley was wearing his Jesus sandals. He had been complaining often, but he continued to come up with new, inventive methods for fastening and tying the laces around his toes and ankles to alleviate friction and chafe. Each shift in his shoe tying strategy seemed to work for a day or two, but then he'd have to come up with a new one. It didn't help that neither of us had new pairs of shoes readily accessible. It was a decision that needed to be coordinated well in advance, and at the moment, neither of us were handling these shoe challenges well.

We asked the hikers sitting around the McDonald's parking lot about hiker boxes, and a few of them said we should check out the nearby hotels across the highway. Dreams of hiker boxes holding new shoes filled my mind as we crossed the overpass.

The first hotel turned up empty. The second had nothing of interest, just a few Ziploc bags of unwanted food. We thought about giving up but, in a state of desperation and hope, decided to pursue the final hotel across the street.

I couldn't believe what I found! Buried deep inside one of the boxes was a lightly worn pair of yellow and black Altras, an expensive trail running shoe with a solid reputation among hikers. They were a size ten and engineered with a properly wide toe box, exactly what I needed for my swollen feet. I smiled as I laced them up and looked toward

Bradley as he shuffled one last time through the hiker box. Unfortunately, he wouldn't find anything to fit him and would continue wearing the latest version of his gladiator sandals.

Nevertheless, he found a few gems to eat, and we left town with a newfound readiness for hiking, my new shoes wrapping my feet like clouds.

Days later, we finally reached Wrightwood and decided it was time to write another email to update friends and family:

May 25, 2015
Mile 367, Wrightwood
Subject: "The Oasis, Deep Creek"

We hope you've been well on your trail. Ours continues to challenge us in so many ways. Physically, our bodies are in pain much of the time as we are still adjusting to the nomadic lifestyle. Let us paint you a picture...

We wake up between 6:30 and 7:30 to the cold desert air. Sometimes the dew point is reached, and we are soaked because we sleep in the open. If we're lucky, the sun is out to ease the transition from lying to standing. We may at this point eat a Cliff bar or just pack up and start walking to warm up. As we walk, our legs and bodies go through many ups and downs. Our feet are blistered, our legs are sore and tight, our minds weak and wandering. Doubts and desires surface and consume us. During the day, we take breaks to rest. We laugh at each other when we start walking after breaking because we look like reborn sheep trying to rewarm our legs up... ha, ha! After fifteen to twenty miles, our walking ends and darkness falls upon us. We cook a meal, maybe start a fire, and then go to sleep under the stars. Repeat.

Although the days may seem long and tedious and uneventful, simple moments start to take on a whole new meaning.

Like a moth trying desperately to escape birds of prey. Or a rattlesnake coiling in defense after almost being stepped on. And sometimes we are rewarded with something really special. Let's add some color to this painting...

Recently, we arrived at Deep Creek Hot Springs: an oasis with a cool flowing river and several hot spring pools in the middle of the desert. We spent nearly two days soaking and swimming with friends, fellow hikers, and locals. We realize the Hot Springs would not have been so wonderful without the cool water to jump into after heating in them. Similarly, this oasis would not have been so magical without the hard work that came before it.

Right now, we're in Wrightwood, the sun's shining, and we feel good. Thanks for the letters and care packages. They're a blessing to read and remind us of the boundless support that surrounds us. We're changing a lot as individuals and learning who we are and who we want to become. It's scary and really exciting. We will never be more ready than now.

Love,
David & Bradley

CHAPTER 14

June 1, 2015
Mile 444, Acton KOA (Kampground of America), (2,206 miles to go)

Descending the switchbacks of the desert hills, I thought I could see a campground nearing in the distance. It had been a long few days of hiking in the desert, and suddenly, sprawled out before me was a green grass field with tents and hammocks set between tree shade. I blinked my eyes to make sure it wasn't a mirage, but it remained.

We entered Acton KOA through a wooden gate beside the highway, set our packs in the shade, took off our shoes, and walked on the soft grass.

This must be the first time I've actually enjoyed walking barefoot, I thought.

A boy holding a frisbee waved. His name was Lucky. Lucky had a wide smile and a wonderful laugh. I would later learn his story, how a year before the trail he'd crashed his car and endured brain trauma that nearly ended his life. He had spent long days in the hospital where he realized life was short and sparked a plan to hike across the U.S. Like me, he traveled with a friend, a boy named Sweet Tea. I could tell there was love and tension between them, the same kind that existed between Bradley and me.

"You guys want to play?" they asked us.

"It's on," we said.

We took sides, and the tossing began. Before long, twenty hikers had joined in, teams formed, and we were all barefoot, sprinting full speed across the field. My body was a well-oiled machine, and without a backpack to hold me down, I was weightless. I couldn't remember the last time I'd run so fast in my life. Despite being given an opportunity for rest, our bodies were becoming conditioned to need exercise. The legs needed to be kept running to stave off the rust.

When the game ended, I milled about the campground sweaty and exhausted until I spotted a bunch of hikers and tourists gathered around a swimming pool. I closed my eyes and shook my head again to make sure what I was seeing was real. When I opened them, a thousand lights were bouncing from the water's surface. My heart skipped, and I rushed to open the gate, dip my legs in at the edge of the pool, and lean back onto the concrete. The ground was hot against my back.

As I stared into the sky, I couldn't help but be reminded of my loneliness. Sure, there was Bradley, and I had met plenty of new friends, but I craved intimacy now more than ever. Touch and sexual encounters were something I had become accustomed to in my old life, even if my relationships were influenced by drinking and smoking.

Women were sparse on the trail, at best one for every four hikers, and most had either started the trail with a partner or had quickly fallen into a trailationship.

It didn't help that everyone was becoming more and more beautiful as the miles passed. The more we walked, the tanner, stronger, and more toned our bodies became. Almost everyone had "the hiker glow," a bright and visible sense of openness and excitement often commented on by towns-people. Despite all these glowing, beautiful women, I hadn't yet found anyone to take away my loneliness, to give me what I didn't yet know how to give myself.

Chapter 14

When I sat up, there was a girl sitting across the pool, her feet dangling into the water. I tried to look away but couldn't. She had long brown hair, brown eyes, tanned skin, a tight and toned physique, and she kicked her legs back and forth, sending ripples across the water toward me. She was well kept with makeup and eye shadow and all the things women on the trail had abandoned miles ago. For this reason, in a world of hikers, she stood out. Apart from her looks, there was something else about her that intrigued me, a knowing that she was the type I liked, that we would get along well. Still, she seemed a bit shy and standoffish, steeped in thought, her brown eyes gazing downward at her reflection.

I thought it strange for such an outwardly beautiful woman to be so pensive and reflective, seemingly concerned with her appearance, but the thought didn't make me any less interested.

As I was staring, she looked up, catching me in my moment of lost curiosity. I looked away, but to my surprise, the few glances she gave the world above the water seemed directed at me. I marked it up to wishful thinking—there must be someone else, something *behind* me she's interested in. And of all the possible objects of attention at her disposal, why would she choose me?

I went back to staring at the sky, but when I returned to observe the pool, the glances became more prolonged and uninterrupted. Soon, there was little doubt in my mind I was the target of her attention.

Her interest drew me nearer to her. I jumped in the lukewarm water and slowly swam toward her, trying to be as inconspicuous as possible, and when I came up for air beside her feet, I introduced myself.

Her name was Elle. Our interaction confirmed my initial belief that she was shy, but much like myself, she lightened up as the conversation progressed and became remarkably easy going.

She was a few years older than me, in her late twenties. Elle had been a track athlete in college and an only child. As we spoke, we were both smiling like fools and biting our lips. I could tell we were both attracted to one another.

She was hiking alone, and when I asked why she had come to the trail, she wouldn't disclose to me what I felt like was a truthful answer. I guessed the reason was too personal for her to share with a relative stranger. She told me she had just started the trail no more than fifty to a hundred miles ago and seemed a bit ashamed of herself for not starting at the border. I told her there was no reason to feel that way, that she was here and should be proud of simply taking the leap. She smiled, then reached up to rub her shoulder.

"Ah! My body is killing me... check these out." She turned to show me bruises on both sides of her hips.

I cringed. "How much does your backpack weigh?!"

"Oh, gosh. It's a lot... want to see it? But you have to swear you won't laugh."

I grinned. "Sure."

"Okay, come."

She took my arm and led me out the gates of the pool to beneath the shade of a nearby tree.

"Here," she said.

The pack was nearly twice her size. She lifted it onto her shoulders and turned in circles like a runway model.

"Let's see," I said. I could hardly lift it from the ground with one arm. I laughed and shook my head.

"So, you haven't had a shakedown yet?" I asked.

"What's that?"

My eyes brightened. "It's a game changer," I said, explaining to her the process.

She blushed. "I'm not sure. So, you want to see *all* my stuff? Even the *personal* stuff?"

Looking through someone's pack was to learn the most intimate details of that person's life. Imagine someone picking up every belonging in your house piece by piece and asking you its purpose. I understood her hesitancy, but from the look of it, she wouldn't last long without lightening her load.

"Only the things you feel comfortable with," I said.

She smiled, knelt down, and began unpacking her belongings onto the grass one at a time. I felt like Steve Climber, the wolverine from kickoff, scanning through all her stuff.

"All right," I said, starting with an obvious luxury item. "What's this?"

"A mirror."

"What do you need it for?"

"My makeup, of course."

A remarkably large bag plopped down from her hands onto the ground between us with a thud. Inside were all sorts of powders, eyeliners, and lipsticks. I feigned a smile, cringing on the inside.

"And what about all this?" I asked, pointing to the heaping pile of clothing she had drawn from her bag.

She shook her head and smiled.

I shrugged. "Well, there must be something we can let go of."

"Hmm, maybe this…?" she asked, pulling out a can of mace.

My eyebrow rose after a laugh. No thru-hiker carried mace on the PCT, at least none I knew of. Mace could be used as a bear deterrent, but the kind she was carrying must have weighed nearly a full pound. To me, it was just a rookie mistake. And then I realized how funny it was for me to think of someone as a rookie.

Maybe I am finding my footing on the trail, I thought.

The can of bear mace wasn't even the worst of it. After she lightened up to potentially ridding herself of the mace, she looked up at me.

"If you think the trail is as safe as you say it is, then I guess there's something else I should show you."

"What's that?"

Next, she pulled out a small pistol from deep inside her pack.

"Is that a *gun*?" I whispered.

"It's for self-defense."

"Do you think you'll need it?"

"Maybe."

I hadn't heard of anyone carrying a gun on the trail. I saw it as distrust and discomfort rather than self-defense. Not only was this pistol incredibly heavy but bringing such a weapon arguably invited further danger into her experience.

I was reminded of how the things we carry tell us of our fears. But who was I to judge? Perhaps carrying a gun gave her a better chance at surviving the trail than not carrying a tarp.

But she eventually agreed it wasn't fully thought through. After some discussion, she decided she'd mail it back home at the next town.

Shortly after the shakedown, I noticed Elle seemed quite interested and trusting of me. It helped me to understand why I had looked up to Steve Climber, still revering his help at kickoff from many miles ago. Showing the parts of ourselves we keep hidden can bring us closer to the people around us.

We spent the rest of the afternoon talking about life, giggling, frolicking, and lying in the grass. But even after a full day's conversation, I still felt like I knew so little about her.

How many days does it take to really know someone? I wondered.

Day turned to night as we lay beneath a myriad of stars. We nestled close together in our sleeping bags and spoke about life and death, joy and pain. As the stars peered out from the blackened canvas above, I tried to kiss her, but she stopped me and giggled.

"Kissing always leads to more," she said. "Is that something you're ready for?"

I laughed. "I'll never know if we don't try."

She narrowed her eyes and gave me a peck on the cheek. "Tell me your story," she said, turning back to the sky, resting her head against my shoulder.

"What do you want to know?

"Everything," she said.

"It's too late for *everything*."

"It's never too late for everything."

I sighed. "But you'll fall asleep."

"Nuh-uh."

I spent some time from the beginning, telling her the best stories about Bradley and me, and she laughed and sighed at all the ups and downs: the barefooting, the dumpster diving, Deep Creek Hot Springs. Slowly, each reaction became quieter than the last. When I finished, the sky was black and her head lay heavy against my chest.

"I told you."

"I'm only shutting my eyes," she whispered. She gazed up into my eyes, her eyes deep brown, swirling portals in the starlight. "Let's hike out together tomorrow morning."

If I'd learned anything from hiking with Bradley, it was that hiking with someone was a big deal. It wouldn't be easy, but my heart was overflowing at the thought of it. As a hopeful romantic, I said yes, and she allowed me a kiss before turning to fall asleep. I was a happy boy, and I slept soundly that night in the open green grass field beside her.

CHAPTER 15

June 2, 2015
Mile 444, Acton KOA

I woke from a lovely dream and a long night's sleep to find myself surrounded by a lively campground atmosphere. Standing, I walked the grass to look for Bradley and found him sitting cross-legged beneath a tree. We hadn't spoken since yesterday morning, and there was much to be discussed. When I told him all about Elle and how she wanted to hike out with us, he laughed.

"She doesn't want to hike out with *us*," he said with a smile. "She wants to hike with *you*. We've all been watching."

I laughed. "Great." I guess it was hard not to notice our playful, flirtatious behavior.

He took in a breath. I could tell there was something he wanted to say.

"What's up?" I asked.

He shrugged. "I'm glad you two crossed paths. I think it was meant to be." He turned away and looked into the desert foothills then back at me. "Hey, you remember the owner we met in the convenience shop, right?"

"Yeah."

"Well, Oz and I offered to fix up a few of his bikes in exchange for a couple of our own. It was an offer I couldn't pass up. Our plan is to leave tomorrow, to head west and get off the trail for a few days… or a couple weeks… everything depends on what we run into."

"Get off the trail?!" I asked.

I could feel my heart splintering into pieces. I knew there was tension between us, but had things really gotten bad enough for him to leave the trail entirely?

He sighed. "My feet have been killing me, bro. You've probably noticed, but these Jesus sandals just aren't cutting it. I'm hoping there's an outdoor outlet on the coast where I can earn some proper shoes. So, with you meeting Elle, and us receiving these bikes… I just think the timing is auspicious."

The latest model of Bradley's Jesus sandals.

"Anyway," he continued, "I think I'm also ready for some change. For the last five hundred miles, it's been nothing but desert! I just don't feel like I'm growing right now, and the trail isn't serving me as it once did. Maybe that means I need to leave for a while." He looked me in the eye. "So, that's the plan. Starting tomorrow, Oz and I are biking to the coast to see the ocean, to visit Santa Monica, Venice Beach, Hollywood—all those places I've heard about but never seen—and hopefully I can snag some new shoes. Plus, I think the time away could be beneficial for both of us." He laughed. "I hope you understand, brother."

In a single moment I felt sad, disappointed, shocked, and betrayed. *After all that talk about finishing the trail together... and now he's leaving?*

And Oz, too! It felt like he had pulled Bradley away from me, that I'd been replaced, tossed to the wayside.

Is he telling me the truth? Is he leaving because of the brutal desert climate and the need for new shoes... or is it because of me?

Apart from a brief moment back in Idyllwild, I hadn't yet fully imagined what the trail would be like without Bradley. Was I really ready to hike the trail without him?

"What do we do about our resupplies?" I asked. "And the tarp, and the cookpot—"

"You keep the cookpot," he said. "Oz has one we can share. And take these maps. They're easy enough that you'll learn to read them. As for our resupplies, take them. I'll find my way."

"So... you're really leaving?"

He nodded. I pressed my lips together, and he reached out and hugged me.

"Don't worry," he said. "If all goes well, I plan on returning."

I noticed myself feeling a bit better.

"I can't promise anything, but I'll try to time it so we meet back up in Kennedy Meadows at mile 702. I'll keep you updated as best I can."

I nodded. It was nearly 300 miles from where we were on the trail today, but having made it 444 miles, at least I knew now I was capable of walking such a distance.

"You're ready," he said. "Be with Elle. Spread those wings and fly!" He stepped back and turned in circles, flapping his arms and cawing.

I managed a grin, but deep down I knew trail plans were not easily kept. Maintaining communication was already difficult since my phone only worked when charging, and Bradley's burner phone rarely received any signal.

But his decision had been made, a decision that echoed the attitude of many hikers. Thru-hikers were leaving the desert in droves, hitchhiking north for greener vistas and the abundant water sources that were rumored to lie beyond Kennedy Meadows, the infamous pack station that marked the start of Central California's Sierra Mountain range.

Others were re-thinking the trail entirely, either returning to their old lives or trying to begin new ones. Maybe Bradley needed this time away. Maybe he needed to discover something new, to walk a separate path. And maybe I did too. When the inevitable day comes, that those we deem to be our guides leave us behind, they do so for our own benefit and because they know we're ready.

The next day's sunrise came from behind the mountains. I woke and searched for Bradley and Oz one last time, but they had left. I imagined their shadowy figures pedaling into the horizon, backpacks stacked against their backs.

It was only Elle and me now.

"Will you miss them?" Elle asked as we began packing up to head into the northern foothills.

I nodded. "Yeah. Maybe it was meant to be... after all, I have you now."

She smiled, and we left the grassy field through the gate, taking the trail north, the campground at our backs.

Despite her massive pack, Elle started off hiking fast. Really fast. She wasn't lying when she said she was a track athlete, and she moved at nearly twice the speed of Bradley with his Jesus sandals. I forced myself to pick up my pace.

Days passed, and even though her pace leveled off to match mine, she remained strong, determined, and stubborn. Her presence did me good.

I hiked nearly two hundred miles with Elle. We progressed through the sun-dried wasteland, passing through endless dirt fields of giant industrial windmills, the slow and powerful spin of their blades cutting through the air. Then more desert. We hiked on top of aqueducts beside fields of cattle and herding dogs. We saw rattlesnakes curled up beside the trail and spent nights nestled beside each other in our sleeping bags beneath the cold. I remember looking up and staring into the constellations together, pointing out the shapes and patterns dotting the skies as we touched cheeks and kissed. The stars were as bright as I'd ever seen them.

It took some time, but history began to repeat itself. I noticed a similar progression to that of Bradley and me: the initial view of perfection, the finding of flaws, the growing tension. It was all there, happening again like a tired and reoccurring nightmare.

I couldn't put my finger on it, but there was something she was hiding from me. I had told her my story, but I still didn't fully understand hers. What little she had told me about her past seemed mysterious and incomplete, as if she was withholding the missing pieces of a puzzle. But perhaps the strangest thing was how she refused photographs of us when others offered them.

First the bear mace, then the gun, the unknown past, and now no photos? I couldn't help but think she had come here to escape something.

I remember coming out with it one afternoon. "Why don't you want to take pictures?" I asked. "Is there more to the story?"

She looked at me and rolled her eyes. "You know I don't want to talk about this stuff."

I pressed the issue. "But, I can see so much beauty inside of you," I said. "You're like a flower just waiting to blossom."

She glared at me sideways. "And a flower cannot be forced open. It must bloom on its own accord."

And later that night there was another discussion, and I tried asking her once again to open up. I gave her some piece of advice I should have kept to myself knowing her prior response.

She shook her head. "Advice shouldn't be given unless it's asked for," she said. "And isn't advice always for ourselves? You're skilled with words, but I'm not looking for a preacher or a therapist. Anyway, that's enough. I'm tired. I'm going to sleep."

We didn't speak for the rest of the night, and thoughts paraded through my mind.

I hated to see our relationship deteriorating in such a way, and I wondered what was happening. Perhaps our problems could have stemmed from any number or combination of reasons: the trail's physical demands, the constant presence of another person, the sacrifices associated with such a commitment, or even the baggage we had brought with us long before the trail began.

In whichever case, I began to witness that the trail and our relationships bring light to the darkest parts of ourselves. The things we most wanted kept hidden, the things we had never cared to look closely at, the things we thought ourselves free from, manifested most aggressively when times got tough. Now, everything had been brought to the surface.

What was coming up for Elle was likely avoidance of her past, a past I will never truly know or understand. As for me, my shadow was playing the role of the preacher, the giver of unsolicited advice. It was a mistake, and whenever it cropped up, it was a sign for me to turn my own advice inward and ask it of myself.

As Elle said, is there something I too am running away from?

The following morning was the next time we spoke. "I'm sorry about last night," she said. "It must be my food supply

—I'm running low. I don't think I've brought enough to make it to the next town."

It was a challenge to know precisely how much food to pack from town to town. Too much meant a heavier pack and too little meant a hungry day or two as the supply diminished nearer town.

"You can have some of mine," I told her. "I have plenty."

When I handed her a cliff bar, she told me she couldn't take it.

"But I want you to have it. We share on the trail. What's mine is yours."

She shook her head. "It makes me feel weak. I won't take it."

I sighed and left it alone. No more advice, I told myself.

It was then another hiker named Tim walked by with his dog, Oakley. He said hello, but I could tell he sensed a delicate situation because he didn't stay long. Before heading up the trail he turned and said, "Did you two say you were low on food? I'm also low, but there's a trail angel about twenty miles up trail where I'm heading. We'd have to hike into the night, but word around the campfire is that he's serving food."

I looked at Elle and smiled. Food was what she had asked for and an offering of food had come into our experience. It seemed almost too good to be true.

When Tim and Oakley continued on, Elle turned to me.

"I don't want to go," she whispered.

I understood she was tired but knew she had the strength to continue.

"We can make it," I said. "You'll see."

Finally, after much resistance, Elle agreed to come along to night hike in pursuit of trail magic. We walked for miles beneath the light of a full moon over the desert hillside. As we tired, Elle began moving slower. I could tell her pack was still too heavy, even with her strength and diminishing food supply.

Weary and exhausted, we came upon the bright lights of a jeep parked beside the trail. The man smiled at our arrival as he was climbing into the car.

"You made it just in time," he said. "I was just about to head out for the night, but I have two more hotdogs just for you two."

Our eyes glowed, staring at the chunks of meat. As he prepared the food, we set out our sleeping spots at a nearby plot of flat land.

When the cooking was finished, he handed the simmering hotdogs to us and drove off into the night, the hum of the engine trailing in the distance.

There were another three hikers who had narrowly earned the same trail magic, and we sat next to them ready to bite into our juicy reward. Just then, another couple approached from the southern darkness with tired faces. They had walked through the night, but they were too late.

"Shoot," they said. "Did we miss it?" Their faces turned long and sad, and they looked in much worse shape than me. After all the help I'd received on the trail, I couldn't allow them to go without that night.

"Here," I said. "Take my hotdog. We'll share." I nodded and gestured that Elle and I would split the other hotdog.

"I don't think that's a good idea," Elle whispered.

"It's okay," I said. "Please, you two enjoy."

The couple looked back at me. "Are you sure?" they asked, skeptical of my decision.

"Yes, please take it. Enjoy."

When I handed them the hotdog and looked back at Elle, her face was bright red. To her, this was the final straw.

She thrust her hotdog into my hand, marched over to our campsite, picked up her sleeping bag that had been set up next to mine, and dragged it to the other side of the tires of an abandoned bulldozer yards away.

I got up and followed her. "What's wrong?" I asked. "You're hungry, aren't you?"

"You didn't even ask me," she hissed.

"Here, you can have it then."

"It's too late. I'm going to bed."

I could tell I must have embarrassed her. "I know you're hungry. Please, just take it."

"Let me sleep."

She thrust her body further into her sleeping bag and zipped it shut around her head. I stood above her still and silent before walking back to my sleeping spot.

It was the first night we slept apart from one another. I lay awake feeling awful for what I had said, my head filling with thoughts. Eventually, I figured the situation would pass by sunrise. Then I slept.

The next morning, as I began to pack up, I glanced toward the distant bulldozer. Elle hadn't moved. I walked over to where she slept and knelt down beside her.

"Are you awake?" I asked. "It's time to get up…"

There was no response.

"Elle, I can't hear you," I said. "Did you say something?" I poked her side through the sleeping bag.

She squirmed. "I'm not going with you."

I furrowed my brow. "What do you mean, you're not coming with me? You can't stay here. We're in the middle of the desert, Elle. What about water and food?"

For a while she said nothing. Then she said, "I'm staying."

"We should really get to hiking," I said. "There's only one way up the trail. I'll see you soon."

"No, you won't," she said. "I'll be moving slowly. Very slowly. Trust me, you won't see me again."

The sun and temperature were rising.

I sighed and waited there for a long time before standing. "I'll see you soon."

With that, I packed and set up the trail toward water. If that was her choice, I would honor it. She could stay behind and avoid me, but I wondered how long it would be before she stopped running from herself. As I walked the desert hills, I had a feeling that would be the last I'd see of Elle.

I hiked from daybreak to nightfall over the landscape, hardly ever stopping. My momentum carried me as I had yet to come across a decent water source. My blood boiled, my eyes watered, and I had the desire to cry as I thought back onto what had happened. We had fulfilled a deep-seated need for each other. She needed protection and security. I needed intimate human connection and touch.

I had once heard a saying: only the immature believe lust and love sprout from separate seeds. I was unsure whether such a saying was true, but there was no chance for the seed to grow without truth passing between us.

Aqueducts along the PCT.

And I couldn't help but wonder...

How much of our relationship was an attempt to avoid the painful feelings of being alone?

Lost in my thoughts, this day became the longest stretch of mileage I'd walked so far on the trail, a thirty-mile day to reach the town of Mojave.

I was alone, the last place I wanted to be. The place I had avoided my entire life. And I soon realized I had never actually been left alone to listen to myself.

CHAPTER 16

June 10, 2015
Mile 609, Lander's Creek Campground (2,041 miles to go)

I fanned the light of my headlamp across the campsite, but there were no signs of life, tents, tarps, or shelters.

"Hello?" I asked.

No response.

I sighed and leaned my backpack against the heel of a pine. Twenty-one miles of walking was enough for one day.

It was strange to see an empty camp. The last month and a half I'd run into tens of hikers every day, but the last two days I'd seen only a few. Not that it mattered. I wasn't interested in spending time with anyone else anyway. There was something I needed to figure out by myself.

I plopped down onto a log. My body ached, but my mind gave me the most trouble. I couldn't stop thinking.

From what I'd heard, I was either days or weeks behind the herd. After the barefooting stint and all those zero-days, I'd have to increase my daily mileage if I wanted to finish the trail before the winter snowfall shut it down for the season.

I both wanted and feared the trail's end. On the one hand, I could easily give up the walking and pain. There'd be nothing better than a long night's rest, a huge breakfast buffet, and maybe one of those massages with hot towels, warm oils, and nice music playing in the background. I'd never had a proper massage before, but that's what I imagined they were like. Then there was that comforting thought of seeing my friends and family. It would mean the world to me to see them again—I missed them more than anything. If only they knew how often I thought of them.

On the other hand, the end of the trail would be the death of me. I had no plans for after the trail, and I knew the truth. After all this was over and done my old self would be waiting for me. I wasn't ready to go back. It would only bring up a whole new list of questions. Who should I be? How should I participate in the world? And after a month and a half, I was feeling further integrated into the trail life. It now seemed like the only life I'd ever known, the only life that truly made sense.

So why *had* I come here?

To run away? To escape? To avoid responsibility? To think things out? To figure out what I should do with my life?

Likely all the above.

But then a new thought came to me—that maybe, and most of all, I had come here to make space for something new. And the more space I could find, the better. In thinking about this, it was the first time I felt grateful for being left alone. Sure, I had been abandoned, but maybe I had asked for it in some strange way. Maybe this had been coming to me. Maybe it was meant to be. And maybe this is why both Bradley and Elle had left—they, too, needed space. Space to search for something new.

As for me, it was better to keep pushing forward into this new space. Plus, it was too late to go back, to return home. I was committed, and I'd go as far as my body would let me. Sure, I was far behind the pack, but I'd made up some ground the past four days. I'd do my best to finish the trail.

I turned off my headlamp, thankful not to be stuck beneath those fluorescent bulbs, behind that desk, staring at that glowing computer screen. Instead, above me were bright stars filling the skies. The chill of darkness ran across my face. The night needed tending to.

I made my way to the middle of the campsite and cleared away a small plot of dirt with my hands beneath the light of my headlamp. I hauled four large rocks from the woods beside the pit and circled them against the eastern winds.

The thinking stopped when work began, and I wondered if this had this always been the culprit—too much thought, not enough work. Or was it too much work, not enough thought? I didn't know.

It was colder than most nights. My hands shook as I shoved them into gloves and went out again into the woods, this time gathering a patch of lichen moss, dried twigs, pine needles, sticks, and logs and carrying them over to the ring. I took a lighter to the moss, which was clasped between twigs and held over a bed of dried pine needles. When it caught, I knelt down and blew life into the fire, sparks flying up and fading into the black. The flames grew, and I added more kindling, sticks, and fuelwood and stared into the twisting flames. The fire did my mind good for some time.

Along with most everything else I'd learned of living in the wilderness, Bradley had taught me how to build fires. I was grateful for that. I laughed knowing I was once clueless on how to properly pack a backpack, fill a water bottle from a stream, or cook over open flames.

Cooking.

Hunger shook me, but I had to wait for the fire to collapse into a bed of coals. Trail life had taught me patience. Everything moved slowly in the desert—rattlers, horned toads, geckos—no living thing had anywhere to be anytime fast. Maybe they knew something I didn't.

When the twigs collapsed, I grouped the coals together with a long stick, added water to the cookpot, and set it on top of the bed. Time passed. When the pot shook, I added my last remaining dinner—a box of noodles stored at the bottom of my food bag—and waited until it was ready.

Then, as I ate, I stoked the fire. The hot noodles slid down my throat and warmed my insides. I could have eaten four more boxes. The spoon clanked against my empty cookpot, and I sighed, shaking off my gloves and holding my hands nearer to the flames, releasing my mind again to the fire. At some point, I realized it was about 9 p.m., so I readied myself for bed.

It was the moment I'd been waiting for all day. My body collapsed inside my sleeping bag, my eyes shut easily, and I stayed completely still, feeling myself slipping into sleep, body pulsing from head to toe, the healing of my beaten and bruised feet—

My feet!

I sprang up and massaged my soles. How could I have forgotten? My feet meant the world to me and needed my daily care and attention. I loved my feet. It was a weird thing to think, but these feet had taken me all this way. It was my feet that would take me to the final goal if it were meant to be. They were filthy, but I didn't care. I pressed my thumbs into my soles for as long as I could stand it before the cold air demanded I shove them back into the sleeping bag.

I reached into the fire and scooped up a hot rock I had placed there earlier. I wrapped it up in a t-shirt and threw it to the bottom of my sleeping bag. The warmth coursed through my insulated cocoon from toe to head. It was an old trick Bradley had taught me miles ago.

"You keep watch," I said to the tree closest to me, speaking as if it understood me quite well.

I looked at the sky one last time. I tried my best that night as I had many nights to watch the skies above in the hopes I'd see a falling star. Some nights I'd see as many as three or five, but tonight there were only clouds. It would be a warmer night so long as the clouds kept their rainfall. My eyelids slipped slowly over my tired eyes.

CHAPTER 17

June 10, 2015
Mile 609, Lander's Creek Campground (2,041 miles to go)

My eyes snapped open. There was a rustling in the woods, a loud cracking of twigs and dry leaves, but I couldn't see anything from inside my mummy sleeping bag. I didn't know if I wanted to, either.

I waited in the darkness, listening. *What is out there?*

I tried feeling the ground beneath me. The sound came again, but this time it was closer. It was clear the sounds were approaching footsteps. My heart beat like a drum as the steps thumped against the earth and drew closer. I could feel a shadow circling above my head. The animal grunted and huffed as it paced around me.

It was either a bear or a mountain lion, and I wasn't sure which was worse. Both were bad. I felt the creature's eyes, deep and black like the bottoms of wells, staring down at me, at this strange, puffy cocoon. While the moments of dehydration and nearly freezing were awfully frightening, at least I could continue to move forward. In this moment, I felt beyond helpless. And for a moment, I accepted death. Of all the ways I could leave this earth, to be eaten on an adventure by some wild beast might at least be memorable!

It was a stupid thought. I wasn't even close to being ready to die. I wanted to see the sunrise, the end of the trail, and my friends and family back home. I thought instead about what I could do.

The beast's face was hovering directly above me, and there wasn't a second to waste. With my hand on the zipper, I unzipped my bag, leapt to my feet, and right as I was about to shout at the top of my lungs, no voice came out.

There was nothing. Nothing but my silent wooden companions standing at attention and the sound of a spring dripping softly in the distance.

I grabbed my headlamp with a shaking hand and shined the light around the campsite and through the cracks of the trees. There were no signs of any tracks or prints in the dirt.

"Hello?" I asked.

I lay back down, shaking, and zipped the bag around myself and listened.

What was that? Was it really nothing?

It couldn't be. The experience was way too vivid to be a dream. Come to think of it, my dreams had grown more intense on the trail than ever before. Some played out as entire narratives like a movie, seemingly speaking to me or showing me something about my life. Others felt like I had lived in them for days and seemed just as real as my waking life. But this dream, if it was one, had crossed the line, blurring the distinction between dream and reality.

I had recently begun to wonder to what degree dreams influenced my mood and emotional states. For instance, it would be either right as I woke up or later on in the day when last night's dream would return to me. I would notice how my bad mood or poor state of mind was in direct alignment with a dream that was frightening, embarrassing, or nightmarish. Similarly, if my dream was the kind where something happened that I always wished might happen to me in the real world, I felt lighter, happy, and calm when waking. Did these dreams dictate my waking life in subconscious ways?

And if so, would the opposite be as equally true? Would my waking life influence my dreams when asleep? How closely intertwined were the two worlds? And if they were intertwined in any way, the importance of dreaming couldn't be overlooked so easily as I had done in the past. Somehow, I had to take control of my dreams, face them, or at least seek to better understand them.

The thought reminded me of my dream to find myself, to understand my life, and to finish the trail. It reminded me of my nightmares of falling short in life, failure, my inevitable death, or even worse, living my life without an understanding of who I should be in the world. Waking or sleeping, I decided I would confront both dreams and nightmares.

I took a deep, conscious breath and shut my eyes. The world faded into darkness once again.

Hours later, I woke to a cloudy twilight. There was only the wind and the soft pattering of raindrops.

Ah, this is why I woke up, I thought.

I pulled my Tyvek groundsheet out from beneath my sleeping bag and wrapped myself in it as if I were a burrito. The rain exploded like fireworks against my shelter. My eyes were wide open. I couldn't sleep.

CHAPTER 18

June 11, 2015
Mile 609, Lander's Creek Campground (2,041 miles to go)

I stretched my legs, pulling myself from a dreadful night's sleep, and groaned. Everything was damp. The earth smelled rich and a Stellar's jay chirped in the canopy above. I peeled the groundsheet off my sleeping bag, stood carefully, and slipped on my shoes before dragging everything into the sunlight.

The fire from the night before had been doused. I lugged the rocks back into the forest, fitting them like puzzle pieces into their original ditches.

Leave no trace.

I snagged my water bottle and walked the footpath to the spring. Water was everything. It was something I had known intellectually my whole life, but the trail had brought a deeper understanding to the concept.

It was a short hike back to the campsite, and I grabbed my backpack like a farmer would a milk bucket and walked it to a fallen tree to take a seat. Inside my food bag was two small oat bars. It was all that remained of my rations and would have to suffice. I stuffed one in my pocket and bit into the other while checking the maps. The road into town was forty miles ahead. Two or three more days of hiking. I sighed.

With the sun balanced atop the pines, my packing routine unfolded like clockwork. Stuffing everything inside my pack, every movement was meticulous and precise as I had developed a subtle understanding of where each piece of gear should live inside a backpack for proper comfort and weight distribution.

After one last glance around the campsite, I threw the pack over my shoulders and tightened the straps. It sparked a familiar feeling. The bag molded against my back, and we became one.

My stomach had thinned since April—any more weight loss and I'd probably looked starved—but the pack fit snugly on my hipbones with the straps tightened all the way. I couldn't gain weight even if I tried, no matter how much ice cream I shoved down my throat.

I found the trail and took it north, starting slow then finding a steady rhythm. It took about a mile before my legs loosened up, and that's when things really got going, my feet falling with perfect placement onto trustworthy earth, avoiding rocks, and stepping over logs and roots without needing to break stride or take breaks no matter the uphill elevation. Miles passed before my eyes in a state of oneness with my steps. It was always a game to balance the flow of hiking with the opportunities to enjoy my surroundings. Sometimes, I convinced myself I could combine the two without stopping.

I was slowly discovering the advantages of solitude. I had the ability to hike when I wanted to hike, rest when I wanted to rest, eat when I was hungry, and stare into the wilderness when it felt right. In my solitude, I was my own master, another experience I'd never truly known.

During this time, I began to observe my mind without even realizing this was what I was doing. Devoid of distraction, left within the constraints of a goal, the mind and my environment were all I had to contend with.

Much of my mind was filled with songs from my childhood that looped in my head like a broken record, and the best way to rid myself of them was to sing them out loud, allowing the mountains to swallow my voice. Beyond this, the potential for creativity seemed infinite. I wrote entire poems and songs inside my head and remembered them by heart. The mind's capacity for memory without the distractions of urban living was much greater than I had ever imagined. I'd always thought of myself as having a poor memory, blaming it on years of college drinking, but solitude brought everything screaming back to the surface.

It then became evident how my thoughts tended to sway back and forth like a pendulum between two distinct realms, the future and the past, and with them came a mental label, pleasurable or painful.

Thoughts, ideas, and feelings bubbled up to the surface of my mind, none of which I would have experienced if it weren't for the solitude. Interestingly enough, the bubbles that came to the surface of my mind were not under my control. What came up, came up. The process of thinking happened as naturally as water traveled down a flowing creek. No one could dictate the path of that water. Metaphorically, I sat at the bank of my mind to watch the river run its course.

But in these moments, the thoughts and feelings didn't feel like bubbles. They were more like knots, and it was usually the first knots to arise that were most complex and in most need of untangling.

There were all the people I had ignored, hurt, or harmed in some way. All the women I had slept with out of lust. All the comfort I had chosen for my life. All the leaps I hadn't yet taken out of fear.

And then there was a girl, one who I had loved in my youth and never told my true feelings. It seemed like an innocent mistake at the time, but looking back, I now saw how inaction could be as equally detrimental as a harmful action, how something as tiny as the fear of rejection had bled into other romantic relationships, resulting in their failure.

I imagined how those women might have felt, trying to build a life with a person still clinging to an unresolved past. They wished to set sail with me, yet I was unknowingly still tied to the dock. It was fascinating to see how even the smallest knots, if not dealt with, could grow into poisonous snakes.

But just as my life was filled with regret, it was equally filled with pleasant memories, long forgotten, that played out vividly like videotapes—memories of the support and love I'd been given by family, friends, and my community. Each memory reminded me of how fortunate I was to be alive in the first place and to have experienced all these profoundly simple moments during my life, no matter how scripted I had once believed my life to be.

Though there was much good within me, there was also hatred, negativity, jealousy, and animosity for people, myself included. Beside the light lived the darkness. Yin and Yang. Chaos and order. Evil and ignorant thoughts could arise without my wanting them, and I wondered if this darkness was left to grow if it would one day spill out onto those around me.

I mustn't let that happen, I thought.

Finding that such negativity existed inside me, as someone who believed myself to be so pure and good and kind, shook me to my core.

All in all, my inner-life was filled with light and blessings, as well as darkness and knots in need of straightening.

But how to straighten them out? How should I reconcile my mistakes, my regrets? Should I act on them, recreate them, or do nothing but observe them?

And what of my blessings and fortunes? If I wanted guilt to be no part of them, how should they be handled?

This became the game, watching it all come up, wondering what to do. Why was I being presented with all my life's past events? Was this what true solitude was like? And if the ultimate solitude were death and dying, would there ever be a better place and time to confront this? Could it be that some people go their whole lives without experiencing death before their time has come?

As I rose along the path, these words came rushing back to me: "Like with any journey, it's not what you carry, but what you leave behind." It was a line from the movie *Tracks* that had come into my head. These words had stuck with me for some time.

Maybe my loneliness and this entire journey were worthwhile because I was leaving everything behind. Maybe the greatest change comes not from the things you do but from the things you stop doing. It's only then, after excess has been removed, that you see most clearly what remains. As much as I loved and missed my family, friends, Bradley, and other hikers, it was meant to be that I leave them and they leave me. I needed the space to search inside myself.

The thoughts ended as I glanced up at the horizon. The sun's descent into the west was coming to an end. I had walked almost all day without stopping, and it was time to eat. I'd soon find a campsite, rest, and continue to walk with the rising sun.

CHAPTER 19

June 12, 2015
Mile 651, Walker Pass (1,999 miles to go)

As I hiked into the next day, the forest thinned and the path opened up to a large campground with picnic tables and out-houses. There were hikers around, but I continued through and found an interstate highway that split the trail.

I sat by the edge of the road on top of my foam pad and checked my phone. There was no signal, so I lined up my paper maps with the road in front of me. A westward hitch would take me into Lake Isabella, a small lakeside town settled beneath the desert foothills where I could re-supply and get back on my way to Kennedy Meadows.

From the pass, the landscape was but empty winding roads meandering along the valley. I lay down and shut my eyes.

A humming brought me to my feet, but it faded into nothing. The road was empty. I'd be waiting for a while.

I ate my last oat bar, threw off my shoes, turned my socks inside out, and lay back against my mat. My bare feet rested over the edge of my backpack, tingling and pulsing as new blood flowed into my heels, soles, and toes. The wind blew. There was the chatter of hikers in the southern campground. I closed my eyes again.

Something was approaching. I opened my eyes, sat up, and listened. It growled in the distance. The sound grew louder, and I stepped to the edge of the road with one thumb up to the sky, waving my other hand high above my head. It was a shiny white sedan of the expensive sort, and it came to a screeching halt where the trail met the road. The driver side window rolled down halfway.

Sunglasses covered the man's eyes, and his face was chiseled and framed by long blonde hair.

"Where to?"

"Lake Isabella. I think it's about fifteen miles west of here."

He glanced at his watch and sighed. "A bit out of the way. If you don't mind coming along on some quick business, I can take you into town afterward. Your call."

I turned to the campground. *Maybe someone else wanted to come along too?*

"I'm in a hurry," he reminded me. "Hop in, or I'll have to move on."

I nodded. "Okay, one sec."

As quickly as I could, I slipped on my socks and shoes, packed my bag, ran around the car, and hopped in the passenger's seat. My pack sat atop my lap like an overgrown dog as we pulled onto the highway. I noticed I'd forgotten to buckle up, but figured the pack would be a fine enough airbag.

"Nice car," I said.

He nodded, smiled, gripped the steering wheel with both hands, and slammed on the gas. My pack smacked me in the face and sandwiched me against the seat. I tried acting casual as the speedometer tilted over eighty, then ninety. My heart beat fast, and I was sure we would die at any second. The cliff-side roads made me nervous, but the thrill of time travel had taken me.

"What's with the pack?" he asked.

"I'm hiking north."

He nodded and didn't ask much else, but he had a lot to say about himself. I soaked up his stories like a sponge as the highway curved against the mountainside before dipping down into the valley below. It felt safer at ground level, with miles of barbed wire fences and prairie fields.

Suddenly, the roof peeled back, folding like an accordion into the trunk. The wind beat against my eardrums.

"You mind?" he yelled.

I shook my head. I didn't have much choice, but I didn't mind it either. My hair flapped in the wind as we soared down the country road.

Eyeing the road with one eye, he reached across me, rifled through the glove compartment, grabbed a pack of cigarettes, and lodged one between his lips. Then he lifted his hips and plunged his hand into his pocket to dig for a lighter. In the time it took him to do so, I was sure we'd run off the road and explode into flames. Navigating with his knees on the wheel, he ducked below the dash to light the cigarette and returned upright for a long exhale.

He held the pack out to me and nodded, but I waved it off.

"No thanks, but thank you."

He shrugged and threw the pack to the floorboard.

The car slowed after a while, and we hung a right onto a dirt road, taking it all the way to a tall iron gate. The doors swung open slowly and automatically.

"This won't take too long," he said. "Just some quick business, then you'll be on your way."

I kept quiet and watched as the dirt path traveled across the plain, the hills beside the road filled with scattered blocks of stones amid crumbled towers. Weeds grew up and around the dormant stones.

"You see that tower?" he asked.

I turned. "Yeah."

"Many years ago, this land belonged to the natives. It's a shame what happened to them, really, but I guess all good things come to an end."

I nodded.

"You know what's weird, though? They weren't the natives anyway, at least not in the sense that everyone thinks they were. It's a common misconception, the word 'native'. Everything takes from that which came before it."

I nodded.

"I find artifacts every now and again," he said. "But I'm trying to keep a piece of what the natives held dear."

"What's that?"

He exhaled smoke from his cigarette. "The celebration, appreciation, and gratitude of life. We're building something special here. A new beginning. And soon, it'll be complete."

"Building what?" I asked him.

He grinned. "You'll see."

The road followed a manmade stream, and he pointed toward some of the denser brush.

"A mountain lion lives there, but he keeps to himself. We've made peace with him."

The terms of the agreement seemed unclear to me.

The road opened up past the hills and brush. We parked in front of a building he called the main complex. Then he led me away from it, nearer the valley where I could see what he was constructing.

There were dozens of people here, milling about, carrying boards, saws, and tools among stacks of wooden planks and other raw materials neatly piled here and there.

First and most imposing was the largest bonfire pit I'd ever seen, and surrounding it was six massive tipis, each large enough to comfortably sleep six and each equipped with beds, side-tables, lamps, and rugs. Shipping containers were being welded into bathrooms, and farther into the valley stood three giant wooden stages with huge plots of land in between each.

"It's a festival grounds," he said. "There's space for hundreds of people to sing and dance."

I nodded. It was fascinating what people chose to spend their money on.

"Come," he said. "I want you to meet some people."

He led me back to the main complex and walked me through the door.

"Should I bring my backpack in?"

He turned and gave it a glance. "It'll be safe out here."

I hoped he was right, and I stashed it beneath the awning because it was cloudy.

He led me into the kitchen. The room was warm, and a dozen men, women, and children stood around stoves and counters amid the clanging of pots and pans and the popping of fatty meats.

"You hungry?" he asked. "You're looking a bit... thin."

I stared at the array of food: fluffy pancakes, scrambled eggs, and strips of bacon sizzling in the pans. The aroma of melted butter and hot syrup crawled into my nostrils.

"I can always eat."

He grabbed me a plate and walked me toward the dining room where I ate with the others. I took a back seat to their discussions of various ongoing projects, and it seemed oddly normal for guests to show up in this manner. The food was delicious, and I could have eaten three more plates. After I was done, the man handed me a towel.

"There's a shower in that room if you want it."

My eyes grew wide. "That sounds amazing."

"Do you need laundry too?"

As kind as all the offers were and as grateful as I was, I was also ready to get going sooner than later. Time was passing, and the trail was waiting.

"No, thanks. The shower is perfect, though."

He nodded and headed back into the kitchen.

Cold water ran across my face and splashed against the tile. Dirt poured down my legs in waves as it always did, and it took a rough scrubbing to clean my skin and a hard massaging of my scalp to rid my hair of tangles. My feet were given special attention.

I walked out reborn. The man was waiting, and he took me back outside into the festival grounds, showing me more construction projects including a side house, a backyard pool, a bathroom, and a workshop.

He stopped and sat in a chair. He nodded, gesturing for me to sit across from him. I sat, and he lit a cigarette and removed his sunglasses, his green eyes staring at me.

"Do you like it here?" he asked.

I nodded. "It's a nice place."

He leaned far back in his chair, then forward again.

"I'd like to extend an offer to you," he said. "I'm not sure what you're doing exactly, walking this trail and whatnot, but it seems like you're wandering. If you're looking for a place to stay, to settle down, there's a lot that needs to be done around here. There are more tipis that need building, additions to the complex, pools to be cemented, and river channels to dig. Like I said, everything we're doing here is very purposeful. Everyone has their place, some role to fill, something to manifest from nothing. I know that's difficult to find out there in the world."

He took another puff. "I want you to think about it. This could be a nice home for you."

The man leaned back into his chair, folded his hands in his lap, and looked across the plains into the valley, the long grass of the fields bending to the wind.

Apart from the creepy, cultish vibe I was getting, the offer at face value was difficult to pass up. There was free food, living, and lodging. I could imagine settling down for once and working for something purposeful. But I also had this inexplicable feeling, a knowing that this wasn't where I was supposed to be. I didn't think twice about it. There was no way I was staying.

"Thanks," I said, "but I need to get back to the trail. Whenever you're ready, I'm ready to head into town."

The man stared at me for a few timeless moments. He sighed.

"If you're going to leave, take these," he said. He dug into his pocket and handed me some business cards. "Just set up your account online, and we'll be in touch. It's practically free money." He stood and extended his hand. "Ernesto will take you into town this afternoon. Until then, make yourself at home by the complex."

"Thanks."

I smiled politely and waited beside the front door of the complex.

In my memory, this was the only opportunity I'd turned down in my life. Maybe that's how you know you're on the right path, when the path you're walking carries more purpose than anything else, no matter what you're offered.

I reviewed the card. Having worked in marketing before and knowing a decent amount about business, his was clearly a multi-level marketing scheme. I was quite familiar with these strange and mischievous organizations, and it only solidified that I had made the right decision.

When the grounds fell still that afternoon, I caught a ride from a man named Ernesto and headed toward Lake Isabella.

CHAPTER 20

June 13, 2015
Mile 652, Lake Isabella (1,998 miles to go)

"Happy trails," I said to Ernesto before he drove away and disappeared down the road.

When I turned toward the general store, a fleeting thought crossed my mind. I hoped today wasn't Sunday. It was the one day of the week when post offices were closed. I realized how infrequently I thought about the days of the week since each day had become as equally meaningful as the last.

Inside the general store were aisles of chips, snacks, and canned foods. Fridges were stocked with sweet drinks and ice-creams, but I made my way straight to the front counter. A woman emerged from the back room.

"Hey, is your post open today?" I asked.

She nodded politely. "It's Monday, sweetie."

I smiled. It was the first time in my life I'd felt grateful for a Monday.

I slid my ID over the counter and asked if there was any mail for Smart or Lovell.

After disappearing into the back room, she reappeared holding a package and a letter. The box was heavy as was usual for a food drop, and the letter was from a childhood friend.

I stuck it inside my backpack where it remained forgotten until later that night.

I walked outside, greeting the hikers sitting at nearby picnic tables before heading to an outlet to charge my phone.

It booted up slowly, and I waited, endlessly curious if Bradley had tried to contact me. When it turned on, there were no messages.

Maybe it needs more time to receive the data? Time passed but there was nothing.

Stories flooded my head. I became convinced Bradley and Oz had found trail magic by the beach and settled down for good, or worse, been caught by police sleeping on rooftops or digging through dumpsters. I sent him a text that read something like:

Bradley, I'm at Lake Isabella! Will reach

Kennedy Meadows in a few days. Where you at? What's your plan?

I set down the phone, sighed, and set to opening the resupply with my pocketknife. Inside was everything I'd come to expect: pasta, sardines, nut butter, dried fruits, granola, and stacks of oat bars. Nothing was remarkably exciting, but the reliability was comforting. I took what I needed and brought the remainder, which would otherwise be Bradley's share, over to the picnic tables.

"Are you sure, brother?" asked a hiker when I presented them the food.

"Take it," I said.

It's what Bradley would have done too.

After waving goodbye to some new friends, I walked the road north, my thumb to the sky.

* * *

The failing daylight retreated behind the mountains as I arrived at camp that evening. There were other hikers, and I sat with them beside their fire to eat and chat until the skies turned black. It was nice to be among hikers again.

Just as I was going to bed, I remembered my friend's letter from the post and pulled it from my backpack. There was something magical about letters. Coordinating locations with the outside world was difficult, and it forced the sender to exert a lot of effort into timing the arrival of letters. It seemed most letters were thoughtful and filled with the sort of honesty only shared in writing and between people separated by long distance. Every word was precise, strung together like the notes of a song. I'd never forget the letters sent to me on the trail.

I wiped a tear from my eye, then penned a few words of my own into my journal, reading my friend's letter one last time before surrendering it to the fire. Flames crawled toward my fingers before I tossed in the paper as it crinkled into smoke.

When the fire died, the coals pulsed a glowing red. I lay beneath the sky inside my sleeping bag and battled sleep just long enough to see the bursting tail of a shooting star.

The following days were of the same routine I had become accustomed to: eat, walk, rest, and repeat. Anticipation grew as I neared Kennedy Meadows.

The trail had become oddly but refreshingly green and beautiful the last few miles, like the desert finally might be coming to an end. The trail led me through meadows, over bubbling brooks, and across downtrodden green grass fields. I had never seen so much water in so few miles. I stopped to watch a family of deer beside the trail. They seemed human, the way they looked back at me with curious, black eyes, and I wished I could speak with them.

Chapter 20

The moon was full, and I walked the dirt road east passed a barn, coming to a sign reading:

KENNEDY MEADOWS, ONE MILE EAST

My heart skipped. I was close.

I continued down the moonlit road and noticed music playing in the distance. Following the tune through a thicket of woods, I emerged from the shadows to a gathering of hikers, a lone guitar player plucking at the strings.

It took a moment for recognition to dawn on me. The singing voice was familiar, one I knew better than most, one I had sung with during long desert days, and a single glance confirmed my suspicion.

It was Bradley.

I stood back as he finished playing to the crowd's applause, passing the guitar to the next player to begin a new tune. Then he glanced up. When he saw me, his eyes brightened, and he came over for an embrace.

"Good to see you, brother."

"You too."

We stepped back, nodding. It was difficult to even know where to begin.

"I feel like there's a lot to discuss," I said.

He laughed. "No kidding… I'm sure it will all come out in time."

I glanced down at his feet. He was wearing brand new trail runners.

"Nice shoes," I said.

He shrugged and smiled. "They better take me a hell of a long way! Spent a small fortune on these guys."

When the music settled and the crowd dispersed, we headed over to the campsites. There were tents everywhere in all the spaces as far back as the path seemed to lead.

"There's a good group of hikers here," Bradley said. "Lots of 'em too. I think we've caught up to the herd."

"Really?" I couldn't believe it.

He nodded. It was great news. After all our challenges with barefooting, snow, and numerous zero-days, we'd somehow found ourselves back in line. It was fascinating how a solid week or two of consistent action was enough to regain momentum.

The herd at Kennedy Meadows.

We stayed up near the campsite to feed the fire, allowing things to come up naturally.

"Any highlights from the journey west?" I asked.

"Where to begin?" he said, grinning. "The ocean was beautiful, Hollywood was a trip, but, to be honest… I missed the trail. There's something special here."

We nodded.

"I see you're alone," he asked seriously. "Where's Elle?"

"I think I scared her away."

Bradley laughed. "Nah, I'm sure she went through the same things I did. And look at me. I'm back."

"Yeah. It's probably for the better," I said. "Where's Oz?"

Bradley pointed into the woods. "I think he went to try and kill a snake with Patch."

"Oh… right."

It was a classic Oz thing to do.

"Ah," he said. "I've got some good news."

My eyes lit up. "Go on..."

"It's better I show you." He fetched his backpack and tossed a familiar orange sack onto my lap.

"The tarp!"

He nodded. "It arrived at the general store yesterday. So, no more worrying about wet nights."

"Thank God..."

"Also, we're required to carry a bear canister through the Sierra to store our food. They're a bit expensive, so I only bought one, but I found this scent-proof bag for any food that doesn't fit in the canister. You can use it. I'll carry the canister, and you take the tarp?"

"Deal," I said.

We shook hands.

"Oh! And I almost forgot..." said Bradley.

"Yes?!"

"I have a new name."

My brows lifted. "A trail name? What is it?! Tell me!"

"Well, it happened last night," he began. "Everyone was playing music and singing, and this woman stood up demanding that everyone stop playing so we could listen to her sing. Now, you know me. I saw it as an attempt to monopolize the group's attention. So, I'd been given an egg shaker, the musical instrument, earlier in the night by a girl—that's another story, you'll have to meet her tonight—and every time she started singing, I'd start shaking this egg as loud as I could. Everyone but the woman was dying laughing, but the message got through. She lightened up eventually. Anyway, this girl told me my trail name should be... Shake."

"Shake...?"

He nodded. "I like it, man. Think of shakedowns, shedding weight, shedding our old selves."

"Dang. That's a good one."

"Yep. Plus, I got to keep the egg."

He rattled it in front of my face.

"Great." It wasn't annoying at all.

He laughed. The egg shaker would remain in his backpack, and its rattle would signal his approach from a mile away.

Leaving the egg aside, I noticed jealousy brewing inside me. The news of his new trail name rekindled a sleeping desire within me to find my own. Bradley turned and looked off into the trees.

"Want to check out the general store?" he asked.

"Isn't it closed by now?"

"Yeah.... but Applesauce might be there."

I chuckled. "Is this the girl you were talking about?"

He nodded. "She's got a friend."

I glanced at the night sky and sighed. I was ready to sleep, but I could tell Bradley was excited and meeting women was such a rarity that I couldn't pass it up.

"Alright. Let's go."

We left the meadow, and Bradley led me to the Kennedy Meadows General Store, a large wooden building with a wide deck. A few remaining headlamps shined atop the porch, and a short climb up the steps led us to the picnic tables where two women about our age were shuffling cards beneath dim headlamp lights.

"Shake!" shouted one of them. "Get over here, we're just about to play!" She waved us over to the table.

"Hey, Applesauce," Bradley said while squeezing her.

Applesauce was a tall brunette with a bright smile. "You must be David!" she said. "I've heard all about you. Good to meet you. I'm Applesauce." She was upbeat and carried the excitement and playful attitude of a puppy. I could tell we would all get along.

"And I'm Rambo," said another girl sitting across from her. Rambo was shorter, had shoulder-length hair, glasses, and a much calmer demeanor. "Have you played gin before?" she asked.

I shook my head.

"Well, do you wanna learn?"

"Sure," I said, sitting beside her. "I'm ready."

"Ready to lose, that is," Bradley said, gazing up at me.

We played card games with the two girls well into the night, learning they were childhood friends and section-hikers. Applesauce was a teacher and only had a month before she needed to get back to ready herself for the school year. The two had planned out a relaxed hiking schedule of no more than ten miles a day. The lower mileage also made sense since they didn't have seven hundred miles under their belt. It was nice to be around friends and females, and I could tell Bradley was taking a liking to Applesauce. I didn't mind the situation at all. Rambo was intelligent, well read, attractive, and I sensed there might be a connection between us.

Stars filled the sky, and it was time to sleep.

"So, are you guys hiking out tomorrow?" Rambo asked.

Bradley shrugged. "I think we'll be ready to head out by then. What about you two?"

Rambo looked at Applesauce. "Yep! Want to hike with us?"

It was the question he'd been waiting for, and Bradley didn't wait a second. "Let's do it."

The girls laughed.

"We'll see you in the morning then," Applesauce said. "Sleep well, you guys!"

"You too," we said with one final squeeze before everyone departed to their campsites.

"I see what you're doing," I said as I readied my sleeping bag.

He laughed.

"Did they say they're hiking less than ten miles a day?" I asked. "Don't you think that's a little slow?"

"Yeah... we'll play it by ear. If you don't mind, I think I'd like to get to know them a bit better."

It was a slow pace, but I nodded. I felt the same way.

"Night, Bradley... I mean Shake."

He laughed. "Night, brother. Good to see you again."

"You too. Glad to have you back."

I closed my eyes, looking forward to the days ahead. We were out of the desert, among friends, and things seemed to be looking up for once. The only other thought that came to mind before I slept was how I, too, wanted a trail name...

CHAPTER 21

June 16, 2015
Mile 702, Kennedy Meadows (1,948 miles to go)

We departed Kennedy Meadows at dawn along with our new friends Applesauce and Rambo. Their large packs bobbed up and down in front of us as we shuffled up the trail together, music playing from their Bluetooth speakers.

Everything was green here—the grass, the rolling hills, the trees—and no more than three miles after leaving town, we come to a flowing creek with waterfalls and swimming pools.

"Let's break here!" said the girls.

We'd hardly made any progress, but the scene was impossible to pass up. Before we knew it, we were spending the day in leisure: swimming, playing, chatting in the water, and lying beneath the sun on top of warm rocks. About two dozen other hikers must have passed the creek that day, laughing about how far we'd gotten. We tried to convince those passing us to join in on the fun—some did, but many continued on their way. If this were our new pace, the herd would be well ahead of us again in no time.

Bradley and I climbed the boulders upstream in the daylight and sat on flat rocks above the pools in meditation for a short time. I didn't know how to meditate, but I sat up tall like Bradley and shut my eyes, feeling the sun's warmth against my skin and feeling my belly rise and fall. Afterward, I examined the scene, looking down onto the girls from above.

"You think they're talking about us?" he asked.

"Maybe."

"They're pretty cool, huh?"

I nodded. Apart from Oz and Nomad, who had since begun finding their own paths, these two girls were the most easygoing pair of hikers we'd met in the last two months. I was thrilled to be around new, engaging friends and even noticed myself developing a slight crush on Rambo. Still, as much as I enjoyed their laid-back attitude, their schedule concerned me.

Rambo & Applesauce.

By nightfall, we packed up and headed out, hiking a grand total of five miles for the entire day. It was almost no progress, a 'nero'-day as hikers called it, the word meaning 'nearly zero'. It was used to describe hiking days of less than ten miles. But I hadn't enjoyed myself so fully since my time at Acton KOA playing with Elle. I wondered what she was up to and hoped she was doing okay.

Chapter 21

The next few days were spent alongside the girls, entertained by their presence and their refreshing outlook on life. We listened to their music and inched along the trail at a pace of no more than ten miles a day.

During an afternoon meal, Rambo revealed she had a boyfriend, initially disappointing news considering how well we got along and our growing chemistry, but I was more than happy to have her as a friend. My feelings weren't as strong for Rambo as they had been for Elle, and I was grateful to simply enjoy her friendship.

Similarly, it was also becoming clearer that Applesauce may not be as attracted to Bradley as he had hoped, a feeling that plagued Bradley at first. But the two would remain friends long after the girls left the trail.

Meanwhile, during the days after Kennedy Meadows, our group was beginning to grow larger.

Bradley and I formed a particularly strong bond with a middle-aged Australian named Richard. We'd first met Richard at trail angel Bob Reiss's house, but he'd grown into a different man since that time. His stomach had thinned, a red beard now eclipsed his mouth and face, and he donned a kilt. The kilt, he said, prevented chaffing and provided a fine breeze, and on more than one occasion he recommended we look into purchasing one. If his kilt wasn't ridiculous enough, he also wore a wide-brimmed adventurer's hat, a bright yellow buff wrapped around his neck, and a massive, expensive camera dangling across his chest. The man looked something like a modern-day Indiana Jones. He also wore a fancy wristwatch that measured temperature and air pressure, giving him the seemingly prophetic ability to predict incoming storms.

Richard's thick Australian accent accompanied his discussions of philosophy and science, strong opinions, and a propensity for cussing—common behavior in Australia, he told us. It was a statement we later confirmed from the small sample of four other Australian hikers we met along the way.

191

Jim & Richard.

Similar to our email list, Richard kept a blog of his photography and ended up writing a funny post about Bradley and me entitled *The David and Bradley Show...*

I met David and Bradley on day zero at the trail angel Bob Reiss's house in San Diego. Their disarmingly personable attitudes accompanied sharp wits and mischievous smiles; I took an instant liking to them. While not readily apparent, they are both highly intelligent. They have many talents, including the ability to approach a complete stranger and build an instant and genuine rapport. This skill's value becomes apparent on the trail when trying to Yogi a ride or some food.

However, to lump them both in the same description is to do them an injustice, for despite their similarities, they are wildly different individuals. Where David is empathetic, sensitive, diplomatic, and caring, Bradley is... well, all those things in a more retiring way but also bolder, and he seems to derive some pleasure from challenging himself and those around him.

Arm wrestling in the grass.

I guess the easy way to put it is to say that when there is a group decision to be made, Bradley would encourage the group to push for a certain goal while David would temper this, taking into account the needs of some of the quieter members of the group. Where David is concerned about the consequences of his words and actions, Bradley is curious.

After seventy painfully slow miles in SoCal, I met up with them again at Pioneer Mail on what was later explained to me as reckoning day.

—Richard on thefakefacade.blogspot.com

And the rest was history. Richard and his British friend Jim—another crass, heavy-set, middle-aged bachelor—would become our wise and experienced group patriarchs. The photographer and professional diver played off each other quite well, shouting quips from the back of the circle as we ate, rested, or hiked in single-file line. It was alleviating to have a strong sense of humor following the group.

Richard in particular was an experienced outdoorsman. To our relief, he taught us how to properly tie knots and set up our tarp. We would eventually name him Mr. Walker, a fitting trail name since his last name was Walker.

Examining the scene.

Our group was traveling together, the sun was setting, and the campsite was filled with the soft droning of fired-up gas stoves and boiling water.

Bradley was always the first to share whatever concoction we mashed together, passing around our cookpot to the rest of the group around the campfire. We did this to share but also because our mouths watered for more delicious dishes around the fire, knowing our friends would have little choice but to reciprocate such a kind gesture.

Mr. Walker rolled his eyes. "You've got to be kidding me, Shake…"

"What?!" Bradley laughed. "You haven't even tried it yet! It's sooo good!" He took a bite and closed his eyes, chewing with great delight.

Mr. Walker wasn't dumb. He knew what we were after. His resupplies were always filled with these expensive, pre-packaged, freeze-dried, gourmet backpacker meals. And if only we could get a couple bites from them, we'd sleep well that night.

"Get that disgusting shit out of here, Shake," Mr. Walker said, passing back our cookpot and smiling.

Everyone laughed. They'd caught onto our plans, but the intention was too powerful a force. Eventually, everyone felt inspired, and before long, there were huge potlucks shared among our tribe, a rarity for hikers who, for good reason, remained protective over their precious food. For us, the diverse diet was more than welcomed. And so were the friends.

We were moving slowly, and the herd was gaining distance. Still, everyone enjoyed each other's company. As far behind as we were falling, we simply didn't want to leave Rambo and Applesauce. It reminded me of our time back in the desert with the Poodle Dog Boys. We'd had a good group back then, but this was different. This was the first time I really felt at home away from home. And it wasn't just me. Together, everyone felt like we had found family on the trail. Days before, they were strangers. Now they were my trail family.

Trail family in the Sierras.

CHAPTER 22

June 21, 2015
Mile 740, Guitar Lake Basin (1,910 miles to go)

Days later, I woke with my sleeping bag frosted over from the cold night's dew, and I crawled out from under the tarp to view the grassy basin. Tents were scattered across the land, a nearby lake shimmering in the morning sunlight. Marmots stood on hind legs, dashing between white boulders, and the mountain towered high above us all, framed by the skies.

It was Mt. Whitney, the highest peak in the continental U.S. Even though it wasn't technically part of the trail and required a few miles of off-trail hiking to reach its basin, we'd heard the experience couldn't be passed up. We had climbed into such remote wilderness that the only way into town was climbing eastward over high mountain passes to reach plunging mountain roads where we could hitch a long ride to the bottom of the barren desert valley, which boasted a few small towns. It was unlikely we'd ever find ourselves in the area again, and so Mt. Whitney made it to the top of our agenda.

My stomach dropped as I stared at the peak. It was the highest thing I'd ever seen. Garnett Peak from way back in the desert paled in comparison. I had only mildly overcome my fear of heights while hiking through Southern

California's mountain ranges and peering across the expansive vistas, but my legs couldn't help but tremble at the sight of the mountain.

The only good news I'd heard was that the summit was hike-able—no ropes or harnesses necessary. And from the basin where I stood, the trail was just a few miles' jaunt to the peak. Otherwise, there was no way anyone could have convinced me to climb that thing.

I headed toward the lake's edge for water but it was too shallow to fill my water bottles. A nearby log jutting out into the water caught my attention.

That'll do the trick, I thought.

I walked it step by step, one foot in front of the other, not a trace of doubt in my mind. My legs were infallible.

The water against my fingertips was frigid, but I plunged my hand in any way. The bottle gulped in the water.

As we had done in the desert, Bradley and I drank from water sources without filtering, a controversial decision which some hikers saw as an unnecessary risk for contracting giardia. As for why we hadn't yet gotten sick, I still to this day am unsure. All I can point to was how carefully and intentionally I studied each stream, choosing the spots where the flow was strongest and the rocks and leaves might offer a natural filter of their own. Perhaps the greatest reason was how much we trusted the water, maintaining strong beliefs we wouldn't get sick.

Returning to our campsite, Bradley and I stowed our backpacks in Mr. Walker's tent. We wouldn't need the added weight for the hike up. And since we wouldn't be returning to the basin until evening, our packs would be safer from marmots inside a tent.

After stuffing a couple of cliff bars into my pockets and snagging my water bottle, our group found the trail leading toward the mountain. The path ramped upward against the mountainside to form a switchback, and the temperature dropped the higher we climbed.

Shake stalking a jackrabbit.

Before long I found myself sprinting up the mountain, leaving behind Bradley and the others. I was weightless without a backpack and filled with energy after days of slow movement. I leapt crevices with ease, scampered passed the portal entrance, and greeted the slow and struggling day-hikers who had climbed thousands of feet from the other side of the canyon.

As I flew up the trail, my heart beat heavy against my chest. Whatever the reason, I felt I couldn't stop or it would burst, something I wouldn't allow to happen. Or at least not yet. The rising emotion carried me like a roaring bullet train up the final mountain switchbacks.

Suddenly, there was no more trail, only rocks and patches of snow lining the mountaintop. The peak stood a few more paces ahead. There was no one else around.

Heaving, I slowly stepped to the edge of the cliff and looked down to the valley. My eyes blurred and narrowed as I gazed outward, adjusting to the shapes and shadows beyond. Broken mountains unfolded against the landscape in all directions. Grassy basins and rocky plateaus flowed from the mountain's feet, and distant snow-capped mountain peaks shaded the horizon and pierced the clouds. For the first time on this sojourn, I could see just how far I'd come.

I couldn't hold the emotion any longer. I burst, collapsing to my hands and knees. The rock was cold beneath my palms as tears flowed down my cheeks. I was shaking, sobbing. How long had I been holding back my tears? It felt like crying was something my body had wanted for so long. I allowed it to happen, even wanting it to keep going. It was the first time I'd wept from joy.

I didn't understand why this was happening to me, only that it felt right. It was undoubtedly the most beautiful image my eyes had processed during my lifetime. Whether my crying was the result of too much sensory input, a feeling of accomplishment, or a releasing of something unknown, something I'd kept inside me for too long, I may never know. But I smiled as I wept.

Huddling beneath the shade of a rock at the cliff's edge, I felt the thud of my heartbeat begin to calm. A hand came down onto my shoulder.

"You alright?" he asked.

I turned back to look.

It was Bradley. Tears were still streaming down my face.

I nodded. "It's... beautiful."

It was all I could say. He understood.

What could have been minutes or hours later, our friends and other hikers had reached the top, and I returned to equilibrium, my body feeling lighter than ever. I stared off into the canyon unseeingly, surveying the curvature of the earth that spanned the horizon.

"Can you hear me?" The voice came from a hiker a few paces away. He was talking on his cell phone.

Is there cell signal up here? I waited until he was done and asked the man if I could borrow his phone. He agreed, and I dialed a number.

The line rang, and he picked up.

"David!" my dad said.

I couldn't remember the last time I'd heard my father so excited to hear from me. I hadn't spoken to him in days, but I knew this wasn't the reason for his upbeat tone. It wasn't out of the ordinary in my college and working days for the two of us to go weeks without speaking so long as everything was going well. No, the reason for his excitement was that I had finally begun to keep him updated in my life, calling him and my mom at every town I reached along the trail. It was because I had finally begun to make an effort to build that connection.

"Hey, Son. How's the trail? How are you? What are you up to? Is everything okay?" It seemed he had a hundred questions for me.

Mt. Whitney (14,505').

I smiled. "Yeah. Everything's fine, Dad." I paused to catch my breath. I hadn't thanked him in years, maybe not ever.

Today was the perfect day to do so. "I just wanted to tell you that I'm standing on the peak of Mt. Whitney, the tallest mountain in the U.S., and I couldn't help but think of you on your special day. Happy Father's Day, Dad. I love you. Thanks for everything."

"I love you too." I could sense him smiling from back home.

We were thousands of miles apart, and yet, I felt more connected to those who I missed than ever before. And I wondered if leaving something behind actually brought you closer to it.

I spent some more time examining the thin layers of cloud that swirled and drifted above the mountain peaks while eating the snacks I had carried in my pocket.

The crew on top of Mt. Whitney.

Everyone joined together at the top: Bradley, Mr. Walker, Jim, Rambo, Applesauce, and all our other hiker friends. I thought of Nomad—my friend from the desert and a member of the Poodle Dog Boys—and of his mission to toss his wife's ashes from this very peak. Seeing out into the distance, I understood why he had chosen this spot. As the sun sank into the western skyline, it was time to head back down to camp and return to the PCT.

Later the next day, we made our way back onto the trail and crossed paths with a couple of familiar faces. It was Chatty Kathy and Sacajawea, the couple we'd met while soaking at Deep Creek Hot Springs in southern California. Reuniting with old friends was always an exciting event as we never knew which conversation might be our last.

We decided to eat together and catch up for a bit before they went on their way to climb Mt. Whitney. Chatty strummed his guitalele as we ate. Then he stopped, tilted his head, and looked at me.

"You know what, David?" he asked.

"What?"

"You look an awful lot like Barry Gibbs."

"Who…?"

He fell back into laughter. "*Seriously*?" He sighed and shook his head. "Now I feel old. You've heard of the BeeGees, right? They have that hit song: *Ahh, Ahh, Ahh, Ahh, Stayin' Alive, Stayin' Alive.*"

"Oh, right." It was definitely a familiar tune.

"That's it!" He stopped strumming and nodded.

"What?"

"You don't have a trail name yet, do you?"

I shook my head. I had almost forgotten about my desire to find one for myself, one that suited me well.

"What about… Stayin' Alive?"

"Stayin' Alive?"

"Yeah."

I nodded. There was a ring to it. It was fun and had the potential to carry some deeper meaning.

"Hmm, I'll try it out."

From that day on, I was known as Stayin' Alive, my resemblance to Mr. Gibbs later confirmed via a quick Google Images search:

Barry Gibbs & Stayin' Alive.

Sierra switchbacks.

We entered deeper into the Sierra mountain range over the next few days. I had seen many beautiful sights so far, but this place was otherworldly. White granite steps led us to the tops of stony mountain passes overlooking wide sprawling basins filled with meadows and lakes. Every climb was more difficult than anything we experienced in southern California, but the ascensions filled us with excitement because each pass led us to overlook a new paradise.

Having survived the ungodly heat and drought of Southern California, we'd been rewarded with a mostly snow-free hike through the Sierra, a range that in years past I'd heard required days of trudging through dense snowfall. The nights were cold, and at times, we hiked through rain. However, the days mostly held sunshine. We swam in lakes—aware of the chipmunks hatching plans to steal our food—forded rivers, gazed at distant waterfalls, bathed in hot springs, and sipped from the snowmelt flowing from the cracks of the highest glacial mountain peaks. The water was pure and crisp.

At night we made fires, shared food, chatted, and set up "bearicades"—huge piles of everyone's bear canisters and cookpots stacked on top of each other at the center of the campsite. This was our rudimentary bear alarm system, should any visit us during the night.

I'd only seen a couple of bears during the hike so far and from a good distance away. They didn't seem the least bit interested in me, keeping to themselves more than anything, scared and skittish when sensing movement. There was only one bear that visited our camp at night that needed chasing away by Sophie, our friend Patch's dog who we had met at the Paradise Valley Café.

But the Sierra didn't come without challenges. There were greater elevation changes, and the climbing up mountain passes was arduous. Higher elevations meant thin air. It was hard to breathe at times, and it took time to acclimatize. It was especially difficult to cook at night, as the temperature would often drop below freezing, and we'd quickly shove our bodies into our sleeping bags. But the desert had conditioned us for the challenge, and my legs finally seemed to be growing strong.

Stayin' Alive & the Bearicade.

We couldn't help but enjoy ourselves in this new playground, walking at an embarrassingly slow pace, forgetting all about the end goal of finishing the PCT. There was one stretch of trail that could have easily been hiked in four days that we dragged out into ten!

Recalling that the last time we had sent an email update to our friends and family back home was in Wrightwood, detailing our time spent at Deep Creek Hot Springs, we decided it was time to fill them in on the new cast of friends we'd been traveling with the past hundred miles or so:

June 25, 2015
Lone Pine, Mile 788
Subject: World Class Characters

Long time, no talk. We've been bushwhacking through the desert and now find ourselves in the high Sierra mountains at mile 788 on the PCT. We've been hiking with some world-class characters we'd like to introduce you to.

Forester Pass (from top to bottom: Rock City, Slingblade, Shake, Applesauce, Clark Kent, Stayin' Alive, Stik, Wolf, Maverick, Rambo, and Jim).

Birth Name {Trailias}: Bio
  Jim {Jim}: 40-year-old Brit recently come to America after teaching scuba diving in SE Asia.
  Molly {Applesauce}: 26-year-old preschool teacher from San Diego.
  Jacob {Rockcity}: Nomad from Detroit.

Richard {Mr. Walker}: Professional photographer, frequent blogger, and ninja enthusiast from Australia.

Mark {Wolf}: 29-year-old rap artist from Cleveland.

Daniel {Stik}: 29-year-old chef from Dallas. Happened to have attended the same high school as Bradley.

Alexandria {Rambo}: 25-year-old juvenile math teacher from Austin.

Michael {Slingblade}: Photographer and surgical tech from Arkansas.

Ben {3-Weight}: 24-year-old master fly fisherman from Philadelphia. Roll Tide.

Nathaniel {Clark Kent}: 23-year-old student with superb calves. Happens to be in the same Fraternity as David and Bradley.

Blue raspberry Hawaiian punch glacial pool.

So, we've been traveling with this group for one hundred or so miles in the Sierra. The other day we came across Forester Pass, the highest mountain pass on the trail at 13,000 ft. We happened upon a small glacial pool with water as blue as blue raspberry Hawaiian punch. We summoned on-comers one by one as they passed, increasing our group's clout. As our power grew, so too did the peer pressure, and these poor souls knew what was in their future as they were beckoned to the rim. Reluctantly, they approached and watched the hiker before them strip down to their skivvies or birthday suits and plunge into the thirty-five degree water. We came out reborn.

You should have seen us trying to swim to shore as we could barely say a word, besides maybe a loud yell. What a fun time!

It only takes one fallen domino to set the rest in motion, and small decisions build momentum in unseen ways. Any suffering that occurs will be short-lived, while the reward will last a lifetime. The beautiful misery of the cold water brought our group together that day.

It was cold.

Later that evening, we dropped below 10,000 feet and built a fire. We gathered the flour we had sent via our last resupply and wanted to make Damper, which is bush-bread in Australia.

Unfortunately, there was a bar of soap in our latest package which infected all of our food, notably our granola (which we properly renamed granoap) and of course the flour, the core ingredient of Damper. The crowd, however, *remained completely unsuspecting, and it took discipline for us not to die of laughter during the cooking process. After making the bushbread, we broke it and passed it out... hilarity ensued. We all ate the soap bread because of our insatiable appetites.*

The Damper meal.

Our group is splitting up today as Jim and Applesauce depart the trail. As we continue this adventure, we can't help but think of what awaits us next...

Wishing you well,
Shake and Stayin' Alive

It was a sad day as our trail family began its break up. Applesauce needed to get back to teaching. Jim planned on taking a break, unsure of his return. Oz was finding himself sick of the trail, understandably so as he'd already hiked the Appalachian Trail the year before, and he headed west for a scuba-diving excursion.

Everyone had mixed feelings about the changes. Both Bradley and I would miss Oz's energy and resourcefulness. Bradley wished Applesauce had shared his feelings for her, while Rambo decided to carry onward without her best friend for some extra miles. The two older gents were quite the dynamic duo, and Mr. Walker would feel Jim's absence.

This email update was the final update we sent to our friends and family back home as we decided the updates took too much time and effort. The trail had pulled us deeper into its experience.

A filthy fireside face-off.

CHAPTER 23

July 5, 2015
Mile 812, Sierra Mountains (1,838 miles to go)

It was a windy afternoon in the high woods of the Sierra Mountains as our group gathered around a flat rock in the shade of a pine to play a game of cards.

We paid little attention to Bradley and Wolf's antics as they ran into the woods to play stickball, a baseball-like game played with rocks and branches. Before long, the card game was in full swing, and as my turn was approaching, I studied which card should be played next while listening to the sweet chirping of birdsong.

At that moment, a loud crack rang through the forest, and I felt a pang against the back of my head. Everything fell black.

My eyelids peeled open a moment later to the sky, surrounded by my fellow hikers crouching over me. A sharp pain was throbbing against the back of my skull.

"Are you okay?!" they asked.

I nodded and rubbed my head. "What happened?"

"Shake's bat broke," Wolf said, looking at me with clenched teeth. "The branch flew thirty yards and smacked you in the back of the head."

Bradley was apologizing endlessly.

I sat up and blinked hard. "No really, I'm fine." Reality was returning to me. "I would have done the same thing to you, Shake."

Everyone laughed.

Bradley slapped my back. "Your trail name really is Stayin' Alive..."

The trail name was no longer a silly joke. As much as I liked the name, the way things had panned out so far, I wondered if the name was more a curse than anything else.

What other sketchy situations will this name attract?

That night was reminiscent of many before it: the laughing, chatting, and sharing of food. I looked around the circle of hikers beneath the dark sky. I'd met so many fascinating people in the Sierra, not a single one alike: rich and poor, young and old, those who had left behind their mundane lives in search of something new. I met some who had sailed across the seas and others who had traveled to the Far East. I'd met teachers, students, scientists, artists, farmers, hunters, musicians, photographers, CEOs, servers, monks, and veterans. I'd met hikers, bikers, trail workers, park rangers, and volunteers. Each inspired me in different ways, showing me new ways to live. It was still so foreign to me that one could create their own life by their own choosing.

Still, none of it helped me figure out what I wanted to do after the trail. So many new doors had been flung open that it only further complicated things. I felt pulled in a thousand different directions. *How do I know which path is the right one? And what are the consequences if I chose wrong?*

I'd been down this route before—another knot rising to the surface of my mind in need of observation. Nothing more could be done. There was nothing I could do for a future that didn't yet exist.

As we continued walking towards the never-ending northern horizon, hikers came and went while some stayed longer than others. But more than any other, there was a special synergy developing between Bradley, Mr. Walker, and me.

While Mr. Walker enjoyed making fun of us because of our word choices ("duuude", "dope", "dank"), he was also a voice of reason, a mediator between Bradley and I when things got tense, and an expert to guide us when the weather turned sketchy. The relationship was solidified on the Day of Commitment.

The infamous day occurred at Mammoth Lakes, a ski village at mile 900 on the PCT. Bradley and I had met many hikers in the past few miles who loved playing hacky sack. It was a fun, practical game—the bag was lightweight, and the game could be played almost anywhere in groups—and we began to spend much of our downtime honing our skills.

We had somehow acquired a hacky sack of our own through some good fortune and had become quite skilled at the sport (if you could even call it that) since leaving Kennedy Meadows.

Hacky Sack Circle from the Sierras.

Our kicks were precise, and Bradley and I could juggle for minutes at a time between the two of us. There were many tricks we performed: between the legs, over the head, high knees, or the famous sky ball where we'd launch the ball high into the air, executing a soft landing atop our shoe, only to begin again.

It was in the Mammoth Lakes village center that the three of us began rallying. Soon, tourists and kids gathered around us, watching the spectacle with bright eyes. When we noticed the attention, we strategically placed Mr. Walker's hat at the outer edge of the circle with a small sign that read: *PCT Hiker Fund*. We figured it was worth a shot!

Shake's skills.

With our trap set, we developed a busking routine and included the passing men, women, and children in on our fun and games. When all was said and done and the evening had passed, a hundred dollars had been placed in the hat!

Everyone was thrilled. In fact, Mr. Walker was so overjoyed by the outcome that he took us out for a sushi dinner that night. It was the nicest dinner we'd eaten in the past two months. There, he informed Bradley and me that he wanted to support our journey north.

Bradley and I couldn't believe what we were hearing. The terms of the agreement seemed too good to be true. It sounded like so long as we continued to be resourceful and helped Mr. Walker hike a faster pace to finish the trail that we wouldn't have to worry about expenses!

This was a huge deal for us since we were constantly reminded of our dwindling finances whenever entering new towns. Apart from enjoying our presence, I think a part of Mr. Walker sensed we were going to finish the trail and wanted to hop aboard that train.

And so it began—the three of us traveling through the Sierras, hiking up and over mountain passes, and passing through meadows and woods with Richard's photography and outdoors skills accompanying us throughout the most beautiful stretch of nature I'd ever seen.

Sierra views.

Shake & Waterfall.

Stayin' Alive & Shake tarp skills.

* * *

When we passed through the Sierra about four hundred miles later, we ended up back in the high desert of Northern California.

One evening, as we walked along a high mountain pass, Bradley, Mr. Walker, and I made out a village nestled deep in the valley beside the shore of a flowing river. We were happy to know we would soon reach Belden Town, a "rave town" known to host music festivals. We'd heard the likelihood of a festival was slim, but since the trail ran directly through the town, we'd soon find out.

As we made our descent, the first sounds of music reached our ears. Deep, resonating vibrations of an electronic bass drum carried thousands of feet upward, bouncing off the mountain walls, echoing to the tops of the peaks.

My heart quickened. *Is there really a concert going on down there?*

Fantasies and dreams of what awaited us ran through my head. It had been far too long since I had heard music so loudly, danced, or even talked to large groups of people who weren't hikers.

As if pulled by the music against our will, we began sprinting to the bottom of the mountain in full force, crossing a pair of rusted train tracks before wandering deeper into the forest, the trail leading us nearer to the music. What we came to was mayhem and could only be described as a tent city or a makeshift shantytown. A hundred tents were packed closely together, hardly any space left between them. Hammocks hung at various levels from the treetops, while couches and sleeping bags were sprawled carelessly about the riverbank. And there were so many people—artists, freaks, hippies, and musicians. They were dressed in brightly colored, eccentric clothing, tie-dye shirts, swimsuits, bikinis, or were otherwise topless, all pouring into the town entrance with smiling faces.

It was now dark, and everything about the festival glowed fluorescent greens, purples, and yellows. We weaved through the chaos of tents through the entrance past bright and colorful lights while posters were hung to display the event's musical artists and name: *Still Dream Festival.*

The trail ran directly through the festival's entrance; we had little choice but to enter. Enchanted and intrigued by the gathering, the three of us continued on and were led to a familiar group of faces.

A host of hiker friends cheered at our approach. It seemed as if everyone we had met had conglomerated here: Eedaham, Saint Croix, Macho Man Randy Savage, DK Shh, and Nomad, among many others!

My friend Lightning, who I had met all the way back in the Mt. Laguna campground, was lifelessly resting on his back against the dirt.

"We've been here for three days," he explained.

"Three days?!" asked Mr. Walker.

"Beware," said another hiker. "This place is a vortex unlike any I've ever seen."

We couldn't believe it.

Three days at this festival and they still haven't left yet?

It seemed like the lot of them were sinking deeper into the vortex. One hiker after the next admitted how they'd been here for days. The reasons for not leaving were many. First, the climb out of this deep gorge was many thousands of feet high, and the thought of tackling such an arduous pursuit left many hikers paralyzed. Plus, the place was filled with wonderful music, performance art, dancing, and kind and interesting strangers. Hikers told us their stories of river bathing, sleepless nights of music, and drug-induced experiences. Since they had arrived, few managed to escape the festival.

Bradley and I glanced at each other. We knew we'd have to be careful.

As we strolled down the tent city, a festivalgoer with a long beard, sunglasses, and a man-bun tied on top of his head ushered us beneath his canopy and presented us with drugs of all kinds, many of which I'd never even heard of before like "moon rocks" and "sassafras". Although we declined his offers, he continued to present his theories for the origins of the universe, a story that involved giant godlike beings rising from the mud and giving life to smaller human beings.

Mr. Walker rolled his eyes. "Are you serious?" he asked. "Where did you hear this nonsense? From where are you getting your information?"

The guy shrugged. "It's from my imagination, man…"

At that point Mr. Walker laughed and threw his hands in the air. "Alright, I'm out," he said.

We giggled at the conversation and departed. As the night darkened, the music grew louder. While Mr. Walker went to sleep, Bradley and I crawled out under the stars to dance. We walked the sand along the river through fog and neon lighting before coming to the stage. Stage musicians bobbed their heads from behind their performance sound booths. There, we jumped and sweat and danced with the crowd.

When all our energy had dissipated, we retired to the tent city campgrounds, finding space on the dirt and shutting our eyes to a sleepless night of bass drums pounding in the distance.

When morning came, I knew we had to get going, or it would be days before we'd make it out. The nearby river, beach, and festivalgoers made for an alluring vortex. It took hours of convincing, but finally I was able to get Bradley and Mr. Walker to take the high bridge over the river and climb the hill. We trudged up the gorge wall, and as soon as we made it atop the climb, we set up camp.

We were nearing the halfway point of the trail, and I was in heavy anticipation of its arrival. Thinking back to all the vortexes we'd entered and escaped, I had never imagined reaching such a significant destination.

I passed out while listening to the pattering of rain against our tarp.

Tent City at Still Dream Festival.

The Belden Vortex.

CHAPTER 24

August 3, 2015
Mile 1,325, PCT Midpoint (1,325 miles to go)

When I came to the trail's halfway point, I couldn't help but laugh. After working toward this moment for the last who-knows-how-many-hundred miles, all that stood before me was a small stone post, a stump just off the side of the trail.

That's it?! I thought.

Halfway...

For whatever reason, I had imagined a towering monument like the one erected at the southern terminus. The halfway point was supposed to bring tears of joy to my eyes and spark deep epiphanies from within me!

Instead, there was only this stone stump.

I slumped down next to it and sighed.

Still, I couldn't help but think how far we'd come. I'd walked blistered, barefoot, and dehydrated through the desert, escaped snowstorms and injuries, lost friends and lovers... the worst of the journey had to be behind me.

I tried smiling, but we were only halfway through the trail and still stuck in California. That was a difficult pill to swallow. If someone had told me California was expanding or Oregon was a myth, I just might have believed it.

Next to the pillar was a small iron box containing a trail log. I flipped through the pages, reading the names of long-lost friends, and wondering about the names I'd hoped to find but didn't see. After some time, I left a short note of my own:

Our journey is halfway full. Here's to another 1.3K miles of discovery, growth, and adventure.

Cheers,

Stayin' Alive

Bradley and Mr. Walker caught up and had their moments, kneeling before the stump in silence, signing and reading through the trail log. We took a short break in quiet reflection while munching from our feedbags. Then, we headed down the trail toward the next town with hungry bellies. Our dried fruits and nuts were becoming increasingly bland, and I was ready for something greasy, creamy, and fatty to fill both of my stomachs to maximum capacity.

The next day in the small town of Chester, we found a restaurant and sat down at a table with high hopes of earning ourselves a proper meal.

"What can I get started for you boys?" the waitress asked. "Waters all around?"

We nodded.

"You boys looking to order?"

She was onto us.

Bradley cleared his throat. "Well, first off, if there's any scraps or leftovers being sent back to the kitchen, we'd be more than willing to take them off your hands."

The waitress flushed red. "Oh. Umm... I'm sorry, I don't think I'm allowed to do that."

"Don't worry, we won't mind," Bradley said.

I smiled.

She shrugged her shoulders. "It's just... I believe it's against our health code."

Bradley nodded. "Don't worry, we didn't see *anything*."

Mr. Walker and I were trying not to crack up.

"I'll let you know, dear," she said before scurrying back to the kitchen.

"I think you embarrassed her."

Bradley shook his head. "I don't think so. I'm not the one in control of her embarrassment."

We nodded. I guessed he had a point.

We scanned the room for potential opportunities to "table dive," as Oz had called it. The diner was empty except for two tables—a middle-aged couple sitting at the table behind us waiting to order and a table of patrons in the corner booth eating burgers, fries, and chocolate milkshakes. They looked on track to finish their servings. Disheartened, I stared at the vanishing milkshake remnants.

I guess I could buy something, I thought. But the money was needed for resupplies, and until Mr. Walker offered to pay, I wasn't going to ask anything of him. Not to mention the rules of the game would be broken: trust our experience and suffer until the moment of inevitable resourcefulness.

I nodded at the door. "Ready to leave?"

Mr. Walker shrugged. Bradley looked around and nodded. Just as we were about to leave, a voice came from the booth behind us.

"You boys hungry?" The middle-aged man asked.

We nodded aggressively.

"I could eat," Bradley said.

"Then come on over," said the woman.

We smiled at each other and joined them at their table.

"Hope you don't mind our fragrance," Bradley said.

"Not at all." The man laughed. "I used to be a Boy Scout troop leader, so I'm used to the smell. Are you boys on the trail?" he asked.

"That's right," Bradley said. "On our way to Canada."

"Canada, huh?" the man asked. "Think you'll make it? Snow's coming early this year."

"Oh, we'll make it," Bradley said confidently.

"My name's Shake."

"Stayin' Alive."

"Mr. Walker."

The couple laughed after each name.

The man turned to the wife. "Trail names," he said.

She smiled. "Of course. I'm Cindy, and this is Guy."

"Good to meet you both," Bradley said. "What brings you two to Chester?"

"We're on vacation," the wife said, laying her head against the man's shoulder.

"The kids are finally out of the house," the man said, "and we're spending the weekend at a Ranch Resort down the road."

"That sounds lovely," Mr. Walker said. "Care if we join you?"

They chuckled.

"Umm, maybe next time," Guy said.

The waitress passed by our table. "How's everyone doing over here?" she asked.

Bradley smiled. "Well, you can hold the scraps for now. It looks like we found some trail magic."

"Oh." She blushed again then took our order, each of us selecting a burger, fries, and a milkshake.

As we ate with Guy and Cindy, we got to know them well. They were on the edge of their seats listening to our stories, responding with shock, smiles, and laughter in all the right places.

When it was time for them to get going, Guy plucked a pen from Cindy's purse and scribbled on a napkin.

"Here. Take this," he said. "We live in Tacoma. If you make it that far north and you're in need, let us know. Since we couldn't get you into the Ranch Resort, maybe we can find another way to help."

We thanked them, said our goodbyes, and watched as they headed out the front doors of the diner.

"What's the note say?" Bradley asked.

I grabbed the napkin from the table. "First, there's a phone number. And then it says, 'call in case of emergency'…"

Bradley laughed. "Emergency, huh?" A huge grin spread across his face.

I already knew what he was thinking. We'd be calling that number no matter what. The possibility of sleeping indoors or finding a home-cooked meal was a great emergency in our eyes!

There'd be trail magic waiting in Washington, but to make it there required another five hundred miles of hiking. We were lifetimes away from thinking too much of it. More of Northern California still lay ahead.

Stayin' Alive & Shake waiting to hitch.

CHAPTER 25

August 14, 2015
Mile 1,598, Mount Shasta (1,052 miles to go)

Our group of hikers had grown once again. A few new friends accompanied us, including Toast, his dog Zwina, and a young couple named Mac and Cheese. Together we climbed through the forests to witness the looming volcano—

Mount Shasta.

The mountain had been visible for the last hundred miles, but we only saw glimpses of the snowy peak above the pines, and only every few miles. It was clearer now at the overlook, its figure beyond impressive. The sun was at high noon, and we spread ourselves out along the cliff to eat and stare at the peak.

Far beyond the pines—but much closer than ever before —the mountain twisted into the clouds. Trees skirted the mountain but disappeared as the peak ascended. It stood alone against the horizon, its shape intoxicating.

"We're climbing that bloody mountain," Toast said in his Scottish accent.

The self-proclaimed dirtbag stood at the cliff's edge inspecting the landscape, his thick dreadlocks drifting in the wind, his tattooed arms bared, and his calloused hands on his hips. He had years of climbing experience, so perhaps the mountain didn't look as intimidating to him.

"Are you joking, Toast?" Bradley asked. "You really want to climb that?"

"Does it look like I'm joking, Shake?" Toast asked, narrowing his eyes.

I laughed. Although Toast and Bradley got along well, the two alphas had been engaged in a friendly feud for miles. Usually, Mr. Walker, Mac, Cheese, and I thought the dynamic was light-hearted enough to not intervene, thinking it nice entertainment.

A small ball of white fur came to sit next to me. Zwina.

Zwina & Toast.

She was soft and regal, a husky dog, too proud and independent to listen to Toast's commands or stay long beside me. She rarely allowed anyone to pet her. Doing so was a rare treat, but she'd warmed up to the group considerably in the last hundred miles.

Zwina was our guardian. Just before we'd arrived at the overlook, she'd been running what we called status updates, sprinting from the front to the back of our hiker caravan, checking to make sure no one was dragging behind. After completing her scouting mission, she would run to the front of the line past whoever was leading our group and sit down in the middle of the trail, a signal to the lead hiker to slow their pace. Zwina would make sure no one was left behind.

When she wasn't running status updates, she was either hiking alongside us, her nose gently nudging against our socks with each step, knowing precisely how fast to walk to not be hit in the face, or darting into the forest after a fleeing squirrel or chipmunk. When she fled into a chase, it was common that she'd be gone for miles.

"Zwina!" Toast would shout. "Zwina!"

Usually there was silence. It was only miles later, when we thought she might be gone for good this time, that she'd come sprinting from out of the depths of the wilderness, falling right back into line. We joked that if Zwina finished the trail, she'd have hiked the PCT three times over. Walking alongside a dog felt primitive and natural, and I was grateful for her presence.

Also joining us atop the canyon cliff were Mac and Cheese. We'd been hiking with the laid-back, easy-going, twenty-something couple from Seattle for the past few hundred miles. They'd funded their trip working as servers the winter prior. Cheese was a fit blonde girl, and Mac reminded me of some of my fraternity brothers back home. It was a rag-tag group, but the lot of us enjoyed each other's company nicely.

Toast's prolonged cliffside gaze toward the mountain was his way of making sure everyone knew of his latest plan to climb it.

"Well, good luck with that," Mr. Walker said. "You can count me out."

"You're coming too, Walker," Toast said. "You won't have a choice. Here, this should help."

Toast had rolled a spliff during an earlier break as he often did, a joint made of tobacco and weed. He lit it and passed it to Mr. Walker after puffing it himself.

"No thanks," said Mr. Walker.

"Shake?" Toast asked.

Bradley gazed at it for a long moment before reaching out and bringing it to his lips. Smoke fumed from his nostrils, and he started to cough.

I looked away. I couldn't stand when they were high. It was like they'd enter into a different realm, checking out of the one I related to.

Toast turned to me.

"Stayin' Alive, what about you? I know you're climbing it with me."

I shrugged. "Eh... we'll see."

I wasn't sold on the mountain just yet. Although Mt. Shasta was just a hair shorter in elevation compared to Mt. Whitney, it looked much steeper and consequently more frightening. And unlike Mt. Whitney, Mount Shasta was fairly dangerous. I tried to ignore the thought, putting it aside to a more pressing concern: the food situation in the upcoming town.

"Anyone know anything about Mt. Shasta and what's in town?" I asked.

Everyone took out their maps or checked their phone apps.

"There's a grocery store," Cheese said.

"Doesn't look like there's any trail angels," Mac said.

"In that case, I'm getting a room," Mr. Walker said.

Bradley's eyes grew big. So did mine. We looked at Mr. Walker with bright faces.

He rolled his eyes. "Yes, there's enough room for you two fools," he said.

"We'll go in on it with you," Mac said.

"Alright then," Toast said. "Let's just get there already!" He cupped his hands to his face. "Zwinaaa! Zwinaaa!"

His voice echoed in the distance, and it took time for her majesty to reappear from the trees.

Finally, we stood and made our way down the trail toward the mountain. It seemed as if it was drawing us closer with some magnetic force. A part of my mind could already sense it. This place was a vortex.

* * *

It was a sunny day as we took the sidewalk into town, gazing through the hazy windows of shop storefronts lining the streets. Crystals, incense, and other trinkets were displayed behind the glass, and posters for palm readings hung outside the doors. It seemed to me hippy merchandise, but I couldn't help but ponder the results of a good fortune telling! Mr. Walker yanked me away from one of the windows, and we continued toward the town center.

People lined the town square, but everyone looked to be passing through as if the place was some sort of purgatory for wandering souls. Vagabonds milled about the alleyways, the homeless slept on park benches, hikers lay on the grassy hills, and tourists gathered near the town's fountain. We fit in well with the crowd.

We were carrying on in search of a hotel room when an old man approached our group. He looked a lot like us. He had matted hair, tattered clothes, wore a large backpack, and held a wilting cardboard sign with illegible writing. The only visible difference between him and us was the intentionality of his homelessness.

"Hey," he said as he fell in line alongside our group. "My name's Joe. Where you headin?" He trotted next to Mr. Walker.

"Just looking for a hotel, mate," Mr. Walker said.

"Mmm," Joe replied. "You're new to town, aren't you?"

Mr. Walker nodded.

"Then you guys haven't seen Bigfoot yet?"

"Nope," Mr. Walker laughed. "Not yet..."

"Have you?" Bradley asked.

"I've seen a whole family of them," Joe said.

"Did they say anything to you?" Bradley asked. He was genuinely curious.

The man shook his head. "They don't speak. Only telepathically."

"Right," Mr. Walker said, holding up his camera. "Did you snap a picture?"

Joe shook his head. "Didn't bother," he said. "The flash scares 'em."

"Of course." Mr. Walker nodded. "Where'd they go then, mate?"

Joe's eyes grew big and serious. "Teleported," he said. "Disappeared in a flash of smoke and ain't seen 'em since. But I'm watchin'."

"Yep," Mr. Walker said, picking up his pace. "Great meeting you, Joe. Best of luck with all that."

Joe waved as we left him behind.

This town kept growing more strange and more interesting in each moment.

During our hotel room search, we came across a small convenience store with pictures of food displayed across the windows.

"Anyone hungry?" Mr. Walker asked.

Everyone set their packs down.

"Let's do this," Toast said.

The familiar artificial chill of the air conditioning blasted our faces as we walked inside the mart. The space was cluttered with shelves of snacks, fridges of drinks, and the aroma of deli meat coming from the back of the store.

As he waited in line for a sandwich, Mr. Walker struck up a conversation with the woman in front of him. "Ma'am, do live here?"

The woman nodded. "Yes, indeed."

"Please tell me you don't believe in Bigfoot."

She laughed. "Oh. Yeah, actually, he does exist," she said. "He hides in the pines at the base of the mountain. And then there's the Anunnaki—you've heard of them, right?"

Mr. Walker was already looking for ways to escape.

"They're the shape-shifting lizards," she continued. "They live in the mountain's caves, but they also roam the world, disguising themselves as the leaders of our country and the beggars on the corner. You just never know. I think they're here to teach us lessons."

Mr. Walker rolled his eyes. "Right, just curious… thanks."

After he had ordered, our group sat together outside the mart. Bradley and I watched the others eat their food, and Mr. Walker offered us bites of his sandwich. After they were done, Mr. Walker stood.

"I'm off to find a hotel," he said. "You guys can go play. Shake, your phone's working, right?"

"Yep. Signal's strong here in this town."

"Great, we'll be in touch then."

Bradley, Toast, Mac, Cheese, and I waved goodbye for now.

"Sounds good," I said.

As Mr. Walker departed, we found a small park and Bradley busted out the hacky sack. Play ensued.

We then noticed a group of kids dressed in black, coated in nihilism and despair, sitting in the grasses nearby. We asked if they wanted to join us, but they declined our offer. We chatted briefly, learning they were train hoppers, but it seemed like they didn't feel the same way about trains as we felt about the trail. We wished them the best and returned to our games. We set out Mac's trucker's hat to collect money from those passing by, earning nothing that day except a tiring workout.

Still dreaming of Mr. Walker's sandwich, I was ready to eat some cheap whole foods that could only be bought at a grocery store.

Eventually, I tossed him the hacky sack.

"Shake!" I said.

Just barely able to look up in time, he snagged the beanbag from out of the air.

"I'm heading to the grocery," I said.

He nodded. "I'll meet you there. I just need to release some more energy."

"Sounds good," I said, turning to leave.

"Stayin' Alive!" He ran up to me from across the park. "Before you go, I wanted to tell you something."

"Sure."

He sighed, and his gaze sank. "Well, it's about money... I'm running low on funds. Realistically, I'm not sure how much longer I can make it up the trail," he said.

"Oh. How low are you?"

His hand lifted and his forefinger nearly touched his thumb. "I know Mr. Walker has been our savior by buying hotel rooms and meals and all, but I have a feeling we'll lose him soon. It's not going to last."

"You think so?"

He nodded. "He was talking to me about it earlier. I think he's set on skipping Oregon, hiking Washington north-bound, then hitching back down again to hike Oregon southbound to complete the trail before the winter snow. I don't know about you, but I'd rather finish the trail outright at the northern terminus. I know Mac and Cheese think we can make it if we just keep going. Anyway, if Mr. Walker leaves us, I can't make any promises for myself finance wise."

I sighed. "How many resupplies do we have left?"

"That's the thing," he said. "There aren't any. I only planned for California to give us some leeway to change our food strategy. I guess we'll have to figure things out as we go."

I looked at the mountain standing far behind him. I couldn't lose him again. We'd come too far together for him to quit now, and I knew what the trail meant to him. He'd shown me the trail, and I'd do my best to bring him to the finish.

"Hey," I said, placing a hand on his shoulder. "I got you, man. What's mine is yours."

He nodded. "Thanks, brother."

"Of course. Plus, those hiker boxes have been good to us. And even if that doesn't continue, we have Mr. Walker to thank. He's helped save me a ton of money. Whatever I've got left, we'll make it stretch to the end."

"Sounds good, brother. Speaking of finances, I'm off to find some batteries for our headlamps. You need some, right?"

"Yessir."

"Good. I'll meet you at the market."

"See ya there, bro," I said, before smiling and turning to locate the market.

The streets ended, and I balanced myself atop the train tracks leading toward the grocery. The place was massive. Aisles of food lined the supermarket, but being on a budget and resisting my ice-cream cravings, I bought an apple and went back outside, finding a spot beneath the shade to lie back on my mat. I placed my hands behind my head and rested my bare feet on my backpack like a proper vagrant.

As I was minding my own business, a small blue car pulled into the parking space in front of me. The driver's door opened.

CHAPTER 26

August 16, 2015
Mile 1,598, Mt. Shasta Town (1,052 miles to go)

Out of the vehicle stepped a town girl with flowing blonde hair who looked to be about my age. I couldn't help but stare. She was beautiful. Maybe her cleanliness had something to do with it. I also noticed she wore no makeup and felt she emitted a certain sweetness.

She slammed the door, tossed her hair, and made her way toward the grocery.

I tried my best not to look directly at her, but she caught me in the middle of one of my prolonged stares, smiled, and waved as she passed by.

Well, there goes another one, I thought. *Another beautiful woman exiting my life just as quickly as she had entered it.*

Just then, she stopped.

Did she forget something?

The pause seemed to last an eternity. Suddenly, she spun around and began heading in my direction. I froze.

Is she coming to talk to me? I sat up against my elbows as casually as possible.

"Hey," she said.

"Hey." My heart was throbbing.

She smiled. "There's a concert tonight at the Inn. You should come." Her sweet demeanor and calming presence permeated every word she spoke.

"Will you be there?"

"Mm-hm. After all, the town's favorite band is playing. They're really good."

"Then... yeah, I'll see you there."

"Great!"

With that, she turned and trotted off into the grocery. I lay back and laughed. I couldn't remember the last time a woman had approached me so directly. It felt refreshing.

It wasn't long before she was exiting the store with grocery bags dangling from each hand.

"Hey," I said. My legs took some time to straighten themselves out to a stand. "I'm not sure I got your name. I'm Stayin' Alive."

I noticed that introducing myself by my trail name to a townsperson didn't feel nearly as strange as it once had.

She set down one of the grocery bags and shook my hand. "Kenzie," she said. "It's good to meet you, Stayin' Alive."

My heart melted hearing how little my name seemed to faze her.

"Well, I'll see you tonight then, Stayin' Alive?"

"Yep. See you then."

She waved once more before stepping into her blue townie car, the bobblehead flower bouncing in the dash. The car veered out of the parking lot over the railroad tracks and disappeared in the distance.

I lay back on my sleeping pad feeling like the richest man in Shasta and closed my eyes.

I felt a thud beside me and turned. Three fresh batteries rolled on my sleeping pad. It was Bradley. He stopped and looked down at me, confused.

"Okay," he said. "What did I miss?" He must have noticed my oddly wide smile.

I told him all about my encounter with Kenzie and the event taking place that night at the Inn. As I recalled the event, he sent me a smile filled with both happiness and jealousy. We had often discussed our desires to meet someone special on the trail, and suddenly I was the lucky one. Although, nothing had happened apart from a short chat, I felt bad I was the only benefactor. Nonetheless, meeting single women had become such a rare occurrence on the trail that Bradley agreed he'd tag along for the adventure that night.

That evening, after a quick and glorious shower at Mr. Walker's hotel room, Bradley and I headed down the western road to wander the streets in search for this tavern they called the Inn.

Bradley halted and grabbed my shoulder. "You're joking..."

I lifted my head. There it was—the first establishment down the road from our hotel in the exact direction of our choosing.

Music blared from inside, and I pushed open the tavern door. A dimly lit crowd swayed and danced to the music, their attention fixated on the stage or on their partners. The guitar twanged, drums boomed, and cymbals crashed. Everything sounded remarkably loud as we weaved through the crowd toward the back of the tavern for some space. Then, two hands slapped down onto my shoulders.

"You came!"

I turned. It was Kenzie. Her face was glowing, and that same bright smile was spread across her face. Her blue eyes shimmered like sapphires in the lights of the dance hall. We embraced.

"Of course," I said. "I wouldn't miss it for anything."

"You know how to dance, right?" she asked.

I laughed. "You may have to teach me. But I want you to meet my friend first."

I glanced over my shoulder. "Kenzie, this is Brad—I mean, Shake."

Her eyes lit up. "Good to meet you, Shake. Don't move. There's someone I want you to meet, too." And with that, she ran off into the crowd.

We looked at each other and shrugged. Kenzie returned moments later, another girl in tow. I smiled at Bradley. He laughed.

"Hi, I'm Sydney." Sydney was a bright and energetic brunette, and as Bradley and Sydney were getting acquainted, Kenzie pulled me toward the dance floor.

"Nice work," I told her.

"You too."

Music filled the hall, bringing us to another world, and we soon found ourselves surrounded by the crowd, taken by the rhythm, swaying and sweating close to one another.

It was between songs that we bounced questions off one another, learning of each other's past and passions. I knew so little of her except for her careful gazes and her delicate hands. Above all, I felt intrigued, feeling she knew something I didn't.

By the end of the night, the music slowed, and she brought her hips close. I could feel my blood pumping as her body pressed against mine. She wrapped her arms around my neck and ran her hands through my hair. Her breath against my neck sent shivers down my spine. She shook the hair from her eyes and looked up to me.

"Can I kiss you?" I asked.

She laughed, looked away, and then bit her lip. She nodded and drew closer.

I pressed my lips to hers. They were soft and gentle, her mouth wet and unbelievably warm. When I glanced across the hall, I noticed Bradley and Sydney had hit it off just fine as well.

It was well past midnight when we stumbled out of the Inn. The four of us had paired off, walking hand in hand down the empty street leading back to our seedy hotel room.

When we pushed the door open, a sliver of light fell into the room. Backpacks lay against the walls, and our friends were wrapped in sleeping bags, eyes shut. We tiptoed around them and slid into the beds we'd claimed earlier that night. The sheets were warm as she snuggled beside me, and her body melded into mine. It had been ages since I'd held another person so close, really caring for someone lying next to me. As she fell asleep with her head against my chest, I wished the night could have lasted forever.

The four of us back at the seedy motel room.

* * *

Our group arrived at Castle Lake the next morning after a short car ride from Kenzie and Sydney. The place was reminiscent of the beauty we'd found in the Sierra. A shimmering emerald lake spanned the basin, nestled beneath the mountain walls. The surrounding crags were like castles rising into the sky. The lake water was cool, but not frigid, and Bradley and Sydney were returning from the middle of the lake, their kayak gliding across the water toward us.

I looked at Kenzie. It was our turn. We commandeered the craft and gently rowed away from the shore. I sliced the water and pressed us forward with the turning of my paddle.

It felt nice to work a new part of the body.

As the sun poured down from above and a gentle breeze flowed across the lake's surface, I rowed us to the center of the lake then set the oar beside me. It was quiet far from the city. The water, although still, seemed to rock us back and forth ever so slightly in its arms. Kenzie lay back against my lap, and I squeezed her. We floated alone in the silence.

"It's beautiful, isn't it?" she asked.

My gaze shifted upward. She was looking away, toward the distant mountain. It stood alone on the horizon, and I thought I could see wind howling around its spire. Mount Shasta.

"Our friend Toast wants to climb it," I said.

"Really?" she asked. Her face was glowing. "Does he really want to? Do you want to?"

"Yeah, he does. I'm not sure, though. We don't even know where to start..."

"I do!" she said, smiling. "There's an outdoor equipment shop in town I can take you to. They'll have everything you need. And when you're ready, I can drive you to the trailhead."

Is this actually going to happen? For a moment I regretted ever bringing it up. Mt. Shasta presented a much greater challenge than Mt. Whitney, but Kenzie's glowing eyes made me think it was possible.

"You should climb it with us," I said.

She laughed. "No, no. I'd only slow you guys down. But it's wonderful that you're climbing it." She sighed and looked into the distance. "So many people in this town have lived beside the mountain their entire lives, but hardly anyone would ever even consider climbing it. And all the sudden you guys show up and want to climb it the second day you're here!"

"I guess we are pretty crazy. But I'm still not sure. It's not like it's my idea or anything."

"Oh... does that make it any less special?"

I shrugged. Thinking back, the entire trail wasn't really my idea. And look where it had brought me.

"You're probably right."

She laughed. "You know, you think too much, Stayin' Alive." She grabbed my hand. "I wonder. Maybe the mountain is calling you and not the other way around. It happens that way sometimes, you know. It's important to listen to that. Maybe you'll only know why you did it once you get there."

I nodded and sat and watched the clouds, thinking about what she had said.

The clouds were ominous, thin, and white, circling the distant peak, and we watched the sky together for some time. Everything was peaceful and quiet.

CHAPTER 27

August 17, 2015
Mile 1,598, Mount Shasta (1,052 miles to go)

The hotel room was filled with the dreadful sound of the 4 a.m. alarm.

BWAHH. BWAHH. BWAHH.

It only reminded me of how little sleep I'd gotten.

"Are we still doing this?" Bradley asked.

There was no answer. I'd heard the question, but I wasn't going to be the first to speak. There was still that slight chance of going right back to bed and forgetting about the whole commitment.

"I'm up," Mac said.

"Almost ready," Toast said.

I sighed.

I rose and began to dress. Clunky climbing boots and maps, each rented from the local outfitter the day prior, were scattered about the floor. From what we'd been told, climbing Mt. Shasta was no laughing matter. They'd tried to sell us crampons, ice axes, and helmets, but as stubborn PCT hikers, we thought a route was all we would need to find our way to the top.

Instead, our preparation the day before was left to what we felt was most important: food. We'd spent hours preparing

our lunch for the climb, and the result was master crafts-
manship: four massive dream sandwiches complete with
turkey, salami, cheese, avocado, mustard, mayonnaise, and
hot Cheetos, stuffed into plastic baggies and stacked on the
corner table. I grabbed mine, shoved it into my mostly empty
pack, and headed out the front door.

Food preparations for Mt. Shasta.

It wasn't even dawn, and a cold wind ran through the town.
The headlights of Kenzie's car shone in the dark of the hotel
parking lot. She peeked out from the window and smiled.
Exhausted and sleep deprived, Bradley, Mac, Toast, and I
loaded in, waved goodbye to Cheese, Richard, and a few
other friends who had decided to stay behind, and went on
our way.

The road led onward. The sky was black and speckled
with stars. I looked over at Kenzie, smiling. I took her hand
above the console and squeezed. The highway climbed, and
we exited eastward, turning onto a forest road. There were
hardly any signs along the dirt road, and we stopped for
minutes at a time to check our maps and search on phones
for information regarding the trailhead.

We drifted further into the woods. I felt a sense of relief as we became lost among the pines, twisting and turning up the dirt roads. I thought maybe we wouldn't have to climb the mountain after all.

"There it is!" Kenzie said, pointing to a large wooden sign. It was the trailhead.

My stomach sank, but the mountain beckoned. We unloaded from the car and tightened our backpacks. As the group started up the mountain, taking the path into the trees, I pressed my lips to Kenzie's before running to catch up. As I ran into the forest, it hit me that this was the first time in two days we would be apart.

Nothing was to be seen amid the forest canopy as the sun had yet to rise. A cold, thin breeze rushed through the trees. We marched as one with Toast at the helm, barreling up the mountain, keeping a quick pace to warm the body. Our footsteps matched our excitement. It was relieving to hike after days without it.

"How long is the hike, again?" I asked.

"Six miles," Mac said.

"Oh," I said. "That's nothing."

"Yeah," Toast said. "But there's also seven thousand feet of elevation."

"Right." It sounded like a lot. Thinking back to the Sierra, a thousand feet of elevation in one mile was a difficult hike. Seven thousand packed into six miles was unheard of on the trail. Nonetheless, the mountain's gradual uphill slope was alluring and filled us with confidence.

"Keep your eyes out for Bigfoot," I said.

"He's out here somewhere," Bradley said, grinning.

"Wait!" Mac shouted.

Everyone stopped.

He pointed up into the trees. "Guys, what the hell is that?"

It was menacing. Floating in the darkness of the treetops was a pair of glowing white eyes. They were round and ghostly, staring down at us with black and beady pupils.

"Uhh… seriously, what is that?" Bradley asked.

"That's the scariest thing I've ever seen," I said.

"Is it… Bigfoot?" Mac asked.

"Guys," Toast said matter-of-factly. "That's a mink."

We laughed and proceeded onward. Bigfoot would have made for a better story.

The first few miles were relatively easy, a steady hike, and we soon ascended above the tree line. There, everything opened up. The mountain's full figure came into view, and a lone snow-capped peak stared down upon us. It was even more daunting from up close than how it had looked from town.

In fact, as I glanced upward, it appeared to be a challenge greater than any I'd faced on the trail. I wondered if the strength I was finding on the trail could be applied to this new domain. My heart pumped as we continued to climb.

The air was still cold in the waning darkness, and although it took some time to see, the sound of trickling water reached our ears. We had found ourselves beside a mossy stream, and there we broke for water, drinking the snowmelt from the ice caps above. The water was cool and crisp as it passed over my tongue. As much as I would've like to stay longer, it was too cold to sit in the early darkness and rising altitudes, so we stood and trudged onwards without filling our water bottles. The extra weight would only make the climb more difficult, we said. We couldn't help but comment on how quickly and easily the ascent had been so far. But as I ran the calculations in my mind, although we'd walked nearly half the miles, we'd hardly tackled any of the gradient.

We passed a grassy basin with what looked like a couple of tents. There would be others climbing the mountain with us today, and we weren't sure whether they were ahead of us or still sleeping. Still, it was comforting to know we weren't the only ones attempting the feat.

Mt. Shasta sunrise.

It must have been another mile when, halfway up the four-teener, the sun first edged the horizon, and bright orange light spread over the valley. Although it was still cold, the new warmth allowed us to shed our jackets. We continued upward. We were on a schedule, and the faster we could complete the mountain, the faster we could get back to town. I thought about Kenzie, but was glad she and Sydney had stayed in town. At our pace, she was right—they would have only slowed us down.

By now, the earth and dirt were far behind us, having disappeared along with the trees. There was only rock, gravel, and scree scattered across the mountain. The grade grew steeper and the rocks loose and slippery. I fought just to get air to my lungs, and my legs began to tighten. But, it was nothing I hadn't experienced before. I glanced up to see how much more remained. The trail was gone.

"Where's the trail?" I asked.

The ranks stopped to peer upward. "No trail," Toast said, pointing to the peak. "We make our own way now."

I nodded. There was no trail, but it was obvious where we needed to go—up. Falling into line, we hiked up the mountain, choosing between various routes that could be distinguished from fallen scree of those who had come before us.

From here, the climb became more of a slow scramble than a hike. The rising elevation was hardly manageable on two legs, and we crawled upward on hands and feet, finding trustworthy steps where possible, as the earth was quick to crumble and cause us to slide back down. Every step forward was two backward, and it took a kind of effort I hadn't yet experienced just to gain ground. I'd entered into new territory, but there was a ridge above that seemed promising.

"How far from the top do you think we are?" I asked the group, bracing myself against the mountain.

Toast glanced over his shoulder. "Halfway," he said.

I sighed. It seemed like we'd made much more progress than that. "Are you sure?"

He pointed to the ridge above. "We can take a break up there to check."

Exhausted, tired, and frustrated, I stepped forward with diminishing confidence. I could feel anger pressing against my forehead. The climb had become much more difficult than anything I'd experienced on the trail.

When we finally reached the ridge, we broke to eat. Although I'd been looking forward to eating my dream sandwich all day, the climb had made me light-headed and taken away my appetite. Nevertheless, food usually improved my mood.

I took mine out and bit into the bread. My chewing slowed to a crawl. The whole thing tasted oddly creamy and awfully spoiled. It was impossible to peel the bread from the meat, as the sandwich had become a soggy, conglomerated mix of mayonnaise, mustard, and hot Cheetos. It made me want to vomit.

"Is your sandwich disgusting, too?" I asked Mac.

"Yeah, man," he said. "Letting that mayo sit overnight without a fridge was a mistake. How's yours, Toast?"

"Finished," Toast said, licking his fingers.

We shook our heads. Bradley had eaten half of his and was well on the way to polishing off the rest. Since there was nothing else to eat, I forced myself to down half the spoiled mess. At least it was better than yucca pods or turmeric oats.

When I was finished, my mouth was both dry from fatigue and fiery from the spicy Cheetos. Pain throbbed against my skull. My water bottle was empty. *Why didn't we fill up more at the spring?*

"Guys, think we'll see any more water on this mountain?" Mac asked.

"Doesn't seem like it," Toast said. "That first stream might have been our only option. We should keep moving."

The sun loomed high over the world, and we rose to our feet to meet the remaining challenge. Our scrambling continued for what seemed like hours up the mountain, and we found ourselves having reached the next ledge above.

Mt. Shasta view, climbing higher.

Each summit was disappointing as we hoped the peak would come into view, but each ledge held another plateau above and another long climb.

The mountain grew even steeper and more difficult with every step. We hadn't yet reached the next ridge, but I hoisted myself onto a boulder where the rest of the group was waiting.

I turned to Bradley. "Why are we doing this?"

His eyes were chasing the distant horizon. "I'm not sure."

I wasn't sure either. The goal seemed purposeless, and I felt like we'd traveled so far from the trail.

Toast must have heard us from above. "Guys, stop that thinking! Look how far we've come."

It was impossible to see the top, but looking onto the landscape, we must have been three-fourths of the way through.

"Don't you think you'd regret it if you quit now?" asked Toast. "It won't be easy, but we didn't come here for easy."

"Yeah," Bradley said, "Remind us, why did we come here?"

Mac and I laughed.

"Mate," Toast said firmly, "I promise you'll remember this climb for the rest of your life. But how you remember it… that's up to you."

Bradley, Mac, and I exchanged looks and sighed. He was right. We'd regret giving up now after all we'd been through.

As the rest of the group made the final push toward the summit, I sat alone, needing the rest because I'd never felt so exhausted.

Finally, I stood and continued to climb far behind the rest of the group, reaching false summit after false summit. The air grew cold and windy as I made my way higher into the sky. The height was unsettling, the route turning sketchy in spots where a slip might send me down a few hundred feet or more.

When I reached the next summit, patches of snow were settled atop the rocks, and my clothes were flapping in the wind. I shivered but continued trudging higher, the mountain sapping me of all my energy.

Just when I felt like I couldn't hike any further, I looked up. There it was. The peak. Standing above me surrounded by blue skies and sunlight.

Unlike the ridges below, this one was undoubtedly the final summit. I began to make my way toward the spire, but when I looked around, the route I had been walking was completely gone. Anything closely resembling a path had suddenly vanished!

Which way do I go? I could see the summit above me, but there was no path to walk to where I could reach it.

"Come on up."

It was Bradley. His voice coming somewhere above me on the peak. It was faint and hardly pierced the gusts of wind.

I cupped my hands beside my mouth. "Are you all at the top?" I strained my ears, waiting for a response.

"… Yeah…"

"Which way do I go?" My shirt was flapping in the wind.

"… To… the… right…"

I could hardly make out the words.

"What?"

This time there was nothing. The winds drowned out any potential sound.

Is the trail really to the right?

All I saw was a cliff dropping off into thin air. No way in hell I had to climb over the edge and up to that peak.

This time I yelled as loud as I could. "Are you sure it's to the right?"

No answer.

Studying the final ascent, it looked like a long crack that split the mountain. My heart was slamming against my chest. I saw no other options.

With a deep breath and my legs shaking, I held onto a large rock, slowly lifted my right foot over the edge of the cliff, and planted it against a foothold carved into the face of the cliff.

I pushed my jittery foot against the spot over and over again to test it, to make sure it could hold my weight. It seemed solid.

With my right hand, I reached across the cliff and grabbed hold of a rock, yanking it to ensure it wouldn't crumble. With right hand and right foot reaching over the ledge and steadied on new rocks above the precipice, I began to climb.

The precipice was high above, and I grasped the rocks for dear life, my knuckles turning white.

One step at a time.

These words returned to me, the ones following my first steps from the southern terminus of the trail way back in the desert. It was those thoughts that brought my fingers over the final ledge.

I pulled myself up and stood to look around.

This was the peak. Bradley, Mac, and Toast were staring at me from the other end of the summit, their mouths hanging loosely from their jaws.

Everyone began laughing hysterically.

"Stayin' Alive?!" Mac asked. "What the hell are you doing all the way over there?"

They ran over to me and slapped my back before peering down from where I had climbed up.

"No way," Toast said. "That's how you got up here?"

Mac shook his head. "Classic Stayin' Alive."

"Glad you're still alive, Stayin' Alive," Bradley said.

"Yeah."

I could barely speak. My heart was still racing, my mouth dry, and my forehead throbbing from the altitude. I found a spot to rest atop the peak, looking out into the sky, a thin ring of clouds circling the horizon. We sat high above the rest of the world, floating in a sea of blue. I was happy to be alive.

The infamous ascent.

There were others here, too, and we chatted together while enjoying the view and passing around a logbook to sign our names. We spent a long while on the peak recovering, but as the sun began its descent toward the horizon, we stood for the trek downward.

I turned to Bradley. "Hey, I still don't understand how you guys got up here—when I asked how to get to the peak, you said 'to the right', didn't you?"

Bradley laughed. "By 'right' we meant 'continue curling around the mountain spire', not 'climb straight up the cliff'."

"Ah," I said.

The others laughed.

This time, I followed the group down the proper way. It was laughably simple. The route must have been there all along, and I just hadn't seen it.

After departing from the highest spire, the rest was a fast descent. We sprinted down the scree, surfing the loosened rock, gravity pulling us downward as we found our way down to the dirt trail. Going down was a thousand times easier than going up.

Group summit picture, Shasta Crew.

While passing the grassy basins, it was glorious to drink water at the mossy spring. We filled up before walking the final miles of the path back to the trailhead.

What we saw was a beautiful sight. Kenzie, Sydney, and all our hiker friends were standing at the trailhead, smiling as we arrived. After relaying our experience to the group, we hopped in Kenzie's car and drove back to our seedy hotel room for one final night.

As I lay in bed, I felt my eyelids especially heavy after not much sleep and a long day, but I pressed them open for as long as I could possibly manage, knowing we'd return to the trail the next morning.

I couldn't stand the thought of leaving Shasta, of leaving Kenzie. It felt like I'd finally found someone to whom I could give my attention and love, someone to take away my loneliness. Her hair flowed like water through my fingers. One day I'd settle down, build a life, and raise a family. I wished for everything I knew I couldn't have in that moment. Slowly, the night washed over me, and I slept.

Halfway into the night, I felt her warmth leaving my side. "I'll be back when you wake up," she whispered.

"Promise?"

She leaned over and kissed, me and I drifted back to sleep as the door opened and shut.

The morning sunlight poured through the open door. Everyone was stirring, packed and ready to leave, and Bradley's figure stood in the doorway.

I turned. She wasn't there, so I rose to pack my things. When I was packing up, a cheek touched the side of mine. It was warm, and I turned, took her face in my hands, and kissed her.

"I have to go back to work," she said.

"Ah, yeah." I'd forgotten entirely that such a thing existed.

"Here, take this," she said as she grabbed my hand and slid a bracelet made of colorful orb-like stones around my wrist.

"This too," she said, handing me a slip of paper.

I nodded. "I'll write you."

With one last kiss, she departed through the doorway into the sunlight. A slow knowing settled into me. Our paths were separate.

But still, she was right. At the end of every road lay something special. Shasta was an experience I'd never forget, and I hoped I'd meet someone like her again in my lifetime.

Bradley, Mr. Walker, Toast, Mac, Cheese, and I found the path once more with heavy backpacks, but the most noticeable weight was the one settled against my left wrist, the stones glittering in the sunlight.

CHAPTER 28

August 24, 2015
Mile 1,699, California/Oregon border, nearing Highway 5
to Ashland (951 miles to go)

The day had finally arrived—Oregon! I'd expected myself to cry the day we passed into a new state, but sitting just in front of the border sign were the familiar faces of hiker friends. I couldn't muster up any tears in front of a crowd. They greeted us warmly, and I walked over to the sign and kissed it.

Far fewer hikers had signed this trail log compared to previous ones. Hikers were dropping like flies the closer we came to Canada, but the herd was still a great distance ahead of us.

Our group merged with the other one nearby, plopping down beside them right on the trail to enjoy the moment. Zwina ran circles around us all, greeting everyone before returning to Toast's side and nuzzling her nose between her paws.

One of the girls at the front of the trail leaned over and spoke. "Welcome to Oregon," Smokey said, addressing our group. She spoke confidently from atop her sit pad.

"Yeah," Queen B said. "Took you guys long enough!"

The new group of hikers laughed at the remarks.

The Wolfpack.

California/Oregon border.

Colliding with the Wolfpack.

We'd heard of these hikers from recent trail journals, four boys and three girls in total, each signing the trail journals under the name Wolfpack.

Smokey and Queen B seemed to be the leaders of the bunch as they were known for getting up much earlier than necessary, well before sunrise, hiking the day's necessary miles, and then setting up camp well before sunset.

"So," Smokey asked us, "are you guys doing the Oregon Challenge?"

Bradley rose to the occasion. "No question about it."

"What's the Oregon Challenge?" I asked, trying not to seem too embarrassed.

Queen B's eyes darted to meet mine. "It's hiking the entire state of Oregon in two weeks."

It was a challenge many hikers attempted yet few completed. I did the math. Thirty miles a day for two weeks. I'd heard those who completed the challenge did so at their own peril, some having to leave the trail due to injury.

The challenge seemed daunting. Until today, I had only walked one thirty-mile day and it was one of the most difficult days I'd spent on the trail.

And now we're supposed to string together that day for two weeks straight?

But with time running thin, completing the Oregon Challenge would practically guarantee us reaching Canada before the snowfall. Keeping in mind our peak physical shape and matured mental toughness, we accepted the challenge.

I glanced over at Mr. Walker; his eyes sunk to the ground. Meanwhile, Mac, Cheese, and Toast sat up lively, ready for the challenge.

"How about we make things interesting?" Queen B asked.

Bradley laughed. "What did you have in mind?"

"How about... last group to Washington owes the other a town dinner?"

Everyone nodded. We had no idea how this would be enforced, but suddenly, everyone knew the games had begun.

"Deal!" Bradley said, exchanging handshakes.

"It begins in Ashland," Smokey said. "We'll spend one or two zero-days in town before making the push."

Their group began packing and rose to their feet.

"See you there," they said. Their howls echoed through the forest as they headed up the trail. The call to war had been received.

Bradley turned to our group. "Everyone feel good about that?"

We nodded, but Mr. Walker's gaze remained distant. Bradley was right. I, too, felt like we might lose him soon, a thought I wasn't ready to dive into at the moment. Ashland —the first town in Oregon, a small city known for its wayfaring hippies and the nearly year-round Shakespeare Festival—was now within a day's walk. We were so close I could taste it.

I departed shortly after Bradley, who had set off to trail the Wolfpack, walking alone but sandwiched at a distance between our friends.

The miles passed as the track of the sun fell into the west through the forest canopy. I soon came to a junction where a small handwritten note lay in the middle of the trail before me. I picked it up:

"Go right at the road. Follow the clues for trail magic. -Shake"

Glancing to the eastern path, I saw a downtrodden trail leading into the woods. I was skeptical. The last spontaneous off-trail adventure was Garnett Peak, the desert mountain we hiked barefoot, which had nearly killed me. Wanting to avoid a similar catastrophe, I considered ignoring Bradley's note and setting my sights on Ashland alone with the intention of finding us a place to stay for the night. But reading the note again made me curious.

What trail magic had he discovered that was worthy of leaving a note and clues?

I sighed, glancing once more to the woods. I'd give him one more shot at redemption.

I descended the side trail, and after ten minutes of wandering through the trees, my patience ran thin. I'd not yet seen any clues, and without maps, I had no idea where I was heading.

Maybe I passed one of the clues altogether?

Just as I was considering turning around and heading back, there stood a water bottle upright in the distance, placed beside the trail. I recognized it immediately. It was Bradley's. A plastic blue flip-top Smartwater bottle with a colored string tied around the neck, what he called his "identifier", a method we had adopted for personalizing our water bottles so as not to get them mixed up. It was the sign I'd been waiting for.

I left the bottle behind me for the others and continued along the road. Before long, more items began popping up like breadcrumbs along the trail, leading me deeper into the forest. First was a hat he had been given but had rarely worn, then came sticks patterned on the trail in the shape of arrows, guiding me to take new directions. Intrigue flickered inside me with every step.

What is this leading me to?

Then the sound of a drumbeat reached my ears. Memories of Belden town flashed in my mind.

Is this another... rave?

It took some time for the sound to register, but it was different from the one I had heard in Northern California. Yes, soon it became clear this was no electronic drum, but a full drum kit with the crashing sounds of cymbals, high hats, and snares. I matched the beat with my strides, and the music drew closer and louder. Soon the pines gave way to a vast clearing in the forest valley.

Below, parked smack dab in the middle of the field, were ten to twenty people, including the Wolfpack, surrounding a long and colorfully painted school bus! The drum kit and couches sat on the roof of the bus, and everyone cheered when I emerged on the cliff above from the forest shadows.

I squinted to see Bradley sitting on a couch atop the school bus.

"'Hello," he shouted, smiling as I approached.

"What is this?" I asked, laughing from down below.

"Pretty cool, huh? Climb on up."

I nodded then climbed the ladder to join him on the couch.

"So, the note worked out?" he asked.

"Yep. Nice work."

We stared wide-eyed into the open field. I'd never seen anything like it. Carving through the grass was a winding trail with stops that led to a massive trampoline, a jungle gym, and an intricate domed structure.

One by one, our friends emerged from the woods on the distant cliff, and we cheered as they made their way to join us down beside the school bus.

Another movement caught my eye, this one much closer. A young man with red robes and a shaved head had climbed the ladder to the bus roof and extended his hands into the air.

"My new friends!" he said, announcing his presence with a bow. "Welcome to our paradise!"

He plopped down between Bradley and me as if he'd known us for miles and stared into the distant fields.

"Beautiful, isn't it? Name's Otto by the way."

"Shake."

"Stayin' Alive."

"I'm glad you guys discovered us. We weren't expecting visitors after the tea party."

"Tea party?" I asked.

His eyes grew big. "Oh yes!" he said, leaning in close. "It was only a day ago. Hundreds of people gathered around tables stretching far into the forest. It was beautiful! And when night came, we celebrated by playing music and dancing beneath a full moon. What you're seeing is only the aftermath, the post-party," he said, sinking back into the couch. "But it will have to do."

As he spoke, I couldn't help but distance myself. *What sort of person gathers in the middle of nowhere for tea parties and music?*

The first word that came to mind was hippies, a separate breed of human from us thru-hikers! We were the men and women of the mountain, the survivalists and minimalists who carried heavy loads, climbed peaks, and forded rivers. In our eyes, we were tough. We had a destination.

Hippies, on the other hand, well… hippies had tea parties. Yet here they were greeting us hikers and welcoming us into their space.

In a way, the people reminded me of the Shasta train hoppers, those who embodied new lifestyles because the old ones didn't suit their needs.

One woman, who I'd seen earlier hula hooping, sprang from the forest half-robed and readied herself behind a djembe at the foot of the bus. "Let's play, Otto," she pleaded, "Let's play!"

"C'mon, Otto," said another man, lifting a didgeridoo to his lips.

Otto smiled and turned to us. "Excuse me."

With that, he lifted himself from the couch and made his way over to the drum set. The snare rang loudly, and the others soon joined in with their own instruments. Music filled the forest.

Before long, Otto stopped playing. "Won't you join us?" he asked.

"Sure," I said.

I found myself pulled toward a djembe and joined in alongside our new friends, losing myself to the music.

After we were done playing, Otto led us along the trail into the field and showed us the trampoline where we had a few solid jumps, tumbles, rolls, and flips before making our way to the domed structure that we climbed and hung around like monkeys in a jungle gym.

All my preconceptions had evaporated. These were some of the funniest and kindest people I had ever met. As the afternoon slipped away, we sat together sharing food, music, and stories, ours of hiking across the country and theirs of creating an award-winning documentary. The forest had brought together two tribes, neither of whom would have met had we not stumbled off the beaten path.

With night nearing, it was time to get moving. The hikers rose and packed up, ready to head toward town.

"Thanks for having us, Otto," I said.

"Anytime, brother. Anytime."

"Jam Qwest" & the Bus.

Everyone hugged before departing, and we waved goodbye to the rest of our hippy friends, retracing our steps back into the woods. If we were quick about it, we'd reach Ashland the next morning shortly after the rising sun. But, as Bradley and I had discussed, I wasn't looking forward to losing another friend.

Ollie & some of the Jam Qwest crew.

CHAPTER 29

August 27, 2015
Mile 1,727, Ashland, Oregon (923 miles to go)

It was the early morning when we arrived in town, the city of Ashland still covered in darkness. A thicket of clouds had rolled in from the west, extending beyond the horizon, and sheets of rain pelted the streets.

We had been waiting beneath the awning of the local grocery store when Jim's slick rental car pulled into the parking lot. He parked and got out, and we exchanged hugs. It was good to see Jim, our old British friend from the Sierra, but his arrival signaled Mr. Walker's departure. The car was their ride north. The two reunited friends would take Interstate 5 heading toward Washington and continue the trek from there to the Canadian border. They'd fill in the gaps of the trail they'd miss at a later date. My heart sank when the car finally came to a halt.

"You ready, Richard?" Jim asked.

"Coming, mate," Mr. Walker said. "Give me one second?"

"Sure thing."

Mr. Walker had likely made his decision a hundred or more miles ago. My eyes watered slightly as I hugged him for the last time.

We'd walked over a thousand miles together, longer than Bradley and I had hiked with anyone else, and the three of us had become, in his words, "quite the troika." Gone was his experience and wisdom, not to mention the hotel rooms, town meals, and fancy on-trail dinners. Thinking he wasn't up for the Oregon Challenge, Mr. Walker had decided he and Jim would take a different path.

But the Oregon Challenge was something Bradley and I needed to attempt because winter was around the corner. Not making it to the end of the trail was becoming too real of a possibility.

To put things in perspective, it had taken us four months to pass through California's 1,300 miles. Now, we had two months remaining to complete the final two states and their respective 1,300 miles before snowfall shut down the trail. If we wanted to finish, we had to get moving, and fast.

Our friend's departure made me think about how little time we had left in this sojourn, how we had spent more than 120 days on the trail so far and that now we had less than sixty days remaining! Two-thirds of our time gone!

And what exactly have I figured out about what I'm supposed to do in this life? It was too scary to think about for the moment.

Mr. Walker turned to Bradley and me, his eyes glimmering in the streetlight. "I'll see you two idiots again soon?"

"I hope so," Bradley said, "We'll catch up to you two old balls in a couple weeks."

I nodded. "See you soon, Mr. Walker."

We squeezed each other one last time before he hopped into the car with Jim, and the two of them headed out of the parking lot.

Bradley sighed and nodded. "Well, at least we saw this coming."

"Yeah."

As the car disappeared into the rainfall, I had a feeling it was the last we'd see of him.

Later that afternoon, the rain stopped. The Oregon Challenge would begin the following day, so it was important we at least got back onto the trail. That way we could wake with the sunrise and get in a full day's hike.

Hitching out of Ashland with our friends Mac, Cheese, Toast, and Zwina, we made it back to the trail and fell into line. A noticeable presence was missing, but the skies were clearing up for the evening.

We'd made it no farther than a mile up-trail where we found a familiar group gathered beneath the trees, packing up and about to head northbound.

The Wolfpack!

They started howling at our arrival.

We rolled our eyes.

"Well, well, well…" Smokey finally said. "Look who we have here."

Everyone laughed.

"Y'all still game for the Challenge, right?" Mac asked.

"Yeah, don't tell us you've already given up," Cheese said.

Queen B scoffed. A grin spread across her face. "First to Washington wins. And we all know who that's gonna be."

And at that, it began. As darkness fell, we hiked alongside the Wolfpack, bickering and laughing before finding a campsite large enough for both groups. It would be a long day the next day, but we stayed up and chatted while cooking dinner.

That night, our dinner wasn't nearly as hearty or appetizing as it had been for the last thousand miles without Mr. Walker's gourmet backpacker meals. Still, it was delightful to watch our two groups bond through competition. Before long, we were learning everyone's names and sharing food between the two groups.

The Challenge began with the sunrise, our competitive nature rekindled. Three days passed and our groups kept a strong pace, covering nearly ninety miles. I couldn't believe what the body was capable of, but I knew it couldn't last. My legs began breaking down in ways I'd not experienced before. Each morning was filled with loud groaning and stretching. There was hardly time to take breaks, enjoy our meals, or even laugh. Our eyes were glued to the trail, and we walked from sunrise to sunset.

As the hours passed, I worried my ankles might snap at any moment. So much had changed since we'd begun the trail. What was once a journey of self-discovery and adventure had become a race to the finish, a physical and mental battle. If this was what the trail had become, I was ready for it to end.

By the fourth day, we'd lost the Wolfpack and come to the Fish Lake junction, a small stop deep in the basin next to a large lake. The sight was alluring. The town wasn't too far from the trail. There was no doubt there'd be food, drink, and trail magic, but I knew this place was a vortex. We didn't have time for any more inconveniences, and surely the Wolfpack had passed it up.

I turned away from the vista as Bradley came barreling in behind me. He looked down to the basin, thinking the same thoughts I'd just had.

"I say we continue on," I said.

"Agreed."

"Should we tell the others?"

"Yeah."

We plopped down beside the signpost and waited for our group. Shortly after, an exhausted Mac, Cheese, Toast, and Zwina arrived at the junction.

"We think we should keep moving," Bradley said.

The others peered down to the lake.

"We're heading into town," Toast said.

"It's really not that far!" Cheese said, pointing to the sign. "We'll just grab a beer and head back out."

"Yeah," Mac said. "We'll make it quick."

Bradley and I shrugged. Their minds had been made up, and there was nothing we could do.

"Alright," Bradley said. "Meet us at the next water source. We'll wait for you guys there."

"Sounds good," they said. And at that, they traveled down into the basin.

Bradley and I continued the few miles to reach a small pond. The midday sun hung high against the sky as we fell back onto our sit pads. We'd only walked fifteen out of our necessary thirty miles, but I was already bone tired.

"It'll be hours before they're back," Bradley said.

"Yeah." My spine was settling nicely against my sit pad.

"How about this: we'll take a short lunch break, but if they're not back soon, we should continue."

"Sounds good."

After eating an oat bar, a thick fog passed through my mind. My limbs fell heavy.

Looking to the sky, I said, "How about a twenty minute nap? Then we'll get right back to it."

Bradley was already lying down.

"Yeah," he said. "A short nap."

My eyes closed, and the world became black.

I woke to a start, sitting up, shaking my head and rubbing the sleep from my eyes. Bradley groaned and sat up as they approached. Turning back to the trail, Mac, Cheese, and Toast were just arriving, and the sun was dropping into the mountains.

"Sorry we took so long," Mac said.

"What time is it?" I asked.

"Well, it's been six hours since we last split," Cheese said. "The town took longer than we expected…"

Six hours? I turned to Bradley. It was practically a full night's sleep. Daylight would soon end, and there was no way we'd hit thirty miles today.

"We're feeling pretty worn out, guys," Toast said.

We nodded.

"I think our bodies are trying to tell us something," Bradley said.

"What about the Oregon Challenge?" Mac asked.

"It doesn't look like it's going to happen," Bradley said, "but we won't even come close to finishing the trail if we're running ourselves to fatigue like this."

"So, we move at a more sustainable pace and hope for the best?" Mac asked.

Stayin' Alive & Shake beside an Oregon lake.

We looked around at each other, shrugging and nodding.

I fell against my sleeping mat. We'd failed. I imagined the Wolfpack roaring up the trail on their way to Washington. It would be a humiliating defeat, but nothing compared to knowing that finishing the trail was no longer guaranteed. It was humbling and frightening to be thrown into failure even after four months of hiking. We had no choice but to slow down, let go of expectation and plans, and surrender our notions of complete control.

We set up camp beside the lake, deciding to aim for a pace of twenty miles the next day. The rest would be left to the trail, Mother Nature, and Father Time to allow us passage.

As I fell asleep that night, I missed my friends and family, comfy beds, immaculate showers, and warm, delicious foods more than anything. I wanted the trail to be over and done.

CHAPTER 30

September 10, 2015
Mile 1,981, Bend, Oregon (669 miles to go)

With a steady pace, we reached highway 242 where we hitched a ride into Bend, Oregon, a small city on the Deschutes River.

The trip into town was Toast's idea, and I was thankful we went. Toast had spent the previous year living in Bend. His old landlord had graciously sheltered our crew for two nights at her rural home, even driving us to a shopping market in the city for a fresh resupply.

It was the largest shopping mart I'd seen since the days of Walmart or Costco back home. The building seemed the size of a wide meadow, the ceilings as tall as alpines, and the aisles—packed with every kind of packaged food imaginable! The prices were a bargain, too.

Seeing a two-for-one deal for those fitness protein shaker bottles, Bradley and I decided we'd try a stove-less food strategy for the rest of Oregon. Since we were still trying to make significant progress and cooking food took so much time, the plan was to buy only snacks and dinners that could soak during the day and be eaten by night. Leaving the mart, our shopping bags were filled with packets of dried stuffing, ramen noodles, and other dull foods. None of it excited us, but sacrifices would have to be made.

It was late that afternoon that Mac and Cheese rekindled an idea they had been considering for the last two thousand miles—trail tattoos.

I sat on the back deck of the house with the others looking out as the evening sunlight drenched the pastureland, casting a glow against the faraway mountain ranges. Cheese had already begun spreading out the supplies for our "stick-and-poke" tattoos on the porch including a sharpie, safety pins, and a bottle of super cheap black India ink.

Bradley turned to me. "What are you getting?"

We'd had the discussion before and thoughts about getting a trail tattoo had lingered for miles, but I had yet to think up anything specific. My skin was a clean slate and the thought of desecrating my body was a bit intimidating.

"Not sure yet."

He laughed. "Well, think up. I'm going after Mac."

I turned to the rest of the group. "What are y'all getting?"

"The trail provides," Mac said.

Mac formed a teepee with his thumbs and forefingers and held the sign to his thigh. It was a sign started by a few hiker friends of ours. We'd seen the triangle along the trail for the last few hundred miles here and there, carved into the dirt or laid out beside the path with sticks.

As Mac and Cheese traded pokes, each stood up proud and smiling. The teepee had been engrained on their thighs.

Next was Bradley. He shuffled to the edge of the porch deck, hiked up his shorts and carefully brought the sharpie to his thigh, drawing what his fingers had originally outlined. He was slow and methodical, making adjustments with a wet washcloth. After some time, he nodded.

"You're doing mine, right, Stayin' Alive?" Bradley asked.

I laughed. "Alright."

I grabbed the safety pin and bent the needle straight. The sharp point glistened in the sun.

"Do your worst," he said with a grin.

Knowing that a tattoo was for life, I had focused on the process and learned from Cheese's skills. I ran a lighter flame across the needlepoint, wiped it with an antiseptic cloth, and dipped it into the black ink. With one hand, I spread the skin of Bradley's thigh taut and began pushing the pin deep into his thigh, tracing the outline of the sharpie with precise pokes. With each stabbing, I felt a pop as the needle penetrated his skin. He closed his eyes in concentration, breathing deeply but remaining still.

"Does it hurt?"

For a while he said nothing. "Not too bad."

I wiped the blood with a cloth and continued poking along the black lines. Eventually, it was done. Bradley rubbed a wet cloth hard against his leg to reveal only the permanent black dots. We did one more pass through.

"What do you think?" I asked.

He smiled. "Nice work, brother."

Even I was surprised at how professional it looked.

"Did you decide on yours, Stayin' Alive?" Mac asked.

I nodded, picked up the sharpie and began to draw against my thigh. Having hiked almost 2,000 miles, there was no question in our minds that the tattoos needed to be on our legs. The felt tip was gentle and soft against my skin, leaving behind thin black lines. What came out of the process was a footprint—why a footprint, I'm still not exactly sure. The image seemed to flow from me in the moment.

"Ready."

Bradley picked up a safety pin and dipped it in the ink. "Let's begin."

The pokes sent shock waves through my thigh, and it was much more painful than Bradley had made it seem.

When the tattoo was halfway done, a thought came to me. "Wait!" I said, waving him off, "That's a different needle, right?"

Mac & his "Trail Provides" tattoo.

Bradley nodded, too concentrated to bother with the question. "Yeah, you're good."

Shake & I displaying our stick-and-pokes alongside Toast, Mac, Cheese, & our trail angel, Annalise.

I nodded before settling back into the shock waves. It was only much later that Bradley would admit he'd forgotten to change needles.

When he was done, I wiped away the sharpie and only the ink remained. The black dots had already seeped into my skin. At first glance, I loved it. It was comforting to know that long after the trail ended, a piece of it would always be with me, living in my soul and against my skin.

CHAPTER 31

September 14, 2015
Mile 2,043, approaching Olallie Lake (607 miles to go)

Many moons passed as we traversed the Oregon forests at a reasonable pace. The air was thick and hot, and the days were filled with swarms of mosquitos. A thin net veiled my face while my limbs were covered in bites. I often resorted to wearing my rain layer for protection but they always found a way in. The itching persisted beneath my jacket sleeves, which stuck against the sweat of my skin.

Much of Oregon was like walking through a green tunnel of trees as tall as giants. Thick, bright green lichen moss covered the rocks surrounding the path, crawling up trees and dangling from the high limbs, swaying like long, wispy tendrils of drool in the wind. The trees parted every so often to reveal ponds or small lakes covered with idle lily pads, the reflection of the forest painted atop the water.

The trail underfoot was soft and earthen, and it would be this way until the forest fell away and the trail morphed into miles of black lava rock, the aftereffects of exploding volcanoes years ago, the rocks crunching beneath our steps. Then came the burn areas, thousands of blackened trees fanning the hills. Trudging through these lifeless stretches of nature was a sight to behold and reminded me that everything had its end.

One night, the moon was but a sliver, its waning light hardly penetrating beyond the treetops. The lights of our headlamps guided the way and illuminated our cloudy breath.

Bradley and I had somehow become separated from Toast, Zwina, Mac, and Cheese days ago, but we were hoping to see them at Olallie Lake, a small lakeside resort village no more than a few miles ahead. In anticipation of our reunion, we'd walked high mileage days from early morning to late night in order to catch them. Our legs were dead tired, and it didn't help that the temperature at night was always cold, causing us to resent our cook-less food strategy. A warm meal at the end of a long day was something to look forward to, and it was evident that our mushy packaged stuffing didn't provide us with nearly the same satisfaction. Separated from warm meals, the fantasy for bodily warmth was becoming more and more prominent.

"You know what I've been thinking about, Shake?" I asked, turning back to Bradley who was walking close behind me.

We didn't speak much these days. Firstly, the trail had been tough going as it seemed all we did was walk. Secondly, I found after spending so much time with Bradley, all that needed to be said already had, as if we had exhausted every last story, memory, and thought worthy of mention. While tension between us came and went, being around another person in silence was enjoyable.

Bradley looked up. "What?"

"Saunas."

"Oh, man," Bradley said, his eyes rolling back into his head. "Don't tease me, bro. I'd do anything for a sauna right now."

Before long, the trees parted, and our lights shone onto a side path with a signpost pointing us away from the trail.

It was the trail to Olallie Lake!

We followed the path a short distance before coming to an empty boat tied to the bank of the lake. Who knew how large the lake was as it extended far beyond what we could make out in the night, the vast empty space swallowing the light of my headlamp. Turning to our left, our headlamp lights fell upon a small log cabin. It looked to be the general store, but sadly no light came from the windows.

"Is it closed?" I asked.

"Looks like it."

We walked the steps to the front porch and twisted the doorknob. It was locked.

Bradley cleared his throat and knocked against the wood in a pattern. They were the kind of knockings only Bradley's confidence could conjure up.

"Worth a shot," he said.

We waited in the cold, and I prayed we wouldn't have to sleep outside. At the very least, all we needed was to check the hiker log to see if our friends had passed by.

He tried a few more knocks, louder this time. A muffled voice came from inside the cabin, and we perked up.

The door creaked open to reveal the face of a middle-aged woman peering at us from the shadows.

"Hey guys," she said. The woman was remarkably kind and smiled brightly. "You two arrived just in time! I was about to head to bed after turning off the generator. You'll have to use your headlamps, but please, come in."

As she turned to usher us in from out of the cold, Bradley shot me a glance with a giddy grin. Step one complete.

Inside, the shop was lined with shelves of nonperishable goods and treats, but we already knew exactly what we were looking for. The trail log sat atop the front desk beside the register. We flipped to the most recent pages hoping to see the names of our buddies.

I pointed at one of the entries. "Mac and Cheese!"

He read the note then turned to me with wide eyes. "Cabin Six!" He grabbed my shoulders and shook me. It was good fortune once again. We'd be sleeping indoors tonight.

We turned to the woman, smiled, and asked her how we could find cabin six. After receiving the list of directions, we thanked her kindly before heading back out into the night to weave past log cabins, checking the numbers hanging over the doors on the front porches.

As if they'd known our presence was nearing, a cabin door flung open in the distance, and a faint light glowed behind Mac, Cheese, Toast, and Zwina's figures. Zwina darted toward us, her tongue lapping my legs, her fur as soft as could be.

The reunion inside was filled with squeezes and smiles. There were more familiar faces of hikers we'd met long ago but hadn't seen in miles. Joining us was St. Croix who we'd met at Deep Springs Hot Springs; Trapper, a hunter with an endearing southern drawl who we'd traveled with extensively in Northern California; Two-Patch, a tall, scrawny and soft-spoken thirty-year-old; and the playful and attractive Cookie Monster, who was forming a budding trailationship with Two-Patch.

As grateful as I was to see these additional familiar faces, with our added presence the cabin was packed. Our chances of sleeping indoors looked slim.

"You folks have room for us?" Bradley asked outright.

St. Croix smiled and looked around the room. "I think there's plenty of room, boys."

Everyone else nodded.

"Yeah, so long as you're okay with the floor!" Toast said with a smile

No one could deny their hiker family. We'd gotten to know each other too well over these last 2,000 miles.

When the door shut, a toasty warmth flowed over me.

"Wait… how is it so warm in here?" I asked, not at all displeased.

"It's a wood burning cabin!" said Mac. "We've been stoking it since we arrived. Do you guys mind if we keep it going all night long?"

We laughed.

Bradley shot me a smile. "I think we just found our sauna."

It was becoming laughable how things kept working out for us in this way. As I sat beside the cabin's crackling wood-burning stove, I couldn't help but recall the many other auspicious events in our experience thus far: Steve Climber's mentorship, Chef Paul's boiling water to soak our bare feet, Hannah Solo leading us through the San Jacinto mountain snowstorm with her maps, finding that unlikely cabin, our Mt. Whitney summit aligning with Father's Day, Mr. Walker's financial support and wilderness expertise, Elle's arrival when I was lonely, the many hitchhikes we'd gotten into town, Kenzie's presence and facilitating the Mt. Shasta climb… there were far too many to count.

I sensed my skepticism softening. It had gotten to the point where I was beginning to trust my experience and even expect such luck to manifest. More often than not, it seemed whatever we needed was provided.

It made me think more deeply. *Is this happening only because we are on the trail? What is it about the trail that allows for such events to continually find their way into our experience? Could these synchronicities also occur in one's everyday life?* They were questions I put aside for the moment, as the dynamic of freshly reunited friends was too exciting for too much rumination.

After claiming some floor space and spending some time catching up, Bradley turned his attention to the group. "It begins in the morning," he announced. "Everyone's ready for it, right?"

"What are you talking about?" Two-Patch asked.

"Wait," Trapper said, perking up. "Are you guys really going for it?"

Bradley turned to Trapper and placed his arm on his shoulder. "You bet we are, brother."

"Okay…" Cookie Monster said. "What are you guys talking about?"

St. Croix turned to face the couple. "They're talking about the fifty-three-mile day to Timberline Lodge."

Cookie and Two-Patch's mouths fell open.

"Fifty-three miles?" Cookie asked. She was in shock.

"That's crazy," Two-Patch said. "Why the heck would we do that?"

Bradley smiled. "Ah, because of what awaits us on the other side."

He swayed easily to the front of the group.

"Rumor has it that the most delicious breakfast buffet you can think of lies within the Timberline Lodge. I'm talkin' fluffy pancakes, waffles with pools of syrup and melted butter, fresh fruit smoothies, cold cereal, and thick, seasoned slices of ham and bacon—anything and everything you can think of at our fingertips!"

"That does sound good," Trapper said. A string of drool was beginning to fall from his lips.

"I don't know," Two-Patch said. "Fifty-three miles? I'm not sure about you all, but I haven't even hiked anything over thirty miles in a day."

Bradley smiled and rested his hand against Two-Patch's shoulder. "But it's not just any fifty-three miles, Two-Patch—it's the easiest fifty-three miles on the entire trail! There's hardly any incline and decline. So if we sleep now, we'll be well rested. We could even sleep in, let's say 10 a.m., and we'd arrive at 10 a.m. the next morning, just in time to catch the end of the buffet. Guys, this could very well be the most epic thing we do on the PCT."

Everyone looked around to see everyone else's reaction. I knew Bradley had wanted to attempt something like this, recollecting the time he'd wanted to hike for twenty-four hours straight, and finally his chance had come. Knowing we needed to move quickly, I was up for knocking out fifty-three miles in one day as long as we could convince everyone else to join in.

"Well, what do you think, Cookie?" Two-Patch asked.

Her eyes were beaming. "I'm in!" she said.

Two-Patch sighed. "Well, I might have to catch up with you guys afterward. I'm just not sure…"

Bradley placed his arm atop Two-Patch's shoulder. "Brother, tonight we'll sleep soundly, and before you know it, we'll be feasting on that buffet. But we can only do it if we're all in this together. There's strength in numbers."

Two-Patch sighed as everyone stared expectantly.

"Alright," he said. "I'm in."

Everyone cheered, Cookie hugged him, and excitement swirled about the cabin. We did our best to dampen the energy in favor of sleep. Before long, we were sleeping soundly in the cabin's warmth and resting for the big day ahead.

The morning came, and we packed up then circled ourselves outside the cabin. It was ten in the morning, just as we had planned. We first began jumping up and down to wake ourselves, then spent time visualizing the buffet and what it would be like to move up and down the line, filling our plates and devouring everything in sight. The vision was set like stone in our minds.

St. Croix huddled us in close. "Here's the plan. Let's divide the journey into five equal sections. Every ten miles we'll take a short break, then we'll keep walking until we reach our destination and the feast begins."

Shouts of approval filled the forest, and we set off northbound away from the sprawling lake.

The first ten miles flew by with high energy and soaring confidence. We marched up the trail, which was just as flat as we'd expected, in a single-file line with heads down, easily knocking out ten miles.

I remember claiming that the hike was a "piece of cake" after we'd just taken our first break for water and set off again within the hour.

The sun had fallen from its highest point as we'd completed the first ten miles in what seemed like no time at all. We established a more sustainable pace for the next ten, playing word games to pass the time. This kept the group involved and feeling like a single, cohesive unit. Time passed easily, and the trail was smooth sailing as we reached mile twenty in the late afternoon. Finishing what would normally be an entire day's worth of hiking before sunset was something we were not accustomed to, but we felt strong in our accomplishment.

During our brief respite at mile twenty, Cookie's ankle started to swell. It wasn't worth pushing forward and risking injury this far along the trail. We were all sad to lose Cookie's energy, and I could tell Two-Patch felt the worst about leaving her behind. But she urged us to continue forward, saying she would arrive at Timberline within the next couple days. Whether any of us would be there was still to be seen, but Two-Patch would undoubtedly wait. We said our momentary goodbyes and carried on, knowing she'd be okay.

It was after this that the effects of the challenge began to set in. Our word games lost their appeal. Thinking required too much effort. My body grew sore, and my mind fell toward sleep. We sat down at mile thirty by a campsite to cook dinner and recharge, passing around our various dishes in a potluck.

The sunlight was nearly at its end, and an entire night still lay ahead of us, the equivalent of which was another entire day's worth of hiking. It was an unfamiliar but strangely exciting feeling. Our eating lasted an hour, a much longer break than our previous two. Instead of sleeping like any other ordinary day, we rose to our feet to begin again, attempting to rile ourselves up to continue the mission. No matter how distant or ephemeral the goal, all I could think about was that luxurious buffet to drive me forward.

The night had fallen dark long ago, and as we climbed the ridge, sheets of rain began showering the forest. The heavy raindrops soaked the forest floor and dribbled endlessly from the hoods of our rain jackets. We had entered into hell! My vision was blurry, my eyelids heavy, and I felt like I was pressing them open with all my might in an effort to keep from nodding off mid-stride and falling down the side of the mountain ridge to my left. My perception became that of a tunnel, a mere spotlight cast from the light of my headlamp. I could only see about four feet in front of me, the distance between my feet and the next hiker.

It was in this space, staring at the ground and honing my gaze, that my mind began playing tricks on me. Hallucinations of wild colors and shadowy shapes crept in from the corners of my eyes. I would have thought it was a dream if the pain of walking wasn't so real. We marched closely in single file to ensure everyone's safety, our minds weary, shutting down, anticipating the next stop, and hoping for the rain to end.

St. Croix spoke without turning around. "Is Trapper back there?"

We'd all been awfully quiet, but it did seem like we hadn't heard anything from Trapper for quite some time.

"Nope," Two-Patch said.

The line stopped to take roll of the group. Trapper was nowhere to be seen.

"Maybe he's ahead of us?" Bradley suggested.

"Well, it's definitely unlike him to stay behind," I said.

"Did he stop to do his business?" Toast asked.

"In this rain?" Bradley questioned. "I doubt it."

"Well, I hope he's okay," St. Croix said.

We nodded, knowing we had to carry on because walking was the only thing that made the rain tolerable. It was difficult enough having stopped just for a moment as our momentum was lost. I could have keeled over and slept then and there if it weren't for the others around me, but we turned up the trail and bore on north.

Miles passed, and the trail seemed to have forgotten it was supposed to be flat, choosing instead to rise and fall with greater changes in elevation as we climbed higher into the mountains.

Hours came and went and finally we reached mile thirty-seven. The rainfall was now a misty shower, but the night was colder than ever. Group morale was diminishing, and we discussed calling it quits at the next stop. Maybe this wasn't worth pushing through just for a buffet of food...

It was then that we saw the flames of a campfire flickering in the distance and a shadowy figure sitting beside it. When we approached the light, the figure became recognizable.

"Trapper!" Bradley exclaimed.

"No way," St. Croix said.

"Dear God," Trapper sighed. "It's about time you all got here."

I laughed. "We thought you were behind us this whole time."

Trapper shook his head. "I've been here for at least an hour," he laughed. "You guys move so damn slow."

"Dude," Bradley said, finding a spot next to the fire and holding out his hands, "you have no idea how crucial this fire is."

He nodded knowingly and grinned. We immediately plopped down around the fire for a long while, relieved from the weight of our backpacks, waiting for the warmth to revive our spirits. Just then, Bradley started rifling through his pack and presented us with a gift he had kept hidden that he'd been given by some gentlemen in a town prior—coca leaves from the jungles of South America.

A ritual commenced. If this would help get us through the night, we'd do whatever it took. We boiled water in our group's largest pot, added in the coca leaves to stew, and passed around the tea, sipping carefully from the simmering brew. The hot tea slid down my throat and warmed my body to the core. Before long, the effects of the tea were kicking in, and we were ready to walk once again.

The energy and excitement lasted only about five miles more. The night was pitch black. Our minds and bodies were drained of energy as we crossed a highway and found a nice campsite to take our last break.

"How far out are we?" I asked.

"This is mile forty-five," St. Croix said. "So, we're eight miles away still…"

"Maybe we can rest for just a couple hours?" Two-Patch suggested.

"Yeah, just a couple," I said.

"I think that's a bad idea," said Trapper.

"How about we rest for two hours?" St. Croix said. "But no sleeping. Just to rest the eyes."

Trapper held his ground, but he was outnumbered. Lying down, we shoved our bodies into our sleeping bags—only to avoid the cold, we said. It wasn't long before my posture gradually relaxed more and more into the earth. My eyes shut easily.

"Get up! Get up!" Trapper shouted. "The sun is coming up!"

Groans rose from all around me, and my eyes squinted open in a daze to the eastern sunrise.

"Guys, it's been two hours," he said. "We should leave now, or we're not making it."

I tried moving but couldn't budge from the warmth of my sleeping bag. Everyone seemed to be in the same predicament. It wasn't until the faintest sunlight crept across our sleeping bags and onto our faces that we felt revived.

One by one, the healthy peer pressure of the group brought us all to our feet and once again up the trail.

The final climb was long and much more arduous than anything we'd faced so far. After another hour, the group stopped to take a final break, but I pushed onward alone, wanting to reach the breakfast buffet in time. Memories of climbing Mt. Whitney returned to me. I wasn't going to stop until I made it to the top. Climbing over the final steps of the ascent, I could see Mt. Hood, a snowy mountain peak. Rising in the near distance was the roof of a great building that crowned the top of the hill.

Timberline Lodge.

I approached the fortress through the parking lot, smiling at tourists as they climbed out of their luxury vehicles. I felt a strange satisfaction in their not knowing who I was or what I had done.

After walking up the entrance steps, I pushed open the wide double doors of the lodge. There stood a grandfather clock whose hands had not yet reached 10:30.

No more than five minutes later, the rest of the group entered through the doors. They were all exhausted, but I could see the same incredible feeling of accomplishment in their eyes.

We rushed through the main hallway toward the lobby in boundless anticipation of our reward. The room was large, round, and many stories tall, centered around a great stone fireplace stretching from floor to ceiling. It was filled with plush couches and chairs adorned with tasseled pillows. Although the feeling was warm, cozy, and inviting, our immediate attention was stolen by a familiar group of faces lounging on the couches.

The Wolfpack. We'd finally caught up to them.

"Well, well, well," Bradley said. "Look who we have here."

"You guys finally caught up," Smokey said. "Congrats. How'd you do that?"

"We just pulled off a fifty-three-mile day," Mac said.

"Wow," said Queen B, "Nice work you guys. But you're not here for the breakfast buffet, are you?"

"You bet we are," Cheese said.

"Ah," said Smokey. "Sorry to be the bearer of bad news, but you guys just missed it."

"No way," I said.

"Mmhm," nodded Queen B, "They just shut the doors. You can go see over there."

We ran across the room to the two massive, ominous wooden doors. Hanging beside them was a small golden plaque in which the words DINING HALL were inscribed.

Our eyes widened while we read the smaller plaque listing the dining hall hours. The buffet had indeed closed at ten-thirty. Our timing was off, and lunch wouldn't start for another hour.

I nearly collapsed. The news was a knife shoved into our empty stomachs. With the long-desired food slipping from our fingertips, we desperately scrambled to the front desk to question the nice clerks, but they only confirmed our fears.

Exhausted, we returned to the lobby and scattered ourselves about the hall with the Wolfpack, laying claim to the remaining couches. If food weren't an option, sleep would have to do, and we were in desperate need of it.

I plopped onto a long green couch at the far end of the room and stuffed a nice pillow behind my head. Crowds of tourists with cameras strapped around their necks walked slowly on by, observing the grand lodge and staring at us hikers as if we were animals in a zoo. We'd missed the buffet, but our group had successfully made it all the way to

Timberline in one day's work. And we'd caught up to the Wolfpack. These wins were enough to justify the effort.

I noticed the group of tourists had turned toward us and were snapping pictures of us. It was the last thing I saw before my eyes shut and my mind went blank.

CHAPTER 32

September 16, 2015
Mile 2,094, Timberline Lodge (556 miles to go)

I awoke as hungry as I'd ever been, my stomach begging for food with deep growls. I knew we had missed lunch during the hours of sleep gone by, but dinner would be starting soon. I forced down a measly cliff bar in the meantime.

Trotting over once again to the infamous double doors, I peered through the crack that was just wide enough for me to catch a glimpse of the preparations being made for the upcoming dinner feast. The sweet aroma of sizzling meat crept through the slit and invaded my nostrils.

"Excuse me, Sir," said a voice.

I turned. An usher stood guard next to a podium by the doors.

"Please have patience and respect the procedure," he said. "The doors won't be opened for another few hours. It's only four. Dinner begins promptly at six. And don't forget, it's reservations only."

Reservations only?! It was more bad news. I managed to thank the well-dressed man before hauling myself back into a slumping heap over the couch. The possibilities of eating here were growing thin, and the result was dampening my mood. Bradley was awake now, too, and together we decided if we couldn't eat, we should explore the lodge in search of… who knows what. Adventure awaited.

The halls themselves were lined with hundreds of doors and various wooden staircases that spiraled into new, elegantly decorated spaces all worthy of exploration, but the first room that caught my attention was a game room with rows of chairs lining a large projection screen for playing movies. A small chess table sat in the corner between two plush chairs, and in the middle was a ping-pong table with the soft popping of a ball launching back and forth between two smiling little girls. I smiled at the scene and continued down the hallway. We'd be back here.

The corridor led me to a final frostbitten glass door, and I pushed it open to the outside world. The chill of winter ran through my hair as snow drifted gently down onto a covered pool. To my right was the adventure we had been seeking—a steaming hot tub! Just then, the door behind me squeaked open and out walked Bradley wearing hiking shorts and nothing else. At once he scurried from the cold and leapt into the tub.

"How'd you know?" I asked.

A long smile rose into his cheeks. "How'd you not?"

Already wearing my only pair of shorts, I shed the rest of my clothes and hopped in, first dipping my feet into the cauldron before sinking my body into the hot liquid. I lay back as snow landed softly onto my eyelashes. Word of the tub quickly spread. We were soon stewing with a few more friends of ours. We laughed, said nothing, and held breath-holding contests before jumping back and forth between the cold and hot pools, bringing back memories of our time at Deep Creek Hot Springs thousands of miles ago.

After drying off, we headed inside and found a shower in one of the lower levels. Showering being the usual religious experience, my limbs and muscles felt rejuvenated. The only thing that bothered me was my stomach still hadn't forgotten about dinner.

When we returned to the main hall, we decided to sit patiently next to the wooden double doors of the dining hall, hoping magic might come our way. We didn't have to wait long.

Sitting across the room was an old woman with her husband diligently watching the servers set the final dishes and silver trays onto the tables for the evening dinner course.

Bradley turned to me briefly before smiling and standing to approach the couple. Before long, they'd struck up a conversation, and I made my way over to join them.

"Will you two join us for dinner?" she finally asked.

Our dreams had been answered. We happily agreed with not a second to waste, and when the dining hall doors swung open to the public, we followed behind the elderly couple with bright eyes. The servers greeted us warmly, and the woman made it explicit we should order anything and everything our hearts and stomachs desired. Dinner began and large plates full of food came to our table and quickly left empty. We laughed when we looked around as, one by one, hikers had found their way into the dining hall by means of befriending various patrons inspired to hear their stories in exchange for dinner. It seemed everyone would feast that night.

After four delicious courses, each more extravagant than the last, our bellies were satiated and the old man footed the bill. Just as we were thanking them, the woman reached into her purse and handed us two hundred-dollar bills.

"Here," she said. "I want you to take this."

We were stunned. It was enough money to ease our financial worries and resupply us for at least another couple hundred miles!

I felt my heart warming. "Is there anything we can do for you?" I asked.

Her eyes looked deeply into ours. "Your presence was plenty enough," she said. "Plus, you two remind me of my boys. That's all the payment I need."

I don't exactly recall the reason why her sons were absent from their lives, whether it was distant living or having passed, but I could tell they were pleased to be around us. We felt the same way.

The old man, who had said very little up to this point, leaned in with a soft smile on his face. "Sometimes, one doesn't need a reason to give, and today, you don't need a reason to receive."

His statement threw me into a spin. They were nearly the same words spoken by trail angel Bob at the southern border! Thankfully, the dinner was so large that we were sent back to the lobby with boxes filled with hot meats and greens for the hikers who hadn't found trail magic that night.

As excited as we were for everything the night had brought us, the light was fading from the great windows of the lobby room. We'd have to find a place to sleep outside in the cold, as lodging here was far too expensive for us to stay. We were used to it, but having to leave the warmth of the lodge was heartbreaking.

Just then, Smokey approached us. We were expecting some sort of rival challenge, but she informed us that all hikers at the lodge would be sleeping inside tonight, that a kind gentleman and ex-hiker named Snowman had reserved a room for everyone.

Bradley and I glanced at each other and laughed. I could hardly believe the amount of generosity bestowed on us that night.

We thanked Smokey then ran to spread the word to the rest of our hiker friends. Knowing we'd secured a place to catch some sleep, we gathered in the movie room to watch *The Shining*... and it just so happened that the movie was set in Timberline Lodge! I'd never understood the sensational-ism of scary movies as they had seeded more than enough nightmares in my youth (*The Ring, for example*), but I felt braver among the crew and enjoyed the movie.

When it ended, we found our room, claimed our bunk beds, and tucked ourselves into our sleeping bags. Hikers packed the room like sardines. That night, we joked and laughed alongside the Wolfpack, and it was nice getting to know them better. To an outsider, the sleeping situation might have seemed like poor conditions, but for us hikers, it was magical. We shut our eyes and dreamt of the day we'd enter Washington.

CHAPTER 33

September 21, 2015
Mile 2,144, Cascade Locks (506 miles to go)

A couple days later, the Day Hikers—our group now consisting of myself, Bradley, Toast, Zwina, Trapper, Mac, and Cheese—entered into a small town called Cascade Locks before crossing over the Columbia River via a steel truss cantilever bridge known as the Bridge of the Gods. The timing was auspicious as we entered Washington on the day of the Equinox.

Crossing into Washington.

297

A cool, fall breeze tossed our hair as we strolled down the highway in awe of how far we'd come with our band of hopefuls. It had been a four-week passage through Oregon, much longer than our aspired two-week timeframe, and we estimated we had another four weeks before the winter's snowfall shut down the trail, a narrow window considering Washington's terrain was said to be much more challenging than Oregon's and reminiscent of the dramatic elevation changes of California's High Sierra. We couldn't afford any setbacks, and the thought of not finishing occupied most of my thoughts.

We crossed the bridge, but our feelings of accomplishment were remarkably fleeting. With only one state standing between us and the U.S./Canada border, there was still much work to be done.

Red, orange, and yellow leaves fell from the trees and crunched underfoot on the hike out of Cascade Locks. The riverside valley was steep and upward climbing along the mountainside. We hiked ten miles of switchbacks before rising above the tree line and beginning a downhill trod through open fields, past lakes, and across wooden footbridges.

Water was everywhere. We didn't have to carry it or worry about thirst, which was a nice change of pace. Streams and creeks flowed cool and crisp, water dripping from the cracks in the mountainside. I rarely carried any more than half a liter of water, keeping the bottle in my hand to keep the weight off my back. It was faster moving this way.

Despite not leaving town until 11 a.m., we had hiked twenty miles by nightfall. Time was short and high mileage would become the norm. We vowed not to take any zero-days in Washington to increase our chances of finishing the trail. Our priority was walking, and it consumed the majority of our journey. What was once an adventure had now turned into work.

The vow lasted until the next town. Eighty miles later, when we reached the forest road to Trout Lake (mile 2,226), rainfall drizzled from the clouds. Using the gloomy weather as an excuse to rest, we caught a short hitchhike off-trail into town, the rain splattering our faces as we rode in the back of a pickup truck.

There was much more in the cramped general store's hiker boxes than we expected.

The herd must have passed by a few days ago.

We scavenged a reasonable amount and left the rest for those hiking behind us. As far behind as we were, there were still others even farther behind. The least we could do was leave them a few goodies.

A few hikers were lounged outside the store in chairs beneath an awning. The scene was a far cry from our times in the desert and the Sierra where downtime was spent wandering town, throwing Frisbees, or playing hacky sack. Now, all we wanted was rest.

Bucky & that handsome face of his.

It was there we met up again with Bucky, an old friend from the desert. Bucky had grown tan and strong since we'd last seen him, but he was still a good ol' boy from Wisconsin, a dairy farmer about our age who carried a bright smile and a laissez-faire attitude on life. He was optimistic about his chances of reaching the end, a welcomed sentiment to keep close by this late in the season.

Bucky's favorite animals were the chattering chipmunks that threw cracked nuts onto hikers from the safety of treetop perches. I couldn't imagine why he enjoyed them so much, but it made me rethink my frustration with these animals. His second favorite animals were the forest slugs we'd seen in more recent miles. I tried to tell him slugs weren't animals, but he would have none of it.

What separated Bucky from most hikers I had met was that he had not missed a single step on the trail in an attempt to complete the entire trail from Mexico to Canada with continuous steps. This meant even on sections where we would get a hitch into town, Bucky would make sure to walk back across the highway to exactly where he was picked up and continue on from there. It was rare for someone to be so mindful, meticulous, and concerned with completing the trail in its entirety, especially since the feat was difficult enough with the numerous and inevitable trail closures hikers experienced along the way due to fires, endangered species, and invasive plants. But none of them stopped Bucky. He even crossed through sections of the trail that were officially off-limits. We liked Bucky's strategy, approach, and personality, and we quickly became good friends while chatting and waiting for the rain to pass.

The rain continued through the night and into the next morning, but we needed to get moving. A kind local agreed to transport our group of Day Hikers back to the trailhead in his truck bed. Soon, we were heading north, climbing into the Washington Cascades, preparing to walk for 150 miles straight toward the ski resort town of Snoqualmie.

The climb into Goat Rocks Wilderness was unforgiving but filled with beauty reminiscent of the High Sierras. The elevation brought us to high mountain plateaus covered with boulders and green grass as hordes of mountain goats stood proudly against ungodly mountainside inclines. Snow clung to the tops of distant mountain peaks, more so than we had seen before, another sign our time here was running out.

It was a treat to walk with Bucky as he reminded me of Mr. Walker. He served well as a voice of reason between Bradley and me, a role that was becoming increasingly necessary as tensions were once again rising.

Walking long days of many miles was painful, but it also soothed our concerns. So long as we were walking, we had a chance of finishing. There was nothing else we could ask of ourselves. But the trail was wearing on everyone, physically and mentally.

Tough times.

When I came upon them, Bradley and Toast were sitting beside the trail near a grassy basin.

"Are we stopping here?" I asked. It was a fine view, but it didn't make much sense considering we had just stopped a few miles back for lunch.

"Yeah," Toast said. "Spliff break."

I rolled my eyes and looked to Bradley who made no eye contact with me as he unpacked his bag for snacks.

I sighed and found a seat a good distance away from these two, taking out my food bag while Toast rolled up a joint.

I was no fan of these spliff breaks. They were a whole new ritual that had recently been created to support their smoking behavior. To me, it was an unnecessary chore that only slowed us down. I could choose to hike onward, but I wasn't going anywhere fast without Bradley, with whom I shared a cookpot and tarp. Plus, I didn't particularly wish to get too far ahead of the group anyway as this led to me waiting for long stretches of time wondering if and when they'd show up again.

I felt like an outsider looking in, disconnected from these two, left out of this frequent ritual.

I gazed with narrow eyes at Bradley as he smoked. It bothered me he still hadn't kicked his smoking habit. He knew how I felt about it, but the prospect of confronting him was too thick a wall to breach. It was his choice and although it nagged at me, it seemed much easier to let these points of contention slip between the cracks, telling myself I'd address them at more opportune moments.

Finally, Bucky, Mac, and Cheese arrived and joined us in the basin. It was nice to have them around, each of whom rarely, if ever, participated in smoking. It was unfortunate, but I felt a divide widening between Bradley and me, one we had worked so hard to narrow since our early struggles at the beginning of the trail. But now, as the Washington miles came and went, the smoking grew even more frequent, and my time spent with Bradley grew particularly tense.

One night, I went to the bank of a flowing river to fill my water bottles for dinner and when I returned, Bradley was scowling at me.

What now? I thought.

Shake feeding his vice.

"Hey, couldn't you have refilled my water bottles since I'm starting the fire?" Bradley asked.

"Oh... I didn't even think of it," I responded. The words felt uneasy leaving my lips. Reaching for words around him was like walking on eggshells. Any misstep and the problems escalated.

"Oh, that's strange," he said. "Maybe next time you will."

"Yeah..."

It was a genuine error, but even the smallest and most honest mistakes now seemed purposeful, selfish, and done with harmful intention. As if we wished to see the other struggle, each of us was waiting for the other to do something wrong, to react and point the finger.

There were so many shared responsibilities that conflict arose at every opportunity. *Who fills the water bottles? Who gathers the wood? Who starts the fire? Who cooks dinner? From whose pack should we draw from for each meal? And who is pitching the tarp?*

With tired bodies and minds, our communication continued to fail. For example, we placed blame on each other, mostly in absolutes: "you *never* do this, you *always* do that." Absolutes were a dangerous path to walk, but we hadn't made the proper time to address the situation.

The next day, a similar scenario repeated itself, as these things so often did. As I went to the stream, a wholesome thought rose in my mind to fill Bradley's water bottles, but I intentionally chose to ignore it, recalling how he had not helped me set up the tarp the night prior. Of course, I had forgotten he had made the fire and done the cooking. Needless to say, he wasn't happy when I returned and the evening turned sour.

I could tell our passive aggressive behavior was spreading into the group, making the long days hiking even more unpleasant for everyone around us. I sensed even Bucky was distancing himself from us, no longer wanting to get involved in the conflict. I was afraid we might soon lose him. If only Mr. Walker had stayed, he might have been able to mend the situation, but at this point, there was nothing anyone else could do to help us.

Resentment bred distrust. I began watching Bradley's every move like a hawk, attempting to find other circumstances for which he was culpable. And what I began to look for in him, I found. My observations confirmed to me a feeling I had had that there was something he was hiding from me.

One night, although I couldn't confirm it, I thought I heard him eating some food before bed. Thoughts rushed into my mind. *He must be keeping some chocolate treats from me! Or some of those sweet, chewy, and delicious coconut rolled dates...*

The thoughts only led me to hoard my own food, which didn't help bring us any closer.

At other times, I felt it was money he was hiding—
Maybe he really has more than he's admitting to!

Chapter 33

The idea didn't settle well with me since I'd been pay-
ing for much of our resupplies and town expenses ever since
Mr. Walker's departure. Maybe it wasn't that, but whatever
he was hiding, I no longer trusted him. And if he wasn't
going to share, then neither would I.

I began to keep count of all he owed me. *What has he done
for me recently?* I added up what I perceived to be his debts
and kept the counter running at every opportunity.

I stopped doing favors for him, which also meant I
stopped doing favors for either of us. This made him angry,
and although he didn't express it outright, we knew each
other so well by now that we could see into each other's
emotions as through open windows. I knew exactly how to
press his buttons. And just as I pushed his, he pushed mine.
It seemed the more I learned about myself and what hurt me,
the more I also knew what could hurt him.

Just as the two of us no longer spoke to each other during
breaks, we also hiked far apart to avoid the other's presence.
All the while, my mind was reeling as I walked. Deep down,
all I wanted was to get along and finish the trail. I loved him
like a brother, wanted the best for him, and hoped things
would clear up soon.

One morning as I walked through the forest, I could hear
Bradley coming up behind me. It had been a while since we
had spoken kindly to one another. He walked close behind
me for a long minute without saying a word, and I wondered
if he was going to say anything.

Finally, he cleared his throat and mustered up his voice.
"Do you mind moving?" he asked. The guttural words
slipped between his clenched teeth.

I stepped off the trail. He passed without a word, and I
spent the rest of the day trapped in my thoughts.

It was the next day that a similar event occurred, but this
time, I was the one who caught up to Bradley. Even though
I had reflected on how much our last encounter annoyed me,

I still decided to perform the exact same maneuver he had pulled the day before, letting loose the same words.

"Do you mind moving?"

As he stepped off the path, I continued onward. But now, more than ever, something didn't feel right inside of me! I felt anger coursing through my blood, a tight knot pressing against my forehead.

Why did I just do exactly what I resented him doing to me?

I was used to walking in silence, but now my mind was racing. Knowing we hadn't seen anyone for miles and that Bucky was well behind us, I realized this might be the only opportunity to address the problem.

Should I say something? What would I even say? The silence was deafening. I couldn't handle walking with the weight any longer, and something inside me burst. I stopped in the middle of the trail and turned around.

"I think we need to talk."

The world fell silent. He stopped and glared at me with wide eyes. "Mm," he said, nodding. "Let's talk."

We set down our backpacks and sat beside the trail, looking out onto a deep valley of trees. There I waited, hoping something would come from the silence. I still didn't know what I wanted to say.

"I just don't get it," I finally blurted out. "I came here to be happy... whatever that means. But if we can't be happy out here, in the middle of this," I motioned to the wilderness, "then how can we expect to be happy anywhere else?"

I was shocked by my own words. *Is that what I wanted? Happiness?*

Whatever it was, I had come here to find it, and I didn't understand why I was experiencing more suffering than ever. I thought I had left these feelings thousands of miles and months behind. I had thought my corporate life was crushing my soul, but now I began to wonder if it went much deeper than that.

Bradley listened to my every word attentively and with a deep breath, he turned to face me.

"Let's try something," he said, maneuvering into a cross-legged sit. "It's an exercise."

"Okay… what is it?"

"Well, we face each other and look directly into each other's eyes. It's good because we can't hide. Whatever needs to come up… will."

I hesitated. *Stare into his eyes? The eyes of another man? Why the heck would I do that?*

Amid my doubt, he seemed convinced, unflinching. Reluctantly, I sat up cross-legged and faced him with open eyes.

"Whatever comes up," he repeated. "Allow it. Don't hold back your emotions."

And so it began, staring into each other's eyes with serious expressions spread across our faces. It took time to focus as judgments and projections clouded my concentration. The mere sight of his face held a story that was difficult to shed. But the longer we stared, the more the world settled into stillness and silence.

I sensed he was doing the same.

A strange thing began to happen. Beyond his green eyes, the world around him was losing its familiar form, distorting, falling apart, twisting and turning onto itself.

Is my vision deceiving me? Is this experience normal?

My attention fell back onto Bradley's eyes. Things only became more bewildering. The face of my friend was becoming mysteriously and intensely unrecognizable. His face shifted, lost its shape, and what I saw next I would never forget.

Bradley's face stretched into something devilish, his eyes grew narrow, his face fell long and sharp, and his ears came to a point. It was a demonic, ghoulish face, filled with evil.

But I held focus, lost to the trance of this strange experience. In all these moments, time seemed as if it was standing still.

Then, without his face even reorganizing itself at all, I seemed to be staring into my own eyes, into my own face. *Does the image of the devil I saw in Bradley exist within him, or is the evil I saw in him a projection of my own judgments, something living inside myself?*

The dissociation grew even more perplexing, as if a veil of separateness had been lifted from my consciousness. It felt as if there was no difference between myself and the person sitting across from me. There was no more Bradley and no more David. No labels for any of it. In some strange way, the two felt one and the same, and it was like I was staring deeply into my own eyes as if a mirror had been placed between us.

What followed shook me. It was then I somehow knew that by looking directly into him, I was also looking directly into myself. Not only did some part of me exist in him, but the parts I most clearly saw in him were the parts most clearly present inside me. This person was my reflection. And I saw myself through his eyes.

Has life always been like this—a mirror with those closest to me serving as my most direct reflections?

Was everything outside of me just a tool, a test, and a reminder to look inward? And if this were the case—that the trail, the environment, and those around me were nothing but a reflection of what lived inside me—did that mean all of life's problems stemmed from within me?

All the shortcomings I had seen in Bradley—were they my own? Did all my judgments, blame, anger, and tension, which I projected onto him, actually exist inside me?

In those fleeting moments of oneness as I stared into his eyes, I realized how unhappiness was too painful a responsibility to bear alone, to keep to myself, and how it could spread unconsciously onto others, but that I must do my best to walk that path. I had not yet found my happiness and purpose. I had fallen far from it. But at least I now knew where to look.

These thoughts stayed a few timeless moments before I was thrown back into reality. Tears began streaming down my cheeks, and I noticed that Bradley's face was also smeared with tears.

As we wiped away our tears, we nodded. Everything we needed to express was said without words. I knew he had passed through the same experience. We embraced, calmed down, then looked out into the pine-filled valley below.

Finally, Bradley turned to me: "Hey, brother. Thanks for your patience. I'm aware of my choices, the decisions I've been making. It's just that, sometimes these things need to play out. Sometimes we're slaves to our habit patterns, and it takes time before we rid ourselves from them. I promise you, they won't last. All of this will change."

I nodded. "Thanks, man. I know you're right. It will. And it's not just you. We're both working on ourselves. Let's just keep going. We're so close."

Bucky approached us from behind. I'd never been so grateful to see him.

"Are you guys okay?" he asked.

We looked at him and smiled.

"Yeah," Bradley said.

I nodded. "Let's go."

I stood and continued down the mountain, buoyant and drifting toward the valley. My pack somehow felt tons lighter.

It would be another day before Bucky, Bradley, and I would continue onwards, leaving behind the rest of the Day Hikers, parting ways with them at an abandoned radio tower we'd sought shelter in during a heavy snowfall.

It was a difficult decision for everyone, Bradley breaking from the comforts of smoking and all of us leaving good friends and camaraderie, but we hoped walking with our new trio would provide its own benefits.

CHAPTER 34

October 2, 2015
Mile 2,396, Nearing Snoqualmie Pass, Washington (254 miles to go)

"Should we make the call?" Bucky asked.

"Bro, no question about it," Bradley said.

"This is an emergency, right?" I asked.

We all nodded and stared as I pulled the slip of paper from my pocket and handed it to Bradley.

'IN CASE OF EMERGENCY,' read the piece of paper, followed by a twelve-digit phone number.

"He said they live in Tacoma, right?"

"I think so," Bucky said.

"Then it's worth a shot."

Bucky took out his phone and handed it to Bradley, who dialed up the number.

"Hey, Guy. It's Shake, Stayin' Alive, and Bucky. We met in Chester, California and—"

"I figured you guys would call!" came the response with a laugh. "Where are you?"

Bradley was wide-eyed and smiling. "We're on our way to Snoqualmie Pass, about six miles out."

"Right. Let's make a deal, then. If you guys can make it to the pass in an hour-and-a-half, I'll pick you up at the Chevron, and you'll have a place to stay here in Tacoma for a few days."

"We'll be there in an hour!" Bradley said as the conversation came to a close. He turned to us and nodded. "Boys, it's time to book it. We're going to Tacoma!"

Chevron, Snoqualmie Pass.

Guy picked us up in a car filled with cookies, donuts, milk, fresh fruit, and cold water. It would set the tone for the next three beautiful days of rest, relaxation, movies, and home-cooked meals spent with Guy and Cindy in their lovely white-painted house in Tacoma. It was a much-needed break from the trail, and we blabbered endlessly about how difficult the trail had turned since entering Washington. Our hosts must have listened attentively to our concerns because just as we were departing, they offered us all trekking poles that had been lying around their garage. So long as we promised to return them, we could use them for the duration of the trail.

We stared at the sticks with jaws hung loose. Bradley and I had lost our trekking poles long ago, left and forgotten in

311

some desert town. Since that time, we had joked how using trekking poles was cheating as the arm strength provided a nice, noticeable lift for uphill hiking. It was an advantage we had dreamt of having ever since we entered Washington. Thus, we embraced the gift, believing it was meant to be. They were just the tools we needed to make our final push to the border.

Stayin' Alive, Cindy, Guy, Shake & Bucky.

Left at the trailhead, we waved goodbye and headed up the path. I had a feeling Guy and Cindy wished they could have left everything behind and hiked the trail with us.

I, too, was imagining and fantasizing. There was something I found valuable in settling down, in living a normal life in a small white house in the suburbs alongside a family. But they say the grass is always greener. Whatever life held for me after the trail, I was already looking forward to it.

That sentiment rang through my head for many miles to come, and as the days passed, I could feel the end of the trail drawing nearer, less than 300 miles remaining until we reached the northern terminus.

Like a ripened watermelon, my mind was split in two, one half filled with the excitement of finishing the trail and the other packed with the fear of the unknown.

The idea of finishing brought about a sense of accomplishment. It was an achievement I would have never thought myself capable of reaching, much less something I would even be interested in doing.

And yet, resting felt just as meaningful as any achievement. After consistent twenty-mile days, my mind and body were ravaged and my mind lived in places far away from the confines of the trail, brought back only by the beautiful vistas cropping up every few miles. All I wanted was to be somewhere else, to see my old friends, spend time with my family, and experience leisure from dusk to dawn. I had wished the work would come to an end for almost 1,000 miles. It was funny, as that was the same pattern that had occurred in my working life. I had always wished for things to come faster than they were meant to come.

The other half of my mind was packed with fear. I'd finally found some resemblance of purpose in this journey. I had learned to love the trail's beautiful scenery, people, and unmatched sense of adventure. The mere thought of its ending was what I imagined an old man reaching the final years of his precious life must feel like. Death awaited us, and we stepped closer toward it with every sunrise.

And what will happen to me after death?

CHAPTER 35

October 7, 2015
Mile 2,425, 51 miles out from Highway 2 (250 miles to go)

We were less than 200 miles from Canada when thick, dark clouds covered the morning sky, and sheets of rain spread across the mountains. Cold, wet, and miserable, Bucky, Bradley, and I marched uphill in our rain jackets and rain pants through ankle-high water. The freezing water flooded down the trail like a gutter, flowing over my feet and turning them to prickling blocks of ice. Without adequate tree cover, rest spots were few and far between, and we were forced to walk, exposed to the elements.

Each of us had donned two heavy-duty trash bags, one for pack coverage and one to wear as makeshift ponchos as our rain jackets hardly kept us from getting wet, serving more as a protective layer. Even though it was cold and the freezing water chilled my feet, everything from my ankles up heated quickly while walking. Sweat ran down my back beneath my soaked rain jacket.

The rain fell ceaselessly in this way for three days straight. We had not expected it, but should have seen it coming knowing Washington's reputation. We'd hardly dealt with any rain on the trail, and although other hikers had dealt with longer stretches of rain, it was a miserable and unexpected challenge for our troika.

Washington rainfall. Stayin' Alive.

A misty haze shrouded the trail, and the thickening clouds made sunlight an all but distant memory. Unable to sundry our soaked gear and clothes, the miles stretched long, cold, and miserable. I thought back on the desert with fond memories. I would have given anything to see the sun.

Finally fed up with the situation, I said: "This is insane!" to no one in particular.

Bradley stopped and turned to me with a mad look in his eyes and a wide toothy grin.

"Are you okay, Shake?" Bucky asked as he stopped behind us.

I glanced at Bradley. "Yeah. Was it something I said?" He seriously looked like he was going crazy.

Bradley cocked his head back and laughed maniacally. "That's the answer! You said it yourself. Only insane people would do this, right?"

And with that he leapt into a puddle, splashing and stomping, dancing in the rain.

"Shake?" I asked. "What are you doing?"

Bucky and I glanced at each other with eyebrows raised.

"Trust me!" he yelled. "Just try it!"

It took a moment for me while examining his strange behavior to understand what he was doing. He seemed lighter, free from the misery he was feeling moments ago. Was he actually onto something here?

Finally, it made sense. If only insane people would choose to walk such a path, we would have to adopt insanity to make it out.

The playful attitude was infectious. After initial hesitation, I jumped into a puddle, kicked the water and feigned laughter. While the cold itself hadn't dissipated, my relationship to the cold faded nearly instantly. The strategy was working. My eyes widened, and a huge grin spread across my face. This was the way out.

Shake going insane.

"Try it, Buck!" I yelled.

Before long, Bucky joined in, and we were splashing, kicking, and laughing up the trail. We'd gone insane, but madness lifted our spirits.

That night, we found the best camp we could: a sad, soggy, treeless bog where we had no choice but to sleep. We attempted to pitch the tarp using the trekking poles as support, but the poles wouldn't stick firmly into the ground. Pools of water flooded into the space. After many collapses and failed attempts, we finally found a spot devoid of pools and strong enough to stand the rain. Thankful to be out of the rain for the first time that day, we crowded inside and immediately shed our soaked clothes, peeling our clothing from our skin and setting them at the foot of our sleeping bags just out of the rain's reach beneath the tarp's overhang. We changed into our thermals. Slipping into our sleeping bags with dried clothes was like escaping into a whole new world; one I had craved the entire day.

I turned my head when Bradley cussed. His eyes had sunk, and he let loose a deep sigh, holding up his sleeping bag. It was soaked, a shriveled, dripping, lifeless blob.

I gritted my teeth as Bradley examined his bag for failures. Sleeping wet on a cold night sounded both miserable and a real danger at this point.

Bradley looked at us sidelong. "Looks like we're sleeping close tonight, boys."

We nodded. It was his only option for surviving the night. The cold temperature arrived with the darkness, and we huddled close to him as he slid inside his wet sleeping bag.

That night I could hear Bradley breathing loudly as if forcing his breath to warm his body. It wasn't a good sign considering how easily he usually fell asleep. Before long he was shivering furiously between Bucky and me, and we nudged a bit closer hoping he would make it through the night. Eventually his body settled. We hoped everything was all right.

We woke the next morning to the smattering sounds of raindrops against our tarp. A pool of water had gathered by my head, moistening the hood of my sleeping bag, and I scrunched up to avoid the nearing moat.

"You sleep okay last night, Shake?" I asked.

He didn't respond.

"Shake?" Bucky asked. "You okay?"

Bradley shook his head. "Not good," he said. "Thanks for your body heat, though. I'm not sure I would have survived otherwise."

We lay motionless beneath the tarp for a few long minutes hoping the rain would pass. The next town was still a day and a half away. The looming thought of another wet day was dreadful.

The limited food rations were our only motivating factor. We changed back into our wet clothes, slid our feet into cold, damp socks, then shoved those into our frozen shoes. After the tarp was packed away, it felt twice as heavy in my backpack with the extra water weight.

Immediately facing us was an uphill climb over the next ridge. That same gutter of cold, rushing water waited for us as we began to ascend. The energy to muster up our carefree insanity was gone. All that was left was dread, pain, and misery.

Suddenly, as we marched through the flooded trail, I felt a penetrating cold pierce the tips of my toes of my left foot.

Are they freezing?

The sensation crawled higher and turned to a hot burning flow. It was a shocking pain greater than any I'd felt before, far more painful than barefooting.

Stories rushed into my mind of snow-seasoned hikers who departed trails with missing fingers and toes.

Could that happen to me? The thought sent my heart spiraling into rapid beats and my breath turned irregular. The feeling crawled higher up my ankle.

I couldn't hike any longer. I leapt off the path and began to untie my shoe to see what damage had occurred. Just as I felt the pain was at its highest point, I felt a warm light touch the back of my neck. The rain stopped. We looked back into the sky as rays of sunlight fanned down into the basin. The clouds vanished, and warm sunlight filled the world. The pain had left me at the first sight of the sun.

Standing in disbelief, we rejoiced with hands to the sky, then immediately got to work. Not knowing how long the sun would stay, we rushed to unpack our belongings, spreading them atop bushes and shrubs to dry.

I smiled at Bradley as he threw his sleeping bag onto some bushes. He nodded. We soaked up as much sun as we could while the warmth briefly poked through the clouds. We really had embraced the insanity of this journey, but now it was almost over. As our gear began to dry, the sunlight brought us strength and the will to go on.

The sun stayed long enough for us to dry our belongings and not a moment longer. The clouds returned, and the rain fell once again. But it didn't matter. We'd been granted a reset, similar to the feeling after a restful zero-day in town. We were off once again to Canada, closer than we'd ever been before.

CHAPTER 36

October 10, 2015
Mile 2,451, Nearing Highway 2/Stevens Pass/Skykomish,
(199 miles to go)

"I think I'm setting up camp here," Bucky said as he stepped off the path.

Bradley and I stopped, exchanged glances, and turned our attention towards Buck.

"But the next road into town's only another ten miles ahead," Bradley said. "It'll be a late night, but we should aim for it. I have a feeling there's something special waiting for us at the other end."

"You want to reach the Dinsmore's by tonight?" Bucky scoffed, referring to a trail angel's house we had heard about that awaited us in the next town. "But we don't even know if they're open that late or open at all. Plus, you'll have to night-hike, find a hitchhike, and then somehow find out where they live! It just sounds… impossible."

"Impossible?" laughed Bradley. "We've heard that before haven't we, Stayin' Alive?"

I nodded and smiled.

"Okay, maybe not impossible, but unlikely," Bucky settled.

"We can do it," Bradley insisted.

"Go on without me. I told myself I wouldn't do any more night hiking than I absolutely had to. I'll catch up with you guys tomorrow."

"You better," Bradley said.

Bucky gave us a thumbs up as he unbuckled his pack, making his way toward the campsite. It was always difficult leaving others behind, risking never seeing them again. Too many times we had lost friends to the complexities of trail life, and we didn't want to lose Bucky for good.

As Bucky set up his tent, we headed out.

Misty morning mountains.

The night grew dark, and a soft mist fell around us. We hiked for hours through the mountain forests, following the tunnel of light shining from our headlamps. Finally, a loud humming echoed in the distance and bright lights shot through between the shadows of trees. It was highway traffic.

"Skykomish," Bradley said. "Get those thumbs ready!"

Wet and tired, we crossed the highway and stuck our thumbs to the sky. It seemed at first a decently well-trafficked highway as the headlights of cars and sixteen-wheelers flew by one after the next. But the next half-hour passed with the glimmering yellow lights coming out of view as quickly as they had come. Bradley turned to me. Droplets of rain hung in his long, black hair as he smiled.

"Hey, Stayin' Alive," he said, "Do you remember when you asked me how it went when I left the trail back in the desert, and I told you everything was beautiful? "

"Yeah?"

"Well, it wasn't all beautiful. Not everything."

I laughed, but my expression turned serious to match his. "What do you mean?"

"Journeying outside the trail was difficult. Especially at first. But just like the trail, so much of it was filled with anger, sadness, and challenging moments. I guess what I'm trying to say is that the outside world isn't as different as we'd like to believe. Even when we leave the trail, it stays inside of us. This path is so much more than anything physical—it's our inner voice, the one that leads us to our dreams. And that voice only knows the path that's best for us, not the path that's easiest."

I nodded. "Thanks, Shake."

I hoped I would remember his words when the trail was over, figuring they might serve me well, whether we finished or not.

Suddenly, a pair of headlights flickered through the mist. They grew bigger as we waved, but the bright beams flew right by us. We watched the figure continue off into the rain, and we dropped our heads, realizing we might be here all night and that we should have stayed with Bucky.

But then the figure slowed. We looked at each other and looked back up the highway. The car had pulled over onto the side of the road some fifty feet ahead and stopped with the emergency blinkers flashing. We sprang into action, snagging our bags and running as fast as we could with smiling faces to the stopped car. A young woman leaned out the window into the rain.

"Throw your packs in the back and hop in!" she said.

322

The trunk opened, and we leapt into the backseat, thanking them profusely and apologizing for our stench as we buckled up.

"It's really no problem at all," said the woman. "I'm Mary, by the way, and this is Sean. We know a good bit about the PCT. You guys are our heroes! We might even attempt to hike it next year," she said, gently nudging Sean with her elbow. "Plus, Sean doesn't smell too great either. He just got done with a one hundred mile marathon."

My mouth fell open. And we thought what we were doing was impressive! It was nice to have the ego be put in check every once in a while, yet keep distance from comparison. While our daily mileage couldn't compare, comparison itself was a trap. Each journey carried its own value unto itself.

"One hundred miles straight?" Bradley asked in shock.

Sean shrugged with a humble smile. "I had to die a few times along the way…"

We nodded. It was something we could understand.

"So what else do you guys do when you're not busy being superhumans?" Bradley asked.

Mary laughed. "Oh, my job's boring, but Sean's the CEO of a shoe company."

"No kidding?" Bradley asked with a grin.

Oh, no, I thought. I already knew what was coming…

"It's timely you mention that," Bradley continued. "In fact, I've created a proprietary shoe design that you just might be interested in."

I rolled my eyes. *The Jesus sandals.*

"That sounds great to me," Sean said, genuinely curious. "Here's my card. So, where are you guys trying to go tonight?"

"The Dinsmore's," I said. "But we're not exactly sure where they live."

"Oh, honey!" Mary said to Sean. "I know exactly where the Dinsmores live."

Bradley and I smiled as she proceeded to give Sean directions. We patted the middle seat in between us and shook our heads. We couldn't believe Bucky had missed this.

That night we took shelter at Hiker Haven, home of Jerry and Andrea Dinsmore, two wonderful trail angels who had built a hiker house complete with laundry, showers, comfy bunk beds, and the greatest luxury of all—a television with stacks of movies to choose from. We were too tired to enjoy the TV that night, choosing instead to sleep soundly beneath the bunkhouse roof as our clothes and Bradley's sleeping bag tossed circles in the dryer.

Shake, Bucky, and Stayin' Alive trying to hitchhike back on the trail in the Washington rain.

Bucky arrived the next afternoon, shocked by our story of how we had reached the Dinsmore's via some unlikely trail magic, but at the same time, he wasn't entirely surprised.

We elected to stay one more night at the Dinsmore's, enjoying a movie marathon and resting our legs as the rain continued to pour across the mountains. When we removed our clothes from the wash, it was remarkable how little the dirt had faded from our belongings. My yellow shirt was now permanently browned. I stared at it and smiled. It was stained and no washing could remove the trail from within it.

The end of our sojourn was approaching, and we hoped the greatest challenges were behind us.

CHAPTER 37

October 13, 2015
Mile 2,580, Highbridge and bus to Stehekin Café (70 miles to go)

After several more days of hiking, Bradley, Bucky, and I crossed a wooden bridge and caught one of the last shuttle rides of the season down to Stehekin, a sleepy, rustic, remote town on the lip of long Lake Chelan, only accessible by boat, plane, or foot. The shuttle bus, large enough to sit twenty hikers, was all but empty save the driver and us three. It rattled like an empty tin can as it carried us down the hill.

The driver, a friendly old retired man, informed us we'd caught one of the last rides of the season and that the town's bakery—a coveted trail stop for many hikers due to their extravagant pies and cookies—had just closed down the day before. The winter snowfall hadn't come yet, but the trail was slowly shutting down.

We walked the road beside the glassy lake and watched a plane takeoff, gliding across the water, soaring through the canyon window over the mountains, and disappearing into the sun. I imagined how I would soon be riding in a plane, heading home. Thousands of miles ago, a thought like that was the most fearful kind. But today it brought warmth to my heart. As the plane escaped into the sky, it reminded me of the first plane ride we'd taken to arrive at San Diego and how a single leap can change your life. The plane ticket alone could not have brought me this experience. But I sure was thankful for it.

It made me think back onto what trail angel Bob Reiss from day zero had first told us on our drive toward the southern terminus in the Californian desert, how the first step of a journey was always the hardest, and believe it or not, we had already taken that step just by boarding the plane to San Diego.

The idea that the first step was always the biggest and most difficult leap finally made sense to me as my time on the trail was coming to a close. Sure, once we were on the trail, we ran into challenges the likes of which I'd never faced. And it took many steps after the first to reach our destination, but that first step of leaving everything behind was all that was holding me back for the longest time. If I'd had known where it would take me, I might have leapt long ago.

Shake soaring at Stehekin.

At sunrise, we headed inside the Stehekin café for our final proper town meal before hiking out for the last time toward Canada, and we couldn't believe what we saw inside! In the middle of the cozy café, sitting at a long wooden table, were our good friends Walking Home, Nomad (from the Poodle Dog Boys, whose name was now changed to Happy Little Trees), and Mac and Cheese.

Everyone leapt to their feet and hugged. They'd made it on the second to last bus for the season and would be hiking out later that evening.

Knowing my finances had been stretched to last the length of the journey, I ordered pancakes for myself and an omelet for Bradley instead of asking for kitchen scraps. The hotcakes and syrup melted in my mouth as we shared some final giggles with our trail family.

Walking Home, Shake, Cheese, Staying Alive, Mac & Nomad at Stehekin Café.

Before heading out, I asked the waitress if she could take a picture of our group with my cell phone. She agreed and when we saw the result, Bradley and I started cracking up.

"Show us the picture!" Mac and Cheese said.

When we finally revealed the photo to the group, everyone had a friendly laugh at Nomad's expense. We called it the "caveman photo" because Nomad's eyes and mouth were wide open in shock as if he were a caveman who had only just seen a camera for the first time in his life.

After we paid the bill, Walking Home gasped. "Oh! Have you all seen the weather forecast yet?"

We shook our heads, leaning forward in our chairs, anxious to hear the result.

"Sunny for the next five days!" she said smilingly.

We couldn't believe it. Smiles beamed from our faces, and we laughed and hugged. It felt like an enormous weight had been lifted from our shoulders because no rain meant an enjoyable final stretch, and no snowfall meant we would make it safely to Canada.

Rising from the table with newfound confidence, Bradley, Bucky, and I said our goodbyes to Mac, Cheese, Nomad, and Walking Home before heading up the road. As with so many other wonderful friends, it would be the last time we'd see them.

CHAPTER 38

October 17, 2015
Mile 2,644, Hopkins Lake (6 miles to go)

We awoke that final day to find the basin steeped in the soft, golden rays of early sunlight, and the nearby lake shimmering beside us. Ready to hike the final six miles of the trail, I packed my bag but found myself pulled to the edge of the water.

"I think we should jump in," I said.

Bradley and Bucky joined me around the rim. We nodded, stripped, walked in a bit, counted to three, and plunged in. The water was frigid. The lake took away my breath, and I emerged gasping for air with my friends. As I stood, a feeling of nakedness crept across my left wrist. I clasped it with my right hand. The bracelet! It was gone. Kenzie's gift had fallen off into the lake.

My heart beat fast. It had been days or weeks since I had thought of the bracelet. Just like my backpack, it had molded to me and I had often forgotten its existence. And like all important things which remain unappreciated, it's only until after they leave us that we begin to appreciate what we once had. I felt like the bracelet had journeyed too far to be lost now. In a moment of panic, I dove beneath the surface, patting the rocky ground with my hands.

There was nothing but coarse rocks beneath my finger-tips. I tried again, feeling the rocky floor with my feet, but there was nothing. With one last breath and one last try, I dove under, this time feeling something smooth. I grabbed it and came up for air. It was the bracelet. I slid it back onto my wrist and breathed a sigh of relief.

"Everything okay?" Bucky asked.

I must have looked like a fool flailing around in the shallow water.

"Yeah."

I crawled onto the shore and lay against my sit pad to sundry. Some final moments of peace before heading toward the northern terminus.

Bucky & Stayin' Alive.

The three of us hiked out, feeling the end of the trail drawing closer with every step. A nervous excitement filled my body. I knew the others were feeling the same. We all wanted to speak, but there was nothing to say. I tried my best to remain present knowing this exact feeling may never come again.

It was strange to know this life would soon end. My being had grown accustomed to this routine, and despite the daily pain and suffering, I'd learned to love it. In a small way, I felt like I'd learned to love myself, to be okay with whatever pain came up, to go with the flow through all the ups and downs.

With every step, thoughts of what was next for me after the trail flooded my mind, but no single plan stood out. Sure, I recalled Bradley's words that the trail would stay with me, but I had not yet experienced it myself. The uncertainty of what lay on the other side weighed heavy on my mind, more than any backpack ever could.

The trail climbed higher against the side of the valley, and I caught an expected glimpse. A clear cut between the pines. I quickly looked down to my feet and kept walking. I couldn't stand to see it yet. I felt seeing the end too soon would ruin the surprise.

Against my every desire, I lifted my head and peeked again to the north some minutes later. Thankfully, the clear-cut was hidden this time. During my glance, I noticed Bucky was missing. It took me some steps to realize he had hung back to have a moment for himself. I understood completely.

The air was still and cold in the shadow of the valley. Time-less steps drew me nearer to the end. Every moment of the trail ran through my mind like a Rolodex spinning through memories of trail angels and barefooting, snow and sun, dumpsters and oats, hot springs and rivers, best friends and tribes, doubts and dreams, mountain peaks and valleys, music and silence, and pleasure and pain. All of it was nec-essary, every moment a piece of a much larger puzzle scattered about time and space that I may never come to fully comprehend.

Life is like that, I thought.

I wouldn't find all the pieces I needed in every moment. I had to take the time to collect them, and even then, by the time I could begin assembling it, the old pieces will have changed, the puzzle shifted, or the table flipped over. I felt like I was about to have mine flipped for good.

What was most strange was once we arrived, so long as we followed the trail, keeping our sights set on finishing the puzzle, it seemed as if the universe conspired in our favor. Whether by trail families, trail angels, or even strangers, support was there, and we had been carried from the beginning to the end. And the more I left behind me, the more connected to myself I felt.

Suddenly, the trees opened up to a clearing, and I stepped into the emptiness. We waded into the clear-cut that was drawn east to west through the valley. This was the end, the U.S./Canada border, and smack dab in the middle of nature's hallway stood a large wooden monument of posts much like the southern terminus.

Chills ran down my spine, and I began to cry. Bradley turned around and flung his arms around me. I hugged him tightly. After a long embrace, I walked over to the monument, fell to my hands and knees, pressed my forehead against the cold earth, and gently kissed the dirt beneath my face. I felt soaked in gratitude for everything I could think of: my own two legs, my friends, family, angels, and the trail. I stood once more and ran my fingers against the wooden grain of the monument. However dreamlike the moment seemed, it felt real and more beautiful than I had ever imagined.

I remembered my initial feelings of despair before hiking the trail, of wondering if something else was out there for me, wondering if life was scripted.

But hasn't that same script also brought me to this very moment?

Still too overcome to speak, I stood and looked around— a second metal monument stood next to the larger wooden one. I managed to lift the top to find a small booklet hidden inside. A trail log. As we reviewed the entries, Bucky emerged into the clearing. We smiled from a distance, allowing him space to soak in the official finish line before embracing him.

Stayin' Alive & Shake, PCT Northern Terminu.

The log's entries were filled with finishers, friends known and unknown alike. We celebrated the names we knew and wished well the names we expected but didn't see. Then we wrote our own entries. I went first.

10/17—U.S./Canada Border, Mile 2,650

Your experience has led you to a special place. This moment is yours, and no one can take that from you. Today we celebrate because we have achieved great things, and tomorrow we wake up to the next chapter of our lives. May this chapter turn into a novel, and may your novel turn into a saga, one with a clear mind and an open heart. Love it and love yourself. The answers will follow.

Love,

Stayin' Alive

I knew the advice was for myself. I smiled after finishing these words and then allowed Bradley time to write his.

Chapter 38

He finished and placed the book beside him. My curiosity was peaked. Right before we were about to head north toward the nearest Canadian village, I asked him if I could read his entry. I'm grateful he allowed me to do so.

I picked up the trail log, flipped through the pages, and came across Bradley's entry.

When I was finished reading, my jaw fell open. I can't remember what he had written, nor will I attempt to recreate his words, but I recall him mentioning that he couldn't have walked the trail without his rock and foundation, Stayin' Alive.

I sat back against the log wanting to cry again. After all we'd been through, it was one of the nicest things I could have possibly heard from him.

How had I forgotten to mention him in my final note? How had he so easily slipped my mind, while in his entry, I had taken center stage? After all this time, what have I learned? What kind of friend am I?

I thought back onto everything Bradley and I had been through, of all his decisions and my responses... thinking strangely of him for barefooting, my resistance to climbing Garnett peak, my avoidance of hiking twenty-four hours straight, and even my skepticism of coming to the trail in the first place.

Would I have done any of it if it weren't for him? While Bradley pushes the boundaries of what is possible, why do I remain so comfortable? If left to my own devices, am I complacent in my seeking? Is his propensity for risk actually the sort of behavior I need to adopt in my life to further my growth? I mean, maybe not barefooting for seventy-five miles, but surely there is something I'm still avoiding, something I need to confront...

The answer manifested itself just as quickly as I asked the question.

Everything that has been waiting for me since the day I left home.

335

I smiled.

Whether it was work, routine, pain, sacrifice, or imperfection, both the trail and Bradley had taught me that these sources of discomfort must necessarily live within me. Walking brought me no farther from them. Perhaps if I could continue to question what is possible, push beyond myself, confront what is uncomfortable, and look within for the answers, I would be ready for whatever path lie ahead, long after the end of this one.

I stood to hug my friend, companion, and guide, feeling an overwhelming sense of gratitude for the one who had brought me here, who had taught me so much on the trail. Among many other things to remember, I knew I had to hold on to the lesson that sometimes the greatest differences we make in life could be made by simply being ourselves, staying on the path, and offering our love and support to those who surround us.

As we set off to finish the final miles of the trail in Canadian territory, I was still hiking a path, but it was no longer the trail. It was merely a dirt road leading me away from the life I had known and toward a new path that awaited me.

As my final steps pressed against the earth, I thought about how I'd one day find a way to repay him and so many others who'd helped me along the way. I'd find a way to inspire, and remain a light in the darkness, shining brightly among a long and endless path that extended far beyond the dirt beneath my feet.

EPILOGUE

After finishing the trail and reaching Canada, our time spent in the new land lasted no more than a few hours. The same day we finished the trail, Bradley, Bucky, and I caught a hitchhike across the border back to Seattle with a French-Canadian freestyle rapper.

Bradley with our hitchhiking sign. It worked.

I ended up hiking 94% of the total trail from end to end, accepting hitchhikes to skip over small and large sections of California out of convenience. I also avoided burn areas, a couple road walks, and other random closures. Oregon and Washington were hiked in full. At first, the missing trail miles were unsettling, but I eventually came to terms that my self-worth wouldn't be measured in miles. When I looked inside myself, I had no interest in going back to hike the miles I had missed.

Upon returning to the states, we settled in a hotel room in downtown Seattle for a few days thanks to the kindness of Bradley's parents. In an attempt to adapt back into society, we spent far too much time at the local REI. It felt like a second home to us, a middle ground between the trail and the world of old.

To our great surprise, we ran into Steve Climber working at the REI, the wolverine that helped us shed weight from our backpacks at the PCT kickoff. We were overjoyed to see him, and he was amazed to hear we had finished the trail, though not surprised to hear we had given up barefooting. Steve and his girlfriend Amanda offered us a place to sleep for two nights, and we were grateful for their support.

When it was time to leave Seattle on a southbound train, I remembered that Guy, the gentleman whose house we stayed at in Washington, worked as a sergeant in the police force at the downtown municipal court. I decided to stop by to thank him and Cindy for keeping us in Tacoma and to return my trekking poles. As fate would have it, while I was waiting outside the courthouse, Elle, the woman I had met in the desert, happened to now be living in Seattle and walked right out the front doors of the courthouse after resolving a parking ticket. We were both shocked and happy to see each other, sharing a pleasant conversation about synchronicities and fate. I have not spoken to her since, but I wish her well.

Gandalf got back on the trail but did not finish his thru-hike because of his injury. He has continued traveling, seeing the country, and is planning on taking another swing at finishing the trail.

Oz chose not to return to the trail, instead pursuing his aspirations of living on the outskirts of Oregon. He continues to fulfill his mission of being a world traveler.

Stik and Trampon, two hikers from the cabin that snowy night in the woods, were married after the trail, a wedding I attended in October of 2017.

Nomad scattered his wife's ashes from the peak of Mt. Whitney and finished days after Bradley, Bucky, and me.

Bucky, the true hero of this story, completed a continuous thru-hike of the PCT without missing a single step. He continues to live a life of adventure, having spent seasons mushing snow dogs in Alaska, and more recently settling down to run a lettuce farm in Idaho.

Richard ended up completing the sections of Oregon he skipped and currently lives in Australia as the owner of a beachside coffee shop.

As for Kenzie, the woman I met in Mount Shasta, we exchange pleasantries every now and again, but we remain on separate paths. Kenzie, thanks for showing us such a great time in your wonderful hometown. They were days I'll never forget.

Now onto Bradley....

Two years passed after finishing the trail until I saw Bradley again in Jesup, Georgia, where he currently resides and manages a non-profit meditation center. Another great transformation had occurred! His head was shaved, and his grin was just as large as ever.

For ten days, we traded in our hiking shoes for bare feet, our walking for sitting, and sat together with a group of thirty others at a ten-day silent meditation retreat. It's through this inward path that I've found meaning and purpose in life even after losing the purpose of the trail.

The transition from *then* until *now* has been a journey of its own. For me, the trail felt like a dream mere moments after it ended. Like many thru-hikers, I suffered from post-trail depression shortly after arriving home. The trail is simply too different of an experience to easily re-assimilate back into an ordinary life. The body becomes adapted to the novelty of passing wildlife, exposure to the elements, hiking long distances, and the mental fortitude required on the trail —opportunities that are difficult to replicate in urban life. The world of old, upon returning, seemed greyer and drearier than how I had previously left it.

I am still connected with many trail friends via social media to this day. There are Facebook groups for our "class" of hikers, one of my favorites being "airlock" where hikers share their experiences adapting back into society, a difficult path of reintegration. This group has gone quiet the past year, and I hope this is because many of them have found their way. To those just finishing the trail, know that the trail lives inside us. I wish you all healing on your continued journey.

It wasn't long after finishing the trail that I set out to write this book. Reflecting on what made this sojourn special was a difficult and arduous task, one I might have refused knowing it would take three years to complete! It took endless hours to fully absorb what the trail meant to me. I felt like I had ventured through heaven and hell without having to leave earth, like the trail was an entire lifetime of its own. But to die yet still remain was a rare and fortunate experience, something previously unknown to me before hiking the PCT.

Maybe I will never fully understand the meaning behind the sojourn, but I do know this—that the true value of my experience, of any experience, has little to do with any physical trail and everything to do with the person I felt like I was becoming.

Our steps taken went far beyond that of our sandy footprints. They were steps on an inner-path of self-discovery. This involved shedding the thoughts, habit-patterns, and routines of my old self that didn't serve me, and creating this space allowed for something new to grow. I was able to plant new seeds and channel new behavior along the way. I learned to be the recipient of other's good deeds and to pay them forward, to follow my dreams while forgetting the dreams others had made for me, to listen to my inner-voice and intuition, and to be committed to knowing myself. It was not the final destination that brought me any of this, but rather the taking of the steps on the path itself. It was those steps that gave me all the purpose I needed in life.

I believe such steps can be taken without escaping the lives we live. One need not walk for six months across the country for insight. All that's required is that one leave behind doubt, desire, and distraction—the thoughts and behaviors that don't service growth. These live inside us all and prevent us from hearing the voice within and reaching our full potential.

The journey need not and will not end after we reach our destination. There will always be another mountain to climb and a valley to cross. And if we so desire, we can walk many paths throughout one lifetime. Do not worry when one path comes to an end. Another will undoubtedly begin.

The trail also taught me that the wilderness most in need of exploration was the one within me. Here, the wilderness is unbounded and the path never ends. It cannot be quantified in days, measured miles, nor compared to others. May we continue to better understand and chart the infinite territory that lives inside.

No matter where we're at in life, I'm frequently reminded that life itself is drowning in purpose. It just takes a little bit of effort to open our eyes and choose to see it.

May we all venture onto the path within. May we walk into the unknown parts of ourselves, bringing light to the darkness, climbing out from our valleys to stand on mountaintops, if only to see a bit more clearly before the clouds once again return to block our view. We can learn just as much from our valleys as we can from the highest of all the mountains. May we move forward for our own benefit and the benefit of others. The rest we will leave to the trail.

Shake & Stayin' Alive.

ACKNOWLEDGEMENTS

Because I have written and rewritten this book many times, each time trying to dig a little bit deeper inside myself, I have many people to thank. Alex Skold, Michael Aldape, Chuck Klinger, Martha Gaskin, Marcus Corder, Jacob Glenn, Zack Siegert, Tyler Woods, Emily Mendoza, Tanner Critz, Juli Maher, Lori Volkas, John Smart, Charla Smart, Robinson Erhardt, and Bradley Lovell have all enriched the book with their perspective comments and technical edits. It is an understatement to say I am grateful for their help. A special thanks to Brianna Boes for providing professional manuscript edits and thorough copy-editing in the book's final stages.

Secondly, a beautiful book would be nothing without a beautiful cover. Kett McKenna, thank you for the remarkable cover art that graces the front cover of this book. Kett spent countless hours on this design and gave it to me free of charge from the kindness of his own heart. Please consider supporting his work by finding him on Instagram, or reaching out to him via email at kettmckennajr@gmail.com.

A picture says a thousand words, and because my phone hardly worked on the trail but for sending emails in town, I have many photographers to thank, all of whom let me use their work free of charge. Jake Lange, Evan Williams, Liz Donovan, Gracie Ramsdell, Eedahahm, Jaala Freeman, and Will Schmitt all provided photos for this book.

343

I am especially grateful to Richard Walker for his selfless giving both on and off the trail. The majority of the excellent photos contained in this book are his. I highly recommend you visit his blog at http://thefakefacade.blogspot.com/ to see more photos from our trail experience.

I was also given sage advice by those who have come before me. Carrot Quinn, Kyle Rohrig, and Tanner Critz, thank you for offering your time and experience to helping make this possible. These writers each have fantastic thru-hiking memoirs available for purchase on Amazon today.

When this book was only a seed and in its earliest, most fragile stages, I remained wandering and given shelter in the homes of family and friends, without whom I would not have been able to properly tend to its creation in these formative moments. John and Charla Smart, Kim and Kris Lovell, Ryan and Amanda Ashby, Alexandria Hanks, Grant and Natalie Bessac, Jake Wesley & Marlon Figueroa, Jordan-Claire Green, Bonnie Elaine, and Kelsi Golinvaux, Jay Waxse, Morgan Mahoney, Alex Skold, Nick Hughes, Steven Tyson, Brent Longwill, Brittney Buss, Michael Aldape, Pat & Ryan Cink, Rebecca Davis & Andrew Spurlin, Brian Till, Connor Perkins, and Lauren McKenzie & Matt Simpson, thank you for your open-hearts, generosity, and for sharing and multiplying abundance.

A special thanks to my parents for their boundless love, patience, and support. I love you, mom and dad.

Finally, I'd like to acknowledge my hiking partner, Bradley. Thank you, brother. And thank you for showing me the path.

FINAL REQUEST

If you enjoyed this book, **it would mean a lot to me if you considered giving an honest review.** Reviews are critical to the success of any indie author's book as readers take reviews into consideration when purchasing and Amazon weighs reviews heavily when ranking the book. Thank you for your consideration in crafting a short review.

If you would like to read more of my writing, you may do so by subscribing to my blog at: thinkingwithdavid.com. I also keep a podcast called Thinking with David, which can be found on iTunes.

Looking forward to hearing from you.

Love,
David (Stayin' Alive)

Lightning Source UK Ltd.
Milton Keynes UK
UKHW012323210223
417410UK00003B/114